DORIS LESSING

DORIS

LESSING

CRITICAL STUDIES

Edited by

Annis Pratt and L. S. Dembo

THE UNIVERSITY OF WISCONSIN PRESS

Published 1974
The University of Wisconsin Press
Box 1379, Madison, Wisconsin 53701
The University of Wisconsin Press, Ltd.
70 Great Russell Street, London

The articles in this volume originally appeared in
Contemporary Literature, Autumn 1973
© 1973 by the Regents of the University of Wisconsin

Printed in the United States of America
ISBN 0-299-06560-X cloth, 0-299-06564-2 paper
LC 74-5909

Contents

Acknowledgments

The editors wish to acknowledge the generous assistance of the University of Wisconsin Foundation, Rosa A. Pesta Estate, San Diego, California, in the production of the Doris Lessing issue of *Contemporary Literature*.

They are grateful to Roy Okada, Managing Editor of the journal, for his attention to many of the details of transforming that issue into a book, to Julie Wosk for her editorial assistance, and to Nancy Pellmann, the journal's secretary, for her added efforts.

Introduction

The Golden Notebook was published in 1962, one year before Betty Friedan brought out *The Feminine Mystique* and before Sylvia Plath, in Doris Lessing's London, put her head into an oven. At a time when the new feminist movement was in its embryonic stages, Lessing's novel brought to consciousness a quality of being which she herself had taken "absolutely for granted." As she asserts and as such critics as Agate Krouse[1] and Ellen Morgan have demonstrated, there is nothing explicitly "feminist" about Anna Wulf: the quality that startled us in her character was not her ironic "freedom" but the fact that (after years of our attempts to identify ourselves with Quentin Compson, Augie March, and the Invisible Man, not to mention Lolita and Franny Glass) we were presented with a novel whose persona was an intellectual, a political activist, an artist, as well as a lover, a mother—a woman.

Nineteen sixty-two marked a period when those who had weathered the political apathy of the fifties were awakening to the civil rights and peace movements, which would eventually teach them about the chauvinism and divisiveness inherent in even the most radical of causes. Like the decade following the French Revolution, the sixties became a time in which an idealistic dawn of the Washington March was followed by the Jacobin riots of Watts, Newark, and Detroit, which illustrated the inexorable conjunction of violence

---

[1] Agate Krouse, "The Feminism of Doris Lessing," Diss. Wisconsin 1972.

and chaos within even the most humanistic of reform schemes. It was precisely this tightrope between idealism and reality, between utopian left-wing visions and human depravity, that Lessing's heroes walked open-eyed, wryly and compassionately commenting upon the havoc.

It was perhaps because *The Golden Notebook* was one of those novels that seemed to speak directly to a whole generation's experience that it has taken ten years and any number of rereadings to sift through our subjective responses and to arrive at an objective criticism that does justice to its structures and complexity. Moreover, the way that Lessing's philosophical quest leads her to break novelistic forms as soon as she has created them has left even the most devoted readers breathless in pursuit. Similarly, her elision of political realism into the worlds of insanity and science fiction has left those unable to make as graceful a leap between realism and fantasy puzzled and confused. It is our hope that the present collection of critical essays will dispel some of this confusion and begin to develop approaches to her total work which will, in turn, add to the elucidation of each individual piece.

John Carey, Evelyn Hinz, and John Teunissen, for example, develop structural and archetypal approaches to the question of the relation between "art," "reality," and "insanity" in *The Golden Notebook* which lead us towards an understanding of the polarity between inner and outer worlds that informs the later work. It may be the strict formalism that we inherited from the fifties that has made it so difficult for us to grasp the integral connection which a writer with as Marxist a background as Lessing would automatically make between the personal and the social. Selma Burkom, in a 1969 essay entitled "Only Connect," was one of the first to note the way that Lessing handles "the individual conscience in its relations to the collective,"[2] and Lynn Sukenick in her study reminds us that Lessing's "habit of mind" is to see "socially, not personally." Insanity, Sukenick points out, takes on a political dimension in that Lessing comprehends it as a rebellion against prevailing "normal" standards of adjustment, a rebellion participated in not only by isolated individuals but by an increasing network of persons whose "breakdowns" Lessing sees as "breakthroughs."

Readers and critics have been put off, as Dagmar Barnouw reminds us, by what they see as the abandonment of an admirable

---

[2] Selma R. Burkom, " 'Only Connect': Form and Content in the Works of Doris Lessing," *Critique,* 11 (1969), 51-68.

"shrewdness" for "uneasy excursions into things to come." It is to the credit of the authors of the following studies that although they represent a diversity of approaches, they agree in taking Lessing's encyclopedic range of concerns seriously, engaging in a "willing suspension of disbelief" in order to elucidate her works. Plunging into a world where consciousnesses interpenetrate and where human beings develop new "ears" to "tune in" to planetary voices, critics like Douglass Bolling, Sydney Kaplan, and Lynn Sukenick provide a perspective on Lessing's vision by pointing out analogues in Western symbolic and literary traditions. Nancy Hardin, similarly, is able to elucidate the later works by analyzing Lessing's adaption in these novels of the concept of the Sufi Way. These critics help us to recognize that Lessing is, after all, hardly the first writer in English letters to forge a link between social criticism, insanity, and apocalyptic vision: Paul Schlueter, whose book is reviewed in this collection, has noticed the similarities between D. H. Lawrence and Lessing, who finds her context in the same prophetic tradition as Blake, Dylan Thomas, Yeats, and Virginia Woolf.

Like these writers, Lessing comprehends her works not as closed forms but as processes in a quest into the hidden places of the unconscious—"the nethermost sea of the hidden self" in Thomas' phrase, "the dark places of modern psychology" in Woolf's, and, in Lawrence's, "the dark continent of the unconscious." In the Blakean tradition, she combats the deification of reason which many consider the crowning achievement of "civilization" and sees the modern ego as a form which must be broken down in order to be forged anew in the crucible of the imagination; or, in Hardin's explication, as the "old villain," a Sufi "name for the patterns of conditioned thinking which form the prison in which we all live."

Ellen Morgan suggests that the very pattern of "conditioned thinking" that she was heralded as challenging was one which Lessing seems to have passed over with a minimum of analysis. "It must be clearly understood," writes Kate Millett, "that the arena of sexual revolution is within human consciousness even more pre-eminently than it is within human institutions. So deeply embedded is patriarchy that the character structure it creates in both sexes is perhaps even more a habit of mind and a way of life than a political system."[3] Michele Zak, in her treatment of *The Grass Is Singing*, suggests that Lessing intends Mary Turner's "schizophrenic disassociation" as a

---

[3] Kate Millett, *Sexual Politics* (New York: Doubleday, 1970), p. 63.

function of her alienation within a male society, but Ellen Morgan points out that the characters in *The Golden Notebook* are unaware of their position as female "outsiders" and unconscious of their internalization of patriarchal norms. This split between any self-conscious feminism on Lessing's part and her detailed presentation of woman's alienation is not so startling when we consider her within the continuum of women's fiction; George Eliot and Charlotte Brontë similarly developed a fiction which is implicitly feminist at the same time that, in their public pronouncements, they renounced any association with the suffrage movement. Anna Wulf's lack of perspective upon the sexist norms she has internalized seems less surprising when we compare her character to that of Eliot's Maggie Tulliver, Chopin's Edna Pontellier, and Wharton's Lily Bart, whose female isolation was similarly depicted without any explicitly feminist analysis of the causality of their symptoms.

If the present collection can be offered as an initial effort in the study of Lessing as a major author in British literature, we can perhaps urge that future critics turn their attention to social and feminist appraisals, as well as to comparisons between her work and that of other authors in the continuum of both women's fiction and of Western literature in general. In this last regard, critics might take note of the striking way in which Lessing's total work fits into the quest pattern and mythical cycle described by Northrop Frye. Lessing's heroes are poised upon a dialectic of openness and cynicism, between "the integrity of the innocent world" and "the assault of experience"; like Frye's they pass through two erotic phases in their quest, an initiation early in adulthood and a later renewal of eroticism before "some cosmic disaster," in which "society break[s] up into small units or individuals."[4] *The Four-Gated City* culminates in an apocalyptic event, after which the world begins anew. Frye's cycle, similarly, "brings us around again to the image of the mysterious newborn infant floating out to sea," while Lessing's *Bildungsroman* ends with the strangely mature "mutant" black boy leaving her island in order to forge a new and better consciousness for the human race. Finally, exactly as in Frye's cycle, we have the ironic mode, in Lessing's works, returning in a cycle to the world of myth.

In pursuing an archetypal and textual analysis of Lessing's fiction necessary to our further understanding of her encyclopedic range

---

[4] See Northrop Frye, *Anatomy of Criticism* (Princeton: Princeton Univ. Press, 1957), pp. 186-203.

and complexity, critics should heed her caveat against those who feel that literature is merely an element of a " 'divine play' or a 'reflection from the creative fires of irony' etc. etc., while the Marthas of this world read and search with the craving thought: What does this say about my life?" Whatever direction future Lessing criticism takes, the prophetic dimension of her works precludes too narrowly aesthetic an analysis, since they are written not for our artistic delight but to warn of satanic mills and to suggest a New Jerusalem. We ought then, in reading and analyzing Lessing, to pay heed to Douglass Bolling's insistence that "We will do justice to [the] fiction not by seeking to judge it within narrowed formalist bounds but by giving ourselves to its values and by keeping our mind's eye open to the sentence of death beneath which our age thinly lives."

Annis Pratt

CONTRIBUTORS

Dagmar Barnouw has written a book on Mörike and articles on Hölderlin and George; Mann, Lukács, and Musil; Bobrowski, Canetti, and Lévi-Strauss.

Douglass Bolling has published essays on Charles Williams, E. M. Forster, Hemingway, Purdy, and Rudolph Wurlitzer, among others.

John L. Carey is Professor of English Literature and Area Head of Literature and Languages at Bloomfield College (New Jersey).

Nancy Shields Hardin, Assistant Professor of English at the University of Wisconsin—Rock County, has published work on Margaret Drabble and Kobo Abe. She has recently received a grant from the Japan Foundation to study the influence of Pinter on Abe.

Evelyn J. Hinz is the author of *The Mirror and the Garden: Realism and Reality in the Writings of Anaïs Nin* as well as articles on Lawrence, Hart Crane, Cather, and others. She is a Post-Doctoral Research Fellow at the University of Manitoba.

Florence Howe, Professor of Humanities at the College at Old Westbury, State University of New York, was recently president of the Modern Language Association. She has published extensively on feminism in literature.

Sydney Janet Kaplan is Assistant Professor of English at the University of Washington. Her book, *Feminine Consciousness in the Modern British Novel,* is forthcoming.

Agate Nesaule Krouse recently completed her dissertation on Doris Lessing and is Assistant Professor of English, University of Wisconsin—Whitewater.

Ellen Morgan has written articles on Hawthorne and on the feminist novel. She is chairing the Doris Lessing seminar for the Modern Language Association convention in 1974.

Lynn Sukenick teaches literature and creative writing at the University of California, Santa Cruz. She has recently completed a book on women's fiction and has two volumes of poetry in print.

John J. Teunissen is Professor of English and Head of the Department of English at the University of Manitoba. He has published articles on The Book of Job, Roger Williams, the literature of the American Revolution, and Poe.

Michele Wender Zak is a graduate student at Ohio State University.

A Conversation
with Doris Lessing (1966)

Florence Howe

I spent a weekday afternoon in October, 1966, with Doris Lessing,
drinking wine and coffee, eating, talking. Whatever questions I might
have had in my head disappeared into my embarrassment about not
being able to operate the small tape recorder I was carrying. But Doris
was, it turned out, as helpless as I, and son Peter had to be called on
for manly assistance. It was a perfectly inappropriate scene. Here was
the allegedly feminist author of *The Golden Notebook*, stirring a great
pot of soup on the stove, calling for her twenty-year-old son to emerge
from his downstairs bed-sitting room to help the American lady (also
allegedly feminist). I don't know what I had expected, but surely not
this friendly, attractive, slightly scattered woman. Surely not this small
and comfortably dishevelled kitchen at the front of a narrow row
house on a working-class street in north central London. Surely not
the half-filled cat's dishes on the floor.

Why not? Why had I not expected to feel comfortably able to
relax for an afternoon of talk—once Peter had made the tape recorder
work? Probably because Doris Lessing's stories don't make me feel
comfortable. They're tough-minded, thoroughly unsentimental, sometimes cruel, often pessimistic, at least about personal relations. What
comedy they offer is painful, black. And though I admire her books,

---

*Part of this introduction was written in 1966, though none of it was ever
published. The *Nation* (March 6, 1967, pp. 311-13) published excerpts from
the conversation but not in dialogue form. The following abbreviations have been
used: *D. L.*—Doris Lessing; *P. L.*—Peter Lessing; and *F. H.*—Florence Howe.
Copyright © 1967 by Florence Howe. Used by permission.

I hardly expected an easy encounter with the person they reveal.

So I was pleasantly surprised—first, by the fact that Doris Lessing likes to talk. Our conversation had no quality of the interview about it. It was monologue, sometimes ramble. Second, our talk was mostly nonliterary, mostly about race relations, violence, Rhodesia and other African countries, politics, education, England, the U.S., and the war in Vietnam. And third, she was as interested in me as I was in her. I don't know how to explain this, except that I had the sense, throughout, that we were two people talking, not simply a book reviewer interviewing a novelist. By the afternoon's end, Doris Lessing could ask me whether I'd been married and why that marriage had failed.

In 1966, no one was interested in the interview. Doris Lessing's following among the literary intelligentsia in the U.S. was minescule. Only the *Nation* chose to print a tiny section of it. In the years that have passed since then, the interview has been used by a half dozen dissertation writers who, one from another, discovered its existence. And now about forty percent of it (including the main "literary" section) appears here in print.

Why is it still a useful piece to read? For some of the same reasons I thought it was important then. In a letter dated January, 1967, to the editor of a literary publication, I described the "random" flavor of the interview that captures aspects of the life and work of an important writer. I had wanted to talk with Doris Lessing because reading her books had mattered to my life: what higher praise can one offer a writer? She had agreed because she wanted to say things about *The Golden Notebook* to American readers. In 1966, her statements about that novel were news. Even today, after her two visits to the U.S., her increasing popularity, her recent statements in *The Partisan Review*, even today, her 1966 conversation contains both surprises and satisfactions.

I had forgotten the feisty quality of Lessing's questioning (and my own timidity, by comparison). I had forgotten her insistence on the impossibility of explaining certain phenomena—race riots, for example, or the emotions that get "sucked in" around the central ones of anger or fear. I remembered that she had called *The Golden Notebook* a "failure" because people had read it *merely* as a feminist statement. Feminism, she was saying in 1966, was nothing new, and certainly not to her. I remembered her pleasure in the fact that the book had, at least in the nonnarrative sections, attempted the complexity that fiction needed to catch and had caught some of it. But I had forgotten the intensity of her insistence that fiction is "always a lie" and "the terrible despair" that follows the knowledge that you have not caught "what you've actually experienced."

The conversation of 1966 reminds us both of the connections between the writer and her work and of the separation between them —the separation that occurs at least because as a writer's life moves on, the books remain. Doris Lessing's life is the source of her fiction. Again and again in the conversation, and even more impressively in the sections not being printed here, Lessing speaks directly of that life, of her own early indoctrination into racist values, her views of the third world liberation struggles, of the class-bound life of her own London neighborhood. Her fiction, up to 1966, came out of that life. At the same time, we catch a glimpse of a person in the process of change. "Yes, I know," she said at one point agreeing with me, "in five years time, I'll be saying, my god, what a fool I was. I really do feel this way about every two years—what a fool I was two years ago."

The critical period may not be two years, but when someone writes the history of Lessing's life and work, that person will find that sometime before or during the writing of *The Four-Gated City* one of those shifts occurred. Lessing notes in this conversation only that she is about to begin her research for the final volume of the *Children of Violence* series, and that she plans to cover a period of ten years in this concluding novel. There is no obvious sign here of the direction taken finally in *The Four-Gated City* and her subsequent work.

We can outline some aspects of that shift: an interest in Eastern thought; the strengthening of a belief in the mind (above and beyond material conditions); most importantly, a change in the political terms of the novel. In *The Four-Gated City* and in *Briefing for a Descent into Hell*, we are either in the future or the past or in both together. Change is a function only of personal, traumatic transformation or of social holocaust. In this conversation of 1966, as in her earlier novels, we are listening to the sensitive, informed, and questioning political consciousness of a woman who happens to be a novelist. We are in the head of a woman familiar with the lives of people, groups, organizations in London or Rhodesia, and curious about the U.S. and other parts of the world. She ranges with ease, in her talk as in her fiction, from race, sex, and class battles, to the Second World War, Vietnam, and the antiwar movement. The conversation helps to illuminate the manner in which political consciousness becomes the stuff of fiction.

F. H. The first day we got to England we read an article in some newspaper about a poor guy who was trying to teach underprivileged kids in the slums or something in London and what a time he was having, because these people didn't know English. This is the sort of thing that people in the States have been wrestling with for ten years, and it just seems to be something new here.

D. L. It goes on quietly all the time.

F. H. And all the race riots you're predicting now, it seems to me, we've already had and are having and will continue to have.

P. L. No, you see our race riots are a symptom of a completely different thing. They're a symptom of the fact that in England we had a class system allied with a feeling of England as top man. We ruled the world and everyone else were damn niggers or foreigners. And we just can't get on with the fact that we're just human like they are. And they've got equal rights.

D. L. I don't think that's true at all. I think it's a direct expression of the fact that the greatest terror of the British working man is unemployment. And this is there the whole time, rationally and irrationally. Every black man is seen by practically every British working man as a threat to his work. And we see under the Labor government that this is probably going to be so, which is an interesting irony. I don't know, there's more to race riots than that obviously.

F. H. But you know that's true in the States, too, and that accounts for why the relations between Negroes and those people called poor whites are far worse than those between middle-class whites and other Negroes. There's really intense hatred. All those riots in Chicago, for instance, this summer—people were just extraordinarily open in their hatred.

D. L. Yes, but the fascinating thing about riots is why do they take place one year and not the next? And that's not such a silly question. I mean, why suddenly race riots on that scale in the United States? Why not ten years ago?

P. L. Because the factors weren't like that ten years ago.

D. L. Yes, I know but you're just making a statement and not answering it. What factors? Where are they? Why do we say we're going to have race riots?

P. L. Hatred is like steam; it has a boiling-over point, and it has to be reached.

D. L. Well, what is the hatred?

P. L. Every human's filled with hatred.

F. H. Don't you think it has to do with a feeling of self as well as of hatred? I'm not for riots, but I think there's something positive about the man who will say, "No, I've just had enough, I can't take anymore of this." At least that's the way it seems to start, with people saying "no" to policemen. From then on maybe it's sheerly destructive. But maybe that's why they start in the first place. They started in the States two summers ago, in 1964.

D. L. The thing is, nobody can explain, and I say nobody, why they started two years ago in that summer.

P. L. All the factors were ripe.

F. H. Well, it had something to do with why, in that particular summer, SNCC, this movement of students, Negroes and whites from the north and south, decided to have a summer project in Mississippi. They've been working since 1960.

D. L. Yes, but you've been having riots in Los Angeles. And you've just had one in San Francisco. They all started with what is known as agitators?

F. H. They all started in precisely the same way, with a policeman either arresting or shooting a young person or pushing a woman or something like that.

D. L. Well, before they would have taken it, but now they riot?

F. H. Yes.

D. L. Well, something has happened.

P. L. Yes, the boiling point's been reached. Fact is they're now saying "no."

D. L. Peter! Yes, but don't you see that what you're saying is simply a meaningless statement? . . .

P. L. No.

D. L. . . . because we don't understand these things very well.

F. H. There are several ways of explaining it. Some people explain it by saying that people are so hard-pressed; they have absolutely nothing to lose, and so they don't care at this point. It's the only way of asserting themselves, and so they destroy.

D. L. You see, since I came to England—I've been here for sixteen years—there's been a complete change. The whole attitude has changed about color—in two ways. When I came, South Africa hardly existed except for a tiny group of left-wingers who went on about it. Now it's in everybody's consciousness. Nobody ever heard of Rhodesia—it didn't exist. And there's a kind of consciousness, of political consciousness, that is new. And the other thing—very strong—is a color prejudice in this country that hasn't begun to show yet. I think we're going to be appalled when it shows. And it didn't exist before, you see. Or if it did exist, it wasn't conscious; it wasn't in the open, the way it is now.

F. H. Don't you think it existed but never was given expression because most English people didn't go to Africa, most Africans didn't come here, and there was no opportunity.

D. L. Yes, something like a million Africans, a million people, you know, with dark skins from the West Indies. It's hardly anything, a million people. . . .

P. L. It's quite a lot.

D. L. No, it isn't, not very much. It can't only be that there are colored faces around and there weren't before. Of course there were before. Always in London.

P. L. But I think the color prejudice goes right back to Victorian times —the fact that we were white and Christian and they were black and heathen. And so one had a kind of moral one-upmanship and one just hated them, quietly. But they weren't around to hate, really. As soon as they actually turn up and they become your next door neighbor and they start having parties, your hatred can come out.

F. H. More than hatred, it's a kind of fear.

P. L. Well, I mean it's black—it's hatred, fear, it's everything—and what's more they're foreigners, everything.

D. L. Well, I do think we tend to forget that, because we're an ex-colonial country, there are very few families that haven't had a member of it at some point out, you know, being a boss somewhere. It rubs off. Which you haven't got. You see, Americans have never had that. At least not till recently. Doesn't prevent your having race riots.

P. L. In America, anywhere, you've got to work hard at whatever you do. I mean you're past the point where you can go back to nature and start taking money for coconut skins. Now you've got to go out as an adviser to a government, with a degree, and then you'll get money, you'll get fantastic money—cause it's a technical age.

D. L. But there's something still that we don't understand about it.

F. H. Let me change the subject and ask you about *The Golden Notebook.* . . .

D. L. That was an extremely carefully constructed book, you know, much care. And the way it's constructed says what the book is about, which very few people have in fact seen. An occasional rare person writes, and I'll think well at last somebody's got the point. What *The Golden Notebook* is taken to be by practically everyone is kind of a latter-day feminism. What I was doing in *The Golden Notebook* is this . . . there are various springs, you know, where books start from. One was the idea that we always take it for granted that a hundred years ago people were thinking the way we think now. . . . I know I'm being controversial but I maintain that most of the ideas that we take for granted are in fact a complex of ideas which could be described as Left—and which were born with the French Revolution. And they're all to do with freedom. They are revolutionary ideas that are no longer revolutionary and have been absorbed into the fabric of how we live. And they're ideas that fit together in a system—broadly speaking, nonreligious, in the old sense, and to do with the individual in relation to his society and the rights of the individual. Which is a new idea and we don't realize how new it is. We take it absolutely for granted. Three hundred years ago it wouldn't have been taken for granted. And in parts of the world now it wouldn't be—they'd just look at you and not know what you were talking about. But we take it for granted. I was a member of the Communist Party under very

unusual circumstances; without going into details which are in fact
boring, there was a time in my life when I was a member of a communist group which was pure . . . they had no contact with any kind
of reality. It must have been blessed by Lenin from his grave, it was
so pure. The thing was, if we had been in any other part of the world,
where in fact there was a Communist Party, the beautiful purity of
the ideas that we were trying to operate couldn't have worked. I mean,
I found this when I came to England and had a short association with
the British Communist Party.

F. H. Was this in Rhodesia?

D. L. Well, the point was there was no Communist Party in Rhodesia.
And for a short period of about three years, a group of enormously
idealistic and mostly extremely intellectual people created a Communist Party in a vacuum of a kind which no real Communist Party
anywhere in the world would have recognized as such. But, you see,
this experience is not so way out as one might think, because if you
talk to other communists. . . . Communism isn't a thing, never has been,
varies from country to country . . . you find that what left-wing movements have in common, I think, and this is true not only of the Communist Party, but certainly true of left-wing Labor; one is always living
in a state of embattled ideas—in fact, nothing is sort of taken for
granted. And an epoch obviously came to an end, well, towards the
end of the fifties. I thought that if I wrote a book about the kind of
experiences that people I knew had had, I would in fact be writing a
book about the kind of ideas people were having—almost as a record.
And this is the interesting thing. I wrote from inside a woman's view-
point, naturally, since I am one. Ideas about equality of women and
so on . . . inside any left-wing group I've always been a member of,
they're always there—being debated in one way or another and fought
out, in private relationships. But they are the ideas you would find—I
don't know—in the *Sunday Times Colour Supplement* in a cruder
form; they're the same ideas.

   What I'm trying to say is that the left-wing idea is not left-wing
at all. Because it always has to do with the individual, the rights of the
individual: Rights. Fair play. Justice. When *The Golden Notebook*
came out, I was astonished to find actually—just shows you how blind
you can be—that people got so emotional about that book, one way
and another, they didn't bother to see, even to look at how it was
shaped. Now I could mention a dozen books by male authors, but you

see, I won't bother. The attitudes to women are the obverse, mirror attitudes, of the attitudes to men but no one would say that these men are antiwomen. They would say, I don't know, this man has a problem or he's screwed up or he has a soul-problem. After all deep problems very often are expressed through sex. But I articulated the same thing from a female point of view, and this is what was interesting; it was taken as a kind of banner.

F. H. Well I think it's such a rich and complex book that most people can't deal with more than one small aspect of it at any given time. And I do think it's more complex than even you make out now as you talk about it.

D. L. Well, the ideas we live with are complex. One idea goes with another idea. Ideas go in groups, don't they? There are some ideas that couldn't possibly fit together, if you tried. The kind of ideas, for example, that are being breathed in at this moment, you know, 1966 in Communist China, would not, any one of them, let's say, fit in the deep South of the United States of America. You couldn't conceive of such a thing. They're different blocks of ideas hanging together because they have an affinity.

F. H. But the feeling that some of your female characters express toward men is not terribly different from the feeling, say, that Negroes might express toward white people who have dominated them or enslaved them or made them feel wretched.

D. L. Yes, well, that's because in the last generation women have become what is known as "free." And I don't want to get into an argument about how free they are; that's not the point. The point is they're still fighting battles to get free, and rightly. And men are still, some men, you know, some men resist it. But what interested me in that book was in fact the ideas and it still interests me because you have to be apart, a little bit, from an idea before you can see it, even in association with another one. What I'm trying to say is that it was a much more detached book. . . . It was a failure, of course, for if it had been a success, then people wouldn't get so damned emotional when I didn't want them to be. . . .

F. H. I don't think it's a failure. . . .

D. L. Yes, it is. What I wanted was to stand back and look. . . .

F. H. Women read it because you express what they feel again and again about their—

D. L. The funny thing is that I just took that absolutely for granted.

F. H. Well, all right, maybe that's why it's so good and so true.

D. L. This must mean that women are awfully dishonest—

F. H. Or frightened—

D. L. Yes, or dishonest, same thing, isn't it? Because they'll say to each other in conversation or to their own private man something they'd never dream of saying for fear of being called antifeminine or something or other. Which is the biggest weapon that men can use against us. And women are so afraid of it that they'll shut up and play what I regard as a very despicable game. But some of my closest friends expressed to me in private the kind of ideas the ladies in that book express. They were angry and disassociated themselves and said that I was antimale. When I bashed it out with them as is my wont and said to them, "Sit down and let's talk about it," some kind of fear came up. . . .

F. H. Their fear? Your fear?

D. L. We have fear. I think this is not a very new remark. The relationship between the sexes everywhere, not just in Western society, is so much of a melting pot, that it's like the color bar, all kinds of emotions that don't belong get sucked in. You know, I'm convinced that all sorts of emotions that have nothing to do with color get associated around the color bar. Similarly with men and women, they . . . any sort of loaded point sucks in anger or fear.

F. H. But your male characters in that book are really very unpleasant, all of them. There isn't a good male character.

D. L. I don't think that's true. What's that doctor's name?

F. H. Michael.

D. L. There were two versions of him. . . .

F. H. Paul, the other one.

D. L. Why is he unpleasant?

F. H. Well, he's marvelous to a point. Then he leaves.

D. L. Well, men do leave, after all. That doesn't make them less marvelous.

F. H. (Embarrassed laughter)

D. L. If you're going to say a man is unpleasant because he leaves.

F. H. (More laughter)

D. L. I was surprised when you said that. I think the male characters are terrific.

F. H. I guess it's because people have gotten very fond of Anna and Ella and when they're left by Michael and Paul . . . I'm sure this is why I feel the way I do. I revealed it . . . I don't like them for doing that.

D. L. Some of the best men one has known have been the men who can't stick with women.

F. H. Right.

D. L. It is true, isn't it? It's like what I said earlier about this race riot business. There's something we don't understand about it. I don't think we understand nearly as much as we think we understand about what goes on.

F. H. I quite liked Saul at the end better than the other two.

D. L. I was trying to condense him. You know, the "Free Women" section, the envelope. I was really trying to express my sense of despair about writing a conventional novel in that. You see, actually that is an absolutely whole conventional novel and the rest of the book is the material that went into making it. Well, one of the things I was saying was, well, look, this is a conventional novel that you can pick up in any . . . God knows I write them myself and doubtless will again. Well, one has this feeling when you've written a novel. There it is, 120,000 words; it's got a nice shape and the reviewers will say this and that. And the bloody complexity that went into it and it's always a lie. And the terrible despair. So you've written a good novel or a moderate novel, but what does it actually say about what you've actually experienced. The truth is, absolutely nothing. Because you can't. I don't know what one does about novels. I shall write volume five with my usual enthusiasm. I know perfectly well, when I've finished it, I shall think, Christ, what a lie. Because you can't get life into it. That's all there is to it, no matter how hard you try.

F. H. And you think you have in *The Golden Notebook,* in the non-novel section?

D. L. Well, at least I think it's more truthful because it's more complex. People are like other people. I mean, I don't think we are as extra-ordinary as we like to think we are. We are more like other people than we would wish to believe. The same people occur again and again in our lives. Situations do. And any moment of time is so complicated. Well, I do like *The Golden Notebook* because at any rate, though I do believe it to be a failure, at any rate it at least hints of complexity.

F. H. But tell me something that we haven't talked about at all. Tell me about the character named Athen.

D. L. Well, he is the only person in that book who's absolutely straight from life.

F. H. He's the best character in the book.

D. L. He's absolutely straight. And I even left the name in: Athen Gouliaris. And everything is as I said it. I put it in and I said to my publisher, "Look, I'm going to put one character in, and is it all right? His name and his exact circumstances." And he said, "O.K.," because Greece, well, it's the other end of the world, and nothing could happen. So I did. He was a real person. He was one of the most fabulous people I've ever known in my whole life. As far as I know, he was beaten up and killed in prison, together with his friends.

F. H. Why was he in Rhodesia?

D. L. He was out training to be a pilot.

F. H. With the RAF?

D. L. Yes, Greek politics during the war were unbelievably compli-cated. There was a point at which the left, but it wasn't entirely com-munist, section of the resistance movement was sort of made O.K. and heroed and accepted because we were fighting the Germans. Right?

During that period, a lot of them were scooped up and trained in various places. One of the places was Southern Rhodesia. Athen was out learning to be a pilot together with a whole group of them—I think about twenty of them. And they were all communists; they'd all been in the resistance. And they were watching the movement of politics in Greece. Of all the stories during the war, sheer cynicism, Greece is just about the worst. I'd forgotten how horrible it was until I went and did some of the reading of newspapers. So when Athen went back to Greece, he knew that it was almost certain that he was going to be killed; he knew that. His plan was to go back to Greece and to go into the mountains, because at the time he went back, there was practically no resistance.

F. H. It's easy to understand how people could survive in the mountains. They're still so inaccessible.

D. L. Yes, he'd stayed in the mountains for a couple of years. He wanted to get back to the mountains. He was obviously scooped up, along with his friends, and at that time—well, it's a very old story, they were beaten up in prison and shot trying to escape, or whatever particular nasty thing it was. But he was a marvelous man, you know. When I think—oh, water under bridges. Fabulous communists I have known, people—half of them were killed by the other side, in communist prisons. Well, he was just a saint, period. There are very few pure saints—he was one of them.

F. H. I admired everything he said.

D. L. He just lived like that. He was a very extraordinary man. He was a tiny, little dark man, very short and thin. He'd been brought up . . . his history was pure politics, sort of like a poor Negro's history. . . . And he'd come out of it with such gentleness and such compassion. I can't remember him ever saying anything bitter or angry or—he was the only one who spoke English well enough to get on with. Oh, he wouldn't have survived in any communist world either. Well, I wrote to this address, not after I got that postcard—I thought it would be dangerous for his family, but I waited until things had quieted down. One can't write to a country, I got your postcard, I understand its message, well how are you? Anyhow I waited till I thought it was safe, and I wrote a series of letters, just in case, at six-week intervals, and I got no reply. I've still got the address somewhere. If I ever go to Athens, I'll look it up. But why bother to do it? I know what happened, he knew exactly what was going to happen. . . . (pause) Those Greeks, you know, the ones with Athen, they were a bloody, moralist lot of men. They were all poor Greeks, all out of the slums, or peasants or something. A rare, marvelous person comes out of these conditions. I suppose the rest get corrupted.

F. H. I like *The Golden Notebook* better than the *Children of Violence* series, but I think that's because Anna is so much more complex than Martha. I'm impatient with Martha.

D. L. Well, she was very young. How would you like to meet yourself at twenty?

F. H. I do meet myself at twenty in Martha all the time, and I don't like it.

D. L. I didn't like her much even then, poor girl.

F. H. I much prefer Anna.

D. L. Well, you see we're all wise and mature now and can afford to laugh. I've been surrounded by kids of this age for the last five years. Oh, to be young again! I'd rather die. What torment. They're terribly brave, aren't they, the kids, this lot? They're very courageous, because they don't shut things out and they look at things. They've certainly more strength than I had.

F. H. They know more. I don't think I knew much until about five years ago, maybe three years ago. But, of course, I've thought that all my life.

D. L. Yes, I know, one does. In five years time, I'll be saying, my god, what a fool I was. I really do feel this way about every two years— what a fool I was two years ago.

F. H. Don't you think that there are things in the *Children of Violence* series, for instance, that are at least as true in the sense of capturing something . . . ?

D. L. Well, yes, but the thing is a conventional novel form. Each volume echoes the other volume. You know, the same kinds of people and things turn up.

F. H. But you changed it in volume four, don't you think?

D. L. What, the character? Yes.

F. H. But even the style is different.

D.L. I've got a feeling it is, but it shouldn't be. Anyway—

F. H. It's much more like *The Golden Notebook* than the other three, maybe because the character is so much more introspective.

D. L. Yes, I haven't answered that question because I can't. It simply means that one's got older. I had the most shattering experience. You know how we forget everything. Well, when I sat down. . . . Before I start writing any one of these volumes I go down and do my homework. I ring up the *Daily Express,* the *New Statesman and Nation,* and I go and spend a week with the files—which is *the* most recurring depressing experience of my life. You go back and you read five years of past history. It is *always* so awful what we've forgotten, the dreadful things that we've forgotten and as Peter says the way we, the world does not learn by experience. It happens over and over and over again. You know, one year it's Arabia; the next year, it's the Congo; the next, Vietnam. And it's always as if you just took the headlines off the spot . . . I swear, it doesn't matter where it is, it's always the same thing. What we've lived through, we people. The astounding thing is that we're not all maniacs, really, I think. Those five years of *Landlocked,* after the war, God, they were dreadful years. Were you conscious in those days?

F. H. No, I don't think so. '45 to '51—I was at college . . . I was semi-conscious.

D. L. Dreadful, dreadful years. So you see, sometime in the next three months, I'll have to go down and do my homework.

F. H. For what? '50 to '55?

D. L. No, I'm going to end it towards the end of the fifties. It's going to be a much longer, looser novel. I'm keeping the shape as it is.

F. H. You're going to cover ten years?

D. L. Yes, and finish it. But it's always very interesting, that week I spend in the newspaper office. I suppose if one didn't block it out, we would all be mad actually.

F. H. It'll all take place in England then.

D. L. Yes, I'm going to make Martha . . . during the first years I was in England, most of the people I knew were actively political. I wasn't. I was writing books and bringing up Peter. I'm going to make her a secretary or something like that to involve her in the kind of left-wing activity that was going on in England then. You know, I knew enough about what some of my friends were doing.

F. H. Well, you write a little about it in *The Golden Notebook.*

D. L. Yes, I suppose I do.

F. H. There's a section in which you're rewriting something. I'm a little fuzzy about it . . . in which you go into an office.

D. L. Yes, that's right; she was working in a communist publishing house. Yes, well I got that from one of my friends. And I had friends who worked for women's magazines.

F. H. Yes, that's what Ella does.

D. L. I was fascinated; I had a woman I wrote about in *The Golden Notebook*—a woman who changed her entire life, actually. A trade union asked her to write . . . and she got hundreds of letters from women every week in such despair. This is an extraordinary thing, this highly organized society, we think, this serviced, expert society. . . . But who do they write to, these women? No doctor. . . . They write these pathetic bloody letters to a woman who dishes out advice. "What can I do with my life?" you know.

F. H. Yes, in American newspapers too.

D. L. Only women. I don't think men do. What do they do?

F. H. Men?

D. L. Get drunk or something?

F. H. I guess. No, I suppose some of them write to newspapers, too, but you're quite right, mostly it's women, or young boys, young men. I don't know what old men do.

D. L. I used to get a lot of letters, but I don't any more.

F. H. Letters about what?

D. L. Asking me "what to do with my life." The most dreadful letters. Drove me into a depression for weeks. People in the most hopeless situations. And not only women, actually. To which there's no reply. I remember one, a working-class woman, not a middle-class woman, married with four children; I think her husband was a miner. It was loneliness. She was literally round the bend with loneliness. She said, "There's nothing wrong with my life." Her children were simply fine, she took it for granted that she never saw her "good" husband (what she meant was that he was good financially), had children in school, and she was going mad, and she knew she was going mad. She said she was lonely and what could she do? And she used to be interested in painting and should she go to art classes? What she'd lost was will. So what do you write back to ten pages of misery? "Dear Mrs. X, why do you not take up a nice hobby?" It was very painful.

F. H. I wonder, why did people write to you? Because they read your things?

D. L. I don't know why. I'm interested in why.

F. H. Well, you've written about lonely women again and again in stories.

D. L. I suppose so. What is interesting is that people think that one can . . . people think that somebody around has got the six magical words for their problem. You know, somebody knows the answer somewhere and they can tell them. Which of course is not the case.

F. H. Well, you don't sound as though you're worried about writing the fifth volume. You'll just do it. I want to ask you about that directly because my experience is so different with writing.

D. L. I don't find it difficult to write. Actually, I'm too prolific. Partly because I agree with Virginia Woolf that everybody should have a private income—what was it, five hundred a year? What would that be now?

F. H. Now it would be more, of course.

D. L. Five hundred a year would have made all the difference to my life. Even now. Well, I've written more than I should because I needed money and anyway I'm naturally prolific; I enjoy writing. I haven't written volume five because . . . well, what it's like being a writer in

England with income tax. I'll tell you the situation because in fact it's amusing. Yes, I've got everything beautifully worked out. I was going to write a film, so I thought. And I was going to earn three thousand pounds in May of this year. It was absolutely certain, nothing could go wrong with it, you see, that was the joke. Then my American publisher, who is a marvelous man called Bob Gottlieb, rings me up and says, "Doris, I've made you a lot of money. I've sold all of *Children of Violence* to paperback." And he wheeled out noughts which sounded much more in dollars than in pounds. Anyway what it amounted to was that I was going to earn another four thousand pounds this year. And he said, "For God's sake ring up your accountant immediately." And I did. He said, "You cannot possibly earn that amount because you won't earn any—this is England. If you earn that four thousand from America, you won't keep one penny of it, not a penny, in addition to the other three thousand. Go and buy something with it. At once." So I went and bought a cottage in Devon which was lovely and marvelous. Then, you see, my film fell through. So I didn't get this three thousand and the four thousand is locked up in the cottage. So, far from writing volume five, which was my intention, I had to sit down and start writing, you know, what you do when you're short of money, write for television. So I have to write for television at the moment. I have nothing against it, you know, it's a job. But I would like to write volume five. It's just ludicrous, isn't it?

F. H. And someday somebody will be digging through your television scripts. . . . Don't you think that's amusing?

D. L. I promised volume five for this year and it's not going to be out. I'll tell you what I have written. Since I knew I was going to face six months of writing television—I've nothing against television, it's just not the same thing—I did a short book to please myself about my two cats. Now this is an interesting cultural difference. When I ring up my English publisher, and I say I've written a book about my two cats— he's so English—"O Doris," he answers, "how marvelous, I simply can't wait to read it." When I told Bob, there was a long silence. He's taken the book and he likes it. But there was definitely a long silence when he was swallowing this unwelcome information.

F. H. What kind of television scripts have you written?

D. L. We've got a series here called "Blackmail" which anything fits into. So I've written two for this program and also a space fiction one.

I postulated a situation where Britain was a colony of Africa, about X-thousand years from now. Britain is a remote barbarous little place; and someplace in Africa is not only the ruler of the world but several planets as well, and I simply reversed everything. My hero, an African, is the son of the president and he's been ordered to marry an English, a white girl to keep the savages happy. He's already got two wives but polygamy is all right, you see. And he doesn't want to marry a white girl; it's very bad to marry a white, horrible, politics. And he comes over and falls in love, you see, not with the girl he's supposed to marry, but with the leader of the resistance movement. And she with him. And that's really all the plot. And anyway, they all sacrifice themselves for the good of their various countries. I don't know why it's space fiction; I would have called it historical fantasy. I adore writing it. I really do enjoy it. I wrote it roaring with laughter.

Art and Reality
in *The Golden Notebook*

John L. Carey

In an interview published in 1964 Doris Lessing stated: "I got angry over reviews of *The Golden Notebook*. They thought it was personal —it was, in parts. But it was a very highly structured book, carefully planned. The point of that book was the relation of its parts to each other. But the book they tried to turn it into was: The Confessions of Doris Lessing."[1] Lessing had already given some clues to her intentions in *The Golden Notebook* on its dust jacket where she explained that the novel was a combination of two projected books, a fictional work dealing with a novelist suffering from a "writer's block," and a book of literary criticism which would employ various styles so that "the shape of the book and the juxtaposition of the styles would provide the criticism" in such a way that the completed work "would make implicitly a statement about 'alienation.' " *The Golden Notebook*, she says further, is "an attempt to break a form; to break certain forms of consciousness and go beyond them."[2] Clearly Lessing is attempting to fuse an unusual content with an original structure. Without its structural plan *The Golden Notebook* could not make the comment on life Lessing desires; without the content the structure

---

[1] *Counterpoint*, ed. Roy Newquist (Chicago: Rand McNally, 1964), p. 418.

[2] These quotations appear on the dust jacket of the British edition of *The Golden Notebook*. In a letter to me, dated January 29, 1965, Mr. Raleigh Trevelyan of Michael Joseph, Ltd., Doris Lessing's English publishers, states that they come from Lessing's letter to his firm.

would be grandiose and bare, complicated rather than complex.

The central character of *The Golden Notebook* is Anna Wulf, a novelist who has not published for many years. She lives on the proceeds of her first book, *Frontiers of War,* a story about the racial situation set in central Africa during World War II. Throughout the period covered by *The Golden Notebook* Anna's writing efforts are concentrated on four separate notebooks which she keeps hidden in her room and which only Tommy, the son of her friend Molly, ever reads: "I keep four notebooks, a black notebook, which is to do with Anna Wulf the writer; a red notebook, concerned with politics; a yellow notebook, in which I make stories out of my experience; and a blue notebook which tries to be a diary. In Molly's house the notebooks were something I never thought about; and certainly not as work, or a responsibility."[3]

The four notebooks, making up the greater portion of the novel, are all written in the first person, and they cover the years from 1950 to 1957. In addition the novel has a fifth notebook, itself called "the golden notebook," also written by Anna in 1957 and relating only the events taking place that year. Besides the notebooks there are five sections entitled "Free Women," written in the third person in 1957 or early 1958 about events that took place in the summer and fall of 1957, in which Anna Wulf serves as a central intelligence. *The Golden Notebook* opens with a "Free Women" section describing a conversation among Anna and her friends Molly, Tommy, and Richard, Molly's ex-husband (*GN*, pp. 9-52). Then the notebooks themselves begin with excerpts from the black, the red, the yellow, and the blue, in that order (*GN*, pp. 53-216). Another "Free Women" section follows. This pattern is repeated four times so that there are four "Free Women" sections, all objective, all written in and dealing with events in 1957 and 1958. Following each section are excerpts from the four notebooks, written during the years from 1950 to 1957. After the last of these four repetitions of the pattern comes the section called "the golden notebook," and then a final "Free Women" section ending the novel. Even from this brief outline the intricacy of Lessing's design reveals itself. Clearly her structural plan depends on the relation between the "Free Women" sections and the notebooks.

---

[3] Doris Lessing, *The Golden Notebook* (New York: Simon & Schuster, Inc., 1962), p. 406. Parenthetical page references in the text will be preceded by *GN*. Copyright © 1962 by Doris Lessing. Used by permission of Simon & Schuster, Inc.

To begin with, some curious discrepancies between some of the "facts" recorded in the notebooks and those in the "Free Women" sections are apparent. A casual reading may leave the impression that the "Free Women" sections represent the objective ordering of experience by Lessing herself. After she has presented Anna Wulf's subjective version of the events in the notebooks, it seems that in the "Free Women" sections Lessing gives us the real "truth" of these events, "truth" which only an omniscient author could know. If this impression is correct, however, then we must wonder why in 1957, in the first "Free Women" section, Tommy is twenty years old (*GN*, p. 13) and in a notebook written in 1950 he is seventeen (*GN*, p. 197). Why, too, at the end of the "Free Women" sections are we told that Tommy goes off to Sicily with Marion, Richard's second wife (*GN*, p. 554) while in the notebooks he marries a young girl (*GN*, p. 468)? Why are Molly, Anna, Richard, and Tommy referred to by the same names in the notebooks as well as the "Free Women" sections and Saul Green, Anna's lover in the notebooks, called "Milt" in the "Free Women" sections? Why is the account of Saul's relationship with Anna so much less developed in the final "Free Women" section than in the notebooks? Possibly these contradictions might be attributed to carelessness on Lessing's part (after all, in the *Children of Violence* series she calls Jackie Bolton "Jackie Cooper" on at least two occasions),[4] or perhaps to her deliberate attempt to mirror the confusion of life in art. Such explanations, however, do not seem very satisfactory.

Anna's passionate self-doubt, her inner torment, her inability to function as a writer are almost completely absent from Lessing's nonfiction, and the volume of her publications over the past twenty years proves that she obviously does not suffer from a writer's block. Thus we must wonder in what way Anna Wulf's personal struggles in both the notebooks and the "Free Women" sections, as well as her lack of detachment and humor, represent Lessing's own difficulties, as many of the reviewers of *The Golden Notebook* seem to believe they do.[5]

---

[4] Doris Lessing, *A Ripple from the Storm* (London: Michael Joseph, Ltd., 1958), pp. 8, 208.

[5] Many of the early reviewers of *The Golden Notebook* treated it as important chiefly as disguised autobiography or as a statement of principle rather than as a novel. See, for example, Kathleen Nott in *Time and Tide*, 43 (April 26, 1962), 33. Robert Taubman, in *New Statesman*, 63 (April 20, 1962), 569, says it is a "document" and not a "creative experiment." In a favorable review in *The New Republic*, 147 (Dec. 15, 1962), 17-20, Irving Howe asserts that Lessing is primarily interested in "personal relationships" and points out the autobiograph-

The clue to the structure of *The Golden Notebook* and to the resolution of these problems comes, I believe, at the end of the section called "the golden notebook." At this point in the chronological sequence Anna Wulf has almost overcome her writer's block and is on the point of composing a new novel. Saul Green gives her the first sentence of that novel: "The two women were alone in the London flat" (*GN*, p. 547). A few lines later Anna in turn gives Saul the first sentence for a novel of his own, which he soon writes and publishes. Nothing is said explicitly about whether Anna does the same. But the first sentence of the first "Free Women" section of *The Golden Notebook* is: "The two women were alone in the London flat" (*GN*, p. 9).

It seems obvious that the use of this sentence indicates Lessing's structural plan for her novel. From it we learn that the "Free Women" sections are not what they appear. They are not the omniscient observations of Doris Lessing; they are the novelized account of a "real" situation as described by Anna Wulf. They are "fiction" and thus may take all the liberties of fiction. There is no reason for the "facts" they contain to agree totally (or at all) with the "facts" in the notebooks. Anna Wulf, the novelist, is free to draw on the "truth" in the notebooks and to use it as she wishes in her novel, to fictionalize the "facts" as she sees fit. By thus attributing the "Free Women" sections to Anna, Lessing carefully distances herself. The "Free Women" sections, in addition to the notebooks, become Anna's responsibility alone. Through the "fiction" of assigning these sections to Anna, Lessing filters herself out of the novel entirely and makes it impossible to equate the person of Anna Wulf with that of Doris Lessing no matter what the external similarities.

Yet once all this has been said, we must be careful not to overlook another and perhaps more important function served by attributing the entire *Golden Notebook* to Anna Wulf. By making Anna her author, Lessing blurs almost totally the distinction between truth and fiction. *The Golden Notebook*, itself, is a novel, a fictional representation. However, some of the situations and the principal character, a

---

ical elements. Some reviewers did notice the basic connection between the notebooks and the "Free Women" sections, notably John Bowen in *Punch*, 242 (May 9, 1962), 733 (though Bowen also emphasizes autobiography). The reviewer for the *Times Literary Supplement* (April 27, 1962), 280, found this connection only confusing. Many reviews, notably Patrick Cruttwell, who savagely attacked the novel in *The Hudson Review*, 15 (Winter 1962-63), 595-98, interpreted it as a totally pessimistic and sex-saturated critique of life.

woman novelist with a small child who has lived in Africa and now resides in England, do correspond closely to Lessing's biography. Still, these "facts" have been so integrated into the novel that the reader cannot possibly know where the literal truth of Lessing's life leaves off and fiction begins. So too in the "Free Women" sections, the "facts" found in the notebooks are adapted and changed and even contradicted by Anna in such a way that we cannot be positive which version is "true." Reality thus comes to be understood as a complex interplay of objective experience and the subjective ordering of that experience by the artist. Life and art are seen as a single unit impossible to split.

As I have indicated, all the "Free Women" sections were written after the notebooks; they might well have been printed together. Moreover, though all the notebooks were written over the same period and each supposedly covers the same time, their subject matter frequently overlaps, and the time described by one notebook often does not parallel the time described in the notebook printed immediately after. The blue notebook, for example, consists of Anna's personal diary. After a session with Mrs. Marks, her psychiatrist (whom she also calls "Mother Sugar"), she breaks off this diary for several years. When the diary is again picked up, we are not immediately made aware of the time that has elapsed since the last entry. To follow all the events treated we would have to read each notebook separately and in its entirety. The effect of this deliberate confusion of time is similar to the repetition of character and incident between the notebooks and the "Free Women" sections. It serves to blur reality, to prevent the reader from identifying the real "truth" of a situation or of a time. By thus destroying our sense of time Lessing impresses on us the chaos behind the seemingly smooth flow of external events. *The Golden Notebook* unfolds not like a traditional novel, but like a motion picture in which a series of disparate, though overlapping, images is flashed on a screen in the form of the notebooks. The producer of this movie is Lessing; but the script writer, insofar as we know her, is Anna Wulf.

The Golden Notebook also contains a number of parodies, both of incidents recounted elsewhere in the novel and of various writing styles. Newspaper clippings referring to real events which have impinged on the consciousness of the fictional characters make up a great part of the blue notebook. Spelling and punctuation are often careless and give the impression of hasty unrevised writing. Characters are described in the notebooks as "real," in the "Free Women" sections as "fictional," and in a novel which makes up a large part of the yellow notebook as "fictional" again. Further, as the time perspective changes, the reader finds himself forced to accept the impact of the work as a whole, of having to balance it all in his consciousness much like Joyce's *Ulysses* or Faulkner's *Absalom, Absalom!* All of these techniques prevent the reader from making any one-to-one equation between what he reads and "reality."

Keeping this general interpretation in mind, we may now examine *The Golden Notebook* in detail and observe how Lessing works out her techniques in practice. Such a detailed examination may help to explain much that critics have found puzzling. In an incident in the first "Free Women" section of *The Golden Notebook*, Tommy, the son of Anna's friends, Richard and Molly, asserts his belief in the social responsibility of the artist. Tommy charges Anna with contempt for her fellow men because she refuses to show her notebooks to the world. Anna counters, saying that she does not dare to publish because to do so would spread to others her own disgust and disillusion. To her the truth about life appears so frightening that she can neither face nor communicate it. Tommy, however, is too astute to let Anna off so easily. He replies:

If you feel disgust, then you feel disgust. Why pretend not? But the point is, you were talking about responsibility. That's what I feel too—people aren't taking responsibility for each other. You said the socialists had ceased to be a moral force, for the time, at least, because they wouldn't take moral responsibility. Except for a few people. You said that, didn't you—well then. But you write and write in notebooks, saying what you think about life, but you lock them up, and that's not being responsible. (*GN*, p. 40)

The time of this discussion is 1957. Insofar as the "fictional" Anna of the "Free Women" sections represents the "real" Anna of the notebooks, she advanced greatly from the complete inability to communicate she felt in the early 1950s. Even now, however, she is willing neither to face the implications of the notebooks nor to accept her duty as a writer.

Why then does Anna keep the notebooks at all? Why does she take the trouble to write words on paper? The explanation seems to be that, at this time in her life, the notebooks do in fact "contain" the chaos for Anna. They keep it under control and prevent it from overwhelming her. She indicates this to Tommy when he asks:

"Do you realise the whole of this notebook, the blue one, is either

newspaper cuttings, or bits like the blood and brain bit, all bracketed off,
or crossed out; and then entries like buying tomatoes or tea?"

"I suppose it is. It's because I keep trying to write the truth and re-
alising it's not true."

"Perhaps it is true," he said suddenly, "perhaps it is, and you can't
bear it, so you cross it out."

"Perhaps."

"Why the four notebooks? What would happen if you had one big
book without all those divisions and brackets and special writing?"

"I've told you, chaos." (GN, p. 233)

Anna's admission here, however, is only a temporary one, and
she continues to look for a way to escape the implications of the notebooks, both by talking with Mrs. Marks and, more importantly, by
inventing new reasons for her refusal to publish. All of these reasons
skirt the real issue, but all are partly true. Two examples are worth
considering briefly to help us understand her eventual success in
publishing and grasp more precisely the way in which Lessing
attempts to "break certain forms of consciousness." On one occasion
Anna tells herself that literature is "analysis after the event" (GN, p.
196). She then speculates that, granted the truth of such a definition,
she finds it impossible to understand how a novel could capture
"reality." To prevent this inevitable falsification she attempts to record
in minute detail all the facts of a single day (September 16, 1954),[6]
beginning with her morning farewell to her daughter Janet and ending
with the wine she drinks before sleeping (GN, pp. 282-314). Even as
she writes, however, she knows she is failing to capture the truth. By
having been conscious of everything that happens she changes the
shape of the day itself: "The idea I will have to write it down is
changing the balance, destroying the truth" (GN, p. 291).

On another occasion when Saul Green suggests she write a short
story he has mentioned, she replies:

"I can't write that short story or any other, because at that moment I
sit down to write, someone comes into the room, looks over my shoulder,
and stops me."

"Who? Do you know?"

"Of course I know. It could be a Chinese peasant. Or one of Castro's
guerrilla fighters. Or an Algerian fighting in the F.L.N. Or Mr. Mathlong
[an African patriot]. They stand here in the room and they say, why aren't

---

[6] There is perhaps some slight echo of *Ulysses*, but none of Joyce's techniques are used. The account is strictly literal.

you doing something about us, instead of wasting your time scribbling."
(*GN,* p. 546)

Saul replies that this is not the truth; the people she mentions would
not feel this way, and Anna admits he is right. She is merely excusing
herself. As a result of these and other experiences Anna comes to feel
that all words, in the final analysis, may be meaningless:

Words mean nothing. They have become, *when I think,* not the form into
which experience is shaped, but a series of meaningless sounds, like nursery
talk, and away to one side of experience. Or like the sound track of a film
that has slipped its connection with the film. *When I am thinking* I have
only to write a phrase like "I walked down the street," or take a phrase
from a newspaper, "economic measures which lead to the full use of . . ."
and immediately the words dissolve, and my mind starts spawning images
which have nothing to do with the words, so that every word I see or hear
seems like a small raft bobbing about on an enormous sea of images. So I
can't write any longer. Or only when I write fast, without looking back at
what I have written. For if I look back, then the words swim and have no
sense and I am conscious only of me. . . . (*GN,* p. 407)

This reflection occurs when Anna is still engaged in psychoana-
lytic therapy with Mrs. Marks. One of the benefits of these sessions is
her developing understanding of the role "words" have played in her
life. She begins to see that if, as she concludes, "words are form," then
without the application of words the individual units of life have no
form of themselves; without this application the possibility of fixing
the chaos does not exist. Unfortunately, as suggested above, Anna
now begins to find that words themselves are no longer enough to
keep the chaos "contained." For many years, as the result of a childhood experience, she has used words, as she says, to "name" things;
she has played what she calls the "naming game." In a long passage in
the blue notebook, which is worth quoting in full, Anna explains what
"naming something" has meant to her:

First I created the room I sat in, object by object, "naming" everything, bed,
chair, curtains, till it was whole in my mind, then move out of the room,
creating the house, then out of the house, slowly creating the street, then
rise into the air, looking down on London, at the enormous sprawling
wastes of London, but holding at the same time the room, and the house
and the street in my mind, and then England, the shape of England in
Britain, then the little group of islands lying against the continent, then
slowly, slowly, I would create the world, continent by continent, ocean by

ocean (but the point of "the game" was to create this vastness while holding the bedroom, the house, the street in their littleness in my mind at the
same time) until the point was reached when I moved out into space, and
watched the world, a sunlit ball in the sky, turning and rolling beneath me.
Then, having reached that point, with the stars around me, and the little
earth turning underneath me, I'd try to imagine at the same time, a drop
of water, swarming with life, or a green leaf. Sometimes I could reach what
I wanted, a simultaneous knowledge of vastness and smallness. Or I would
concentrate on a single creature, a small coloured fish in a pool, or a single
flower, or a moth, and try to create, to "name" the being of the flower, the
moth, the fish, slowly creating around it the forest, or the sea-pool, or the
space of blowing night air that tilted my wings. And then, out, suddenly,
from the smallness into space.

It was easy when I was a child. It seems to me now that I must have
lived for years in a state of exhilaration, because of "the game." But now it
is very hard. (*GN,* p. 469)

By "naming" something Anna had fixed the chaos. By relating
an object, a place, a person to the universe, she had created order and
achieved a moment of rest and tranquility; through words she found
a moment of stasis in the flux. The words were the form that revealed
the pattern of life; they represented, she believed, reality as it was.
Now she begins to understand that in the "naming game" she had
broken life up into fragments; that, despite the ostensible result of the
game, she had compartmentalized life in much the same way she did in
the notebooks. By a great act of the will Anna can still impose a
"name" on certain parts of the chaos and relate them to the whole;
but increasingly she sees that to do this is to do something artificial.
To "name" something is to assume that it (a person, an object, a
place, an attitude) can be categorized as an independent unit, that it
can be split off from the rest of reality and be considered as an entity
whose relationship to the cosmos is fixed and unchanging.

This becomes clearer to Anna in one of her more significant discussions with Mrs. Marks, a discussion in which she brings into the
open one of her symbols for chaos:

Last night I had a recurrence of that dream which, as I told Mother
Sugar, was the most frightening of all the different types of cycles of dreams.
When she asked me to "give a name to it" (to give it form), I said it was
the nightmare about destruction. Later, when I dreamed it again, and she
said: Give it a name, I was able to go further: I said it was the nightmare
about the principle of spite, or malice—joy in spite. (*GN,* p. 408)

Anna describes the principle as a vase which looks like an elf or pixie. It represents something anarchistic, uncontrollable, and destructive. "This was when I 'named' the dream as about destruction." Later she describes it as an old man who "smiled and giggled and sniggered, was ugly, vital and powerful, and again, what he represented was pure spite, malice, joy in malice, joy in a destructive impulse. This was when I 'named' the dream as about joy in spite" (*GN*, p. 408). The dream takes on a variety of shapes, but the element of violent joy is always present. Though Mrs. Marks recognizes the whole experience as familiar from her other patients, Anna, nevertheless, feels she has a personal "responsibility" for it. She concludes by reflecting: "In other words, it was up to me to force this thing to be good as well as bad? That was what she was saying?" (*GN*, p. 409). Here we touch upon the crux of Anna's problem. In "naming" her dream Anna simply confirms her intuition about the chaos of life; the "naming" merely imposes a form under which the chaos remains as it was before. Evil and destruction go their way at the heart of reality and the writer is powerless to affect them.

Slowly, under the pressure both of this insight and of the collapse of her relationship with Saul, Anna's personality disintegrates. During a violent quarrel, she turns on Saul and "names" him in the most despicable way she can imagine. By so "naming" him, she hopes to fix him in his place and in his relation to her and to the universe. Her words are prompted by Saul's wonder that she lets him attack her verbally over and over:

I shouted at him: "Like all Americans you've got mother-trouble. You've fixed on me for your mother. You have to outwit me all the time, it's important that I should be outwitted. It's important to lie and be believed. Then, when I get hurt, your murderous feelings for me, for the mother, frighten you, so that you have to comfort and soothe me . . ." I stopped and looked at him. His face was the face of a child who has been smacked. "And now you're feeling pleasure because you've provoked me into screaming at you. Why aren't you angry? You ought to be—I'm naming you, Saul Green, and I'm naming you on such a low level that you ought to be angry. You should be ashamed at the age of thirty-three, to be sitting there taking this kind of banal over-simplification from me." (*GN*, pp. 496-97)

Anna here uses the "naming game" to place Saul on a level with Dick Turner, Anton Hesse, and Douglas Knowell, characters from Lessing's earlier novels. This time, however, the "name" does not apply. Saul will not accept this relationship to Anna and to the universe. His way of rejecting his "name" is of great significance to Anna when she finally overcomes her writer's block. He counters with the weapon she herself used—with words. He talks continually and compulsively, spouting jargon, bursting forth with cant phrases about war and communism, screaming egocentric statements about himself and his character. His sentences are a meaningless jumble. But they are not fixed, they are not static, they do not allow him to be so easily typed, to be separated, to be categorized, to be "named." He holds off the horror of Anna's "name" by overwhelming it with language, by showing his own complexity in relation to the universe and his intimate connection with that universe. His words are a mixture of truth and falsehood, fact and fiction; they come from no logical, rational attempt to relate things to each other. They simply pour forth naturally. Anna finally breaks into this verbal torrent:

I wondered if it were right, to check this flow of words, since it was being used to hold himself together, to stop himself collapsing. Then, and it was as if a piece of machinery, a crane perhaps, accepted a great strain, I saw his body tense and concentrate and he began speaking, I say *he*, taking for granted that I can pinpoint a personality. That there is a *he* who is the real man. Why should I assume that one of the persons he is is more himself than the others? But I do. When he spoke then it was the man who thought, judged, communicated, heard what I said, accepted responsibility. (*GN*, p. 505)

Having used words to keep himself from accepting the "name" Anna gave him, Saul can now rationally accept his "responsibility" to the world and to be himself, unique, individual, a person in his own right.

Shortly after this incident Anna goes out and buys a new notebook, the golden one. Partly as a result of this scene with Saul, she begins to feel she may be able to put all of herself into a single volume, to reach a personal insight which will allow her to resolve her writer's block. She begins to comprehend how, by words, she can give meaning to the chaos of the universe and find a place for herself.[7] One evening she has a dream (about a tiger prowling in her room) and thinks she must write a play about the tiger, Saul, and herself. Then she goes on to reflect:

---

[7] In the complicated structure of the novel, Anna's insights overlap and her moods fluctuate. She does not move to knowledge in a strictly logical progression. It is the cumulative effect of all her insights, moving from optimism to pessimism and back again, which finally breaks her writer's block.

Meanwhile, with the part of my mind which, I knew, was the disinterested personality who had saved me from disintegration, I began to control my sleep. This controlling person insisted that I must put aside the play about the tiger, must stop playing with bricks. He said that instead of doing what I always do, making up short stories about life, so as not to look at it straight, I should go back and look at scenes from my life. . . . I had to "name" the frightening things, over and over, in a terrible litany; like a sort of disinfection by the conscious mind before I slept. But now, asleep, it was not making past events harmless, by naming them, but *making sure they were still there.* Yet I know that having made sure they were still there, I would have to "name" them in a different way, and that was why the controlling personality was forcing me back. (*GN*, p. 527)

In the golden notebook Anna shortly follows up this insight and goes back to "name" the events of her past life for the last time and in a different way. This "naming" finally resolves her writer's block and enables her to face what she understands as the relation between art and reality.[8]

The clues to this resolution and also to the most complex technical devices Lessing uses in her attempt to "break certain forms of consciousness" are found in the yellow notebook. Most of the pages of this notebook deal with a new novel Anna is writing even as she is undergoing therapy. Called *The Shadow of the Third*, it resembles the "Free Women" sections of *The Golden Notebook*, though it eventually trails off into incompleteness and Anna merely summarizes parts of it. Two things make this book different from *Frontiers of War* and from Anna's literal account of her years in Africa. First, it does not begin with any preconceived pattern or form; its episodes develop organically day by day, growing and evolving out of each other and not from a feverish nostalgia for form such as inspired her earlier works. Second, the novel is neither all fiction nor all fact. It does not split reality into parts and attempt to say this is all of it, this part is the whole, this part can be "named." As we watch Anna reflect on *The Shadow of the Third* and its characters, we see her growing insight into the relation of art and reality. This relation is considerably different from that implied in the "naming game."

In the earlier part of *The Shadow of the Third* Lessing uses traditional fictional techniques to record a love affair between two char-

---

[8] Twice before she had attempted to "name" the past: in her novel, *Frontiers of War*, which eventually she comes to feel is filled with "lying nostalgia" (*GN*, p. 61); and in a literal record of the events from which the novel arose. This also was a failure, full of "nostalgia" (*GN*, p. 135).

acters named Paul and Ella who resemble Anna Wulf and her former lover Michael. Later, however, Anna begins to reflect on the broader implications of this "fictional" affair and her attempts to portray it:

> Five years.
> If I were to write this novel, the main theme, or motif, would be buried, at first, and only slowly take over. The motif of Paul's wife—the third. At first Ella does not think about her. Then she has to make a conscious effort not to think about her. This is when she knows her attitude towards this unknown woman is despicable: she feels triumph over her, pleasure that she has taken Paul from her. When Ella first becomes conscious of this emotion she is so appalled and ashamed that she buries it, fast. Yet the shadow of the third grows again, and it becomes impossible for Ella not to think. She thinks a great deal about the invisible woman to whom Paul returns (and to whom he will always return), and it is now not out of triumph, but envy. She envies her. She slowly, involuntarily, builds up a picture in her mind of a serene, calm, unjealous, unenvious, undemanding woman, full of resources of happiness inside herself, self-sufficient, yet always ready to give happiness when it is asked for. It occurs to Ella (but much later, about three years on) that this is a remarkable image to have developed, since it does not correspond to anything at all Paul says about his wife. So where does the picture come from? Slowly Ella understands that this is what she would like to be herself, this imagined woman is her own shadow, everything she is not. (*GN*, p. 179)

By allowing both Ella's character and the plot of the novel to work themselves out organically and naturally, Anna uses both to help her understand her own relations with Michael, of whom Paul, Ella's lover, is also a projection.[9] Anna's love affair with Michael was the central event of her personal life during her first years in England. Like Paul, Michael is a married doctor who returns to his wife. Through the use of this "fictional" work ("fictional" in the sense that it is written by a "fictitious" character), Lessing performs another intricate step in her attempt to "break certain forms of consciousness." The "fictional" Ella, who has been created out of the conciousness of Anna Wulf, just as Anna has been created out of the consciousness of

---

[9] Anna writes of Ella at one point: "I see Ella, walking slowly about a big empty room, thinking, waiting. I, Anna, see Ella. Who is of course, Anna. But that is the point, for she is not. The moment I, Anna, write: Ella rings up Julia to announce, etc., then Ella floats away from me and becomes someone else. I don't understand what happens at the moment Ella separates herself from me and becomes Ella. No one does. It's enough to call her Ella, instead of Anna" (*GN*, p. 393).

Doris Lessing, helps Anna to understand herself, her world, and the relation of the artist to his creation.

Furthermore, the novel is one of Anna's notebooks. It is part of the chaos and will never be published. But writing it helps Anna to work out her problems, to put them in new perspective. In the novel she externalizes her confusion, accepts it for what it is, and ceases to try to impress an artificial form on reality. *The Shadow of the Third* is not filled with the nostalgia of *Frontiers of War*, nor with the "untruth" of her nonfictional account of her years in Africa. In this new novel Anna is not sure what she will find as she writes. The image of the third, the shadow of Paul's wife, emerges only after several months, as do the other motifs.[10] Nor has Anna here tried to divorce her fiction entirely from the "facts" as she did in her first novel. By implication, it seems to me, Lessing is saying that all artists should do the same: they should include the "real" and the "unreal" so that finally there is no way of telling which is more "true" or "factual." This, perhaps, is the underlying assumption behind the entire structure of *The Golden Notebook*.

Moreover, by allowing *The Shadow of the Third* to develop organically, Anna sees that it is possible to compose a novel which does not twist reality in a preconceived pattern, that does not impose a moral or a message, that does not say that murder is good or bad, that sex for its own sake is good or bad. With the writing of this novel Anna is preparing herself for the other novel she will later write, the "Free Women" sections of *The Golden Notebook*. Before starting this other novel she must learn more about herself and the relation between fiction and life. Her consideration of Ella helps her to do so. It helps her to see how not only the reading of a novel but the writing of one can change a life.

Even more important than these observations, however, in relating *The Shadow of the Third* to Lessing's structural and thematic intentions in *The Golden Notebook*, are Ella's reflections, after a visit to her father, about a novel she herself may one day write:

---

[10] Ella is better able than Anna to cope with her difficulties. After her romance with Paul breaks up she forces herself to snap out of her lethargy: "Well the cure for the sort of condition I am in is work. I shall write another novel. But the trouble is, with the last one there was never a point when I said: I shall write a novel. I found I was writing a novel. Well, I must put myself in the same state of mind—a kind of open readiness, a passive waiting. Then perhaps one day I'll find myself writing" (*GN*, p. 269).

Now, looking for the outlines of a story and finding, again and again, nothing but patterns of defeat, death, irony, she deliberately refuses them. She tries to force patterns of happiness or simple life. But she fails.

Then she finds herself thinking: I've got to accept the patterns of self-knowledge which mean unhappiness or at least a dryness. But I can twist it into victory. A man and a woman—yes. Both at the end of their tether. Both cracking up because of a deliberate attempt to transcend their own limits. And out of chaos, a new kind of strength.

Ella looks inwards, as into a pool, to find this story imaged; but it remains a series of dry sentences in her mind. She waits, she waits patiently, for the images to form, to take on life. (*GN*, pp. 399-400)

Ella realizes what Anna soon comes to know herself: she must accept the dryness and out of it find a new kind of strength. It is vital here to note that the images which forecast her novel do not finally take form in Ella's own mind. They do not even take form as "fiction" in the mind of Anna Wulf. The scene Ella imagines is one which Anna details at great length in the golden notebook, the scene between her and Saul in which they face the chaos and find their way out of it. Yet the golden notebook is not represented by Lessing as "fiction." It is represented as Anna's "true" account of what happened. It becomes "fiction," a novel, only when we distance ourselves from the postulates Lessing asks us to accept before we begin to read and when we realize that the notebooks are not real records of a real person, but the fictional devices of Doris Lessing, the creator of Anna Wulf and her world. Thus once again Lessing illustrates concretely the interplay between "fiction" and life, the unity and the mutual influence between the artist and his creation. By doing so she suggests, as she has done so often in other places and on other themes, that it is impossible to categorize, to stereotype, to dogmatize.

When Anna Wulf composes the previous passage, in the chronological sequence of *The Golden Notebook* she is almost at the time described in the golden notebook when her relationship with Saul Green is reaching its deepest intensity. She is also trying once more to "name" the events of her past life in a new way. In her dreams she sees repeated continually the events of her life in Africa; and her understanding grows that her days there were, as she says, "infected with death." One night she dreams of the hotel in which she lived and watches the building explode in a cloud like the hydrogen bomb. The scene presents itself to her neither as literal fact nor as fiction. Rather it comes into her consciousness more like a motion picture film in which both fact and fiction are mixed. After the explosion the projectionist stops the camera and runs a new part of the film. In it Anna's real world and her fictional world merge, and a man who is a composite of Ella's lover Paul and her own lover Michael appears on the screen. From this figure Anna learns the wisdom she later passes on to Saul Green and which gives them the strength to continue. The man speaks to her:

But my dear Anna, we are not the failures we think we are. We spend our lives fighting to get people very slightly less stupid than we are to accept truths that the great men have always known. They have always known, they have known for ten thousand years, that to lock a human being into solitary confinement can make a madman of him or an animal. They have always known that a poor man frightened of the police and his landlord is a slave. . . . They have always known that violence breeds violence. And we know it. But do the great masses of the world know it? No. It is our job to tell them. . . . The great men . . . know we are there, the boulder-pushers. They know we will go on pushing the boulder up the lower slopes of an immensely high mountain, while they stand on the top of the mountain, already free. All our lives, you and I, we will use all our energies, all our talents, into pushing that boulder another inch up the mountain. (*GN*, p. 529)

The projectionist now runs more film about the incidents in Anna's African experience, the incidents about which she has already written twice. Again she finds herself "naming" the people in them. At the same time, however, she knows with absolute certainty that the scenes are full of "untruth." The projectionist makes this knowledge explicit when he asks her in a mocking voice if "the emphasis is correct." His question hits directly on the final point Anna must resolve if she is again to be capable of writing fiction:

I shouted at the projectionist: "But they aren't mine, I didn't make them." At which the projectionist, almost bored with confidence, let the scenes vanish, and he waited for me to prove him wrong. And now it was terrible, because I was faced with the burden of recreating order out of the chaos that my life had become. Time had gone, and my memory did not exist, and I was unable to distinguish between what I had invented and what I had known, and I knew that what I had invented was all false. It was a whirl, an orderless dance, like the dance of the white butterflies in a shimmer of heat over the damp sandy vlei. The projectionist was still waiting, sardonic. What he was thinking got into my mind. He was thinking that the material had been ordered by me to fit what I knew, and that was why it was all false. Suddenly he said aloud: "How would June Boothby [the

daughter of the hotel owners in Africa] see that time? I bet you can't do
June Boothby." At which my mind slipped into a gear foreign to me, and I
began writing a story about June Boothby. I was unable to stop the flow of
words, and I was in tears of frustration as I wrote in the style of the most
insipid coy woman's magazine; but what was frightening was that the in-
sipidity was due to a very slight alteration of my own style, a word here
and there only. . . . (*GN*, p. 530)

Anna has understood before, and illustrated her understanding
in the many parodies she wrote for the yellow notebook, that a change
of a comma, a few adjectives added or taken away, a slight shift of
tone can cause a whole new picture of reality to emerge; but now this
knowledge strikes her as never before. Truth and lies are so close,
"reality" and "fiction" are only a hair's breadth apart. Again she asks
herself how a novelist can have the slightest faith he is not giving the
"incorrect emphasis," that he is not distorting reality according to his
subjective bias. But now she is on the verge of an answer, an answer
that will satisfy her and allow her to write once more for publication.
For the projectionist in her dreams is, she realizes, Saul Green. Saul,
the "responsible" man, is acting here as her conscience and she understands that in and through her dreams Saul will lead her to grasp the
part writing and words must play in her life. The explanation comes
soon after:

Words. Words. I play with words, hoping that some combination, even a
chance combination, will say what I want. . . . The fact is, the real experience can't be described. I think, bitterly, that a row of asterisks, like an old-
fashioned novel, might be better. Or a symbol of some kind, a circle perhaps, or a square. Anything at all, but not words. The people who have
been there, in the place in themselves where words, patterns, order, dissolve,
will know what I mean and the others won't. But once having been there,
there's a terrible irony, a terrible shrug of the shoulders, and it's not a
question of fighting it, or disowning it, or of right or wrong, but simply of
knowing it is there, always. It's a question of bowing to it, so to speak, with
a kind of courtesy, as to an ancient enemy: All right, I know you are there,
but we have to preserve the forms, don't we? And perhaps the condition of
your existing at all is precisely that we preserve the forms, create the patterns—have you thought of that? (*GN*, pp. 541-42)

This passage is central to Anna's resolution of her writer's block.
Once again she cannot refute logically the chaos she sees in herself as
a person, in the world in general, and in her profession of writing. She
found this chaos in her relationships with Michael and Saul, in her

sessions with Mrs. Marks, and in her attempts to "name" the past. Words cannot describe it; art cannot give it order. "Naming" it in the ways she has previously attempted only surrenders to it. Now, however, through the words of the composite figure, she understands that reality does indeed exist, that it is a blend of the "good" and the "bad," of "truth" and "fiction," and, most importantly, she understands that existence is better than nonexistence. It is better to be a "boulder-pusher," to accept the chaos, to fulfill one's "responsibility," than to "give in." Since this is so, then an essential condition for reality's existence is the almost futile attempt of the artist to give it form. He does this, not by artificially imposing words, but by letting the form grow organically from the whole of "reality," from "fact" and "fiction," dream and waking, the subjective and the objective.

These conclusions may not seem satisfactory to someone looking for neat logical solutions, and certainly they are not original. They rest on intuition and instinct rather than reason. But they clearly seem to be those of Anna Wulf, and, despite our previous attempts to distinguish between their points of view, they seem also to be those of Lessing. They agree both with the positive humanism of her nonfiction writing and with her statements on the dust jacket of *The Golden Notebook*. To exist is better than not to exist, to struggle is better than to give in, to face the truth and live with it is the measure of an individual's maturity. The artist—in this case, the novelist—is one who, as Anna Wulf suspected when she discussed her nightmare with Mrs. Marks, "forces this thing to be good as well as bad"; he is one who, by his refusal to "give in," by his recognition of the inescapable unity of life and art, helps to make existence possible. He does not run from the chaos, nor does he surrender to it. He merely acknowledges it and goes about his business of letting the interaction between it and his work of art form its own patterns. He does not try to find these patterns where they do not exist, nor does he artificially impose them from his own *a priori* conceptions. Through the interaction of "reality" and the work itself, the chaos is truly "contained," not in the "nostalgic" manner of *Frontiers of War*, nor of Anna's literal account, nor of the notebooks themselves.

For one last time the projectionist reruns his film:

Then the film went very fast, it flicked fast, like a dream, on faces I've seen once in the street, and have forgotten, on the slow movement of an arm, on the movement of a pair of eyes, all saying the same thing—the film was now beyond my experience, beyond Ella's, beyond the notebooks, because there

was a fusion, and instead of seeing separate scenes, people, faces, movements, glances, they were all together, the film became immensely slow
again, it became a series of moments where a peasant's hand bent to drop
seed into earth, or a rock stood glistening while water slowly wore it down,
or a man stood on a dry hillside in the moonlight, stood eternally, his rifle
ready on his arm. Or a woman lay awake in darkness, saying No, I won't
kill myself, I won't, I won't. (*GN*, p. 543)

This last running of the film and the fusing of the images helps Anna
to accept fully that reality is all of a piece, that the "emphasis" given
by herself or by June Boothby or Saul Green is all part of the whole,
and that they themselves are one with the peasant, the soldier, and
the woman fighting suicide.

    Soon Saul comes to her again for their last meeting. Both at last
have reached a new level of maturity, a moment of stasis, of peace
with each other and with their lives. Saul promises to write his own
novel if Anna will give him the golden notebook. She agrees because
he asks for it like a fellow human being who "needs" it and not as a
child begging his mother. Anna had intended to put herself in one
piece in the golden notebook; now Saul hopes to do the same. At last
they are "relying" on each other, accepting their "responsibility" for
each other. When Saul leaves, he does so knowing they are, as he puts
it, "part of the team," no matter how few the other members may be.
The golden notebook ends with a summary of Saul's novel, a story
about the execution of a French and an Algerian soldier because they
put human relationships above the politics of war. *The Golden Notebook* itself comes to a close with the fifth and final "Free Women"
section, a section "fictionally" summarizing Saul and Anna's affair
and bringing to a conclusion Anna's description of her friendships
with Molly, Tommy, Marion, and Richard.

    By the end of the novel, Anna, finally, through her sessions with
Mrs. Marks, her relationship with Saul, her love of her daughter Janet,
and, most importantly perhaps, through writing her notebooks, has
come to understand her role as an artist. The "Free Women" sections
of *The Golden Notebook*, a mingling of "fact" and "fiction," a form
based not on nostalgia but on the unity of life and art, are the result.
And Lessing herself, who is "responsible" for the whole novel, seems,
by her intricate structure, by her involved chronological sequence, by
the mutual interrelation between her "fictional" and her "real" characters, to be illustrating this unity. If *The Golden Notebook* finally is
a book about "alienation," as she suggests, it is also a book which in

the end shows us how to accept alienation and live with it. The last sentence of the novel indicates what Lessing seems ultimately to be saying: "The two women [Anna and Molly] kissed and separated" (*GN*, p. 568). Anna Wulf, it would seem, has at last become her own woman; she has accepted herself for what she is and can walk free in her own person. By writing the "Free Women" sections of *The Golden Notebook*, she has fulfilled her "responsibility" as a writer and as a human being; she has fought the chaos and resisted the nostalgia. Now she can go on "pushing boulders"; she can, despite the pressures of society and the more profound and universal pressures of her own human nature, change history, even if only infinitesimally.

The Pietà as Icon
in *The Golden Notebook*

Evelyn J. Hinz and John J. Teunissen

"We can't either of us ever go lower than that," comments Saul Green after his climactic final encounter with Anna Wulf in the chapter of *The Golden Notebook* which gives the work its title. "No," Anna replies in agreement; and her lover concludes, "Well *that's* played out."[1] What it is that is "played out" in the encounter of Anna and Saul is in general terms the subject of the following discussion. More specifically, our concern is with the three aspects of the encounter toward which this interchange seems to direct our attention: first, in what sense what is played out is of the lowest character; second, why there is a formulaic character about the encounter, a quality of re-enactment and necessity; and third, in what way the drama is a thera-peutic one, *i.e.* why it generates relief.

To appreciate this crucial scene it is essential first to have a clear understanding of the nature of the section of which it is the culmina-tion. The Saul Green section of *The Golden Notebook* is the nadir of the psychological process of the novel, for it is in this section that Anna Wulf's impending madness[2] becomes a reality and she becomes

---

[1] Doris Lessing, *The Golden Notebook* (1962; rpt. New York: Ballantine Books, 1972), p. 641. All further parenthetical page references will be to this text.

[2] The term "madness" and its synonyms will be used throughout this essay as words connoting the irrational rather than psychic sickness, since this usage is Lessing's own as well as a central point of the novel in general.

a total victim of the irrational forces of her psyche. This governing information is conveyed in two related ways. First, we discover Anna concluding that Saul Green is insane because he denies having uttered certain words, etc.; the words Anna attributes to Saul, however, are those she had recorded in the earlier sections of her notebooks with respect to her previous affairs and those of her fictional characters. It is not Saul but Anna who is mad; she has lost all power to distinguish between the past and the present, between fact and fantasy. Second, we learn that Saul Green himself is not a flesh and blood character but a projection of a maddened imagination upon a normal, healthy, and good-natured male named "Milt" who appears in the final section of *The Golden Notebook*. We are clued to this situation in the penultimate section by Anna's ironic and inverted puzzlement over the difference between Saul and the type of man she had expected, and the confirmation is provided in the final section when we discover, through the character of Milt, that her defeated expectations embodied the reality.[3] The following scene, then, must be understood as the imaginative construct of a woman who is mad and a projection of and hence an index to her madness.

The encounter of Anna and Saul occurs on the morning following his announcement that he is going to leave her. Anna has wakened first, and seeing the "ill and thin" face of her lover as he lies sleeping she mentally argues that he is in no condition to leave and

---

[3] The Saul Green episode of *The Golden Notebook* consists of two parts: the fourth blue notebook (the blue notebooks being the "diary" section of the quartet) and the golden notebook (designed as the one composite notebook and the end of Anna's departmentalizing—"all of myself in one book"). The two parts are unified by the fact of Anna's madness but distinguished by the nature and degree of her irrationality. In the blue notebook Saul is an antagonistic projection, reflecting Anna's tendency to hold others responsible for the destruction she has experienced; in the golden notebook Anna identifies Saul as her "projectionist" and is brought to admit that the scenes of violence and distortions of the truth that haunt her from her past were "Directed by Anna Wulf." Consequently, Anna's madness has a defensive and hence negative quality in the blue notebook and takes a positive direction in the golden notebook, where she surrenders to the dictates of her unconscious.

This difference between the two parts of the Saul Green episode is obviously important for a total appreciation of the psychology of *The Golden Notebook*, but in view of the failure of so many critics to recognize that Saul Green is a projection and not a "real" character (see, for example, Dorothy Brewster, *Doris Lessing* [New York:Twayne, 1955], p. 147), it has seemed best to concentrate this discussion upon the fact of Anna's madness and its basic direction and to reserve qualifications for succeeding studies of the work.

thus that she cannot let him go. As he wakes, she fights her desire to
say: "You can't go. I must look after you. I'll do anything if only
you'll stay with me." As she sees it, Saul is similarly fighting his desire,
and watching him she wonders what would be their present situation
if at the beginning of their affair some weeks ago he had not unconsciously reached up in his sleep and put his arms around her neck. It is
this that she wants him to do now, at the same time that she troubles
over the recognition that to touch him would constitute a betrayal. The
exhaustion occasioned by the emotional struggle causes her to black
out, and in this unconscious state she surrenders to her desire: "I
cradled him in my arms." He in turn clings to her and murmurs in a
child's voice, "Ise a good boy." As she looks down upon him in this
position, she observes three facial expressions: "first the sentimental
falseness that went with the words; then a grimace of pain; then, seeing me look down, in horror, his grey eyes narrowed into a pure hating
challenge, and we looked at each other helpless with our mutual shame
and humiliation" (pp. 640-41).

The encounter in one sense then can be viewed as the lowest in
that it is at once a parody of the relationship between a mother and
her child and a perversion of the normal sexual relationship between
a man and a woman. Lowest, on the one hand then, connotes the conventional sense of debasement. There is, however, another sense in
which the encounter represents an ultimate low, an archetypal sense in
which low refers to something basic in the individual and collective
psyche, to some primal and eternal image of the relationship between
the male and the female located in the unconscious and known to us
in its projected form in the great artifacts of our culture.

If we focus in visual and objective fashion upon the pictorial
quality of Anna's narrative of the encounter, the following interlock-
ing images appear to be projected: first, a woman gazing down with
pity upon the "lifeless" body of a man; next, the figures in the position
of mother and child. Adopting the method of Anna's psychoanalyst,
"Mother Sugar," we could "name" the first image "woman grieving for
her dead lover or brother," and the second, "Madonna and infant."
More specifically, to the Greek mind the first image would connote
the tale of Antigone and her heroic attempt to give proper burial to
her brother, and one notices that Antigone is one of the names that
Mother Sugar gives to Anna (p. 5). Thus in isolation are projected
the two major faces of woman in her relationship to man: lover—or
sister—and mother. These images, however, are not isolated as Anna

projects them; they conflate, the second becomes a gloss on the text of the first, and a composite third image establishes itself—the image of the young mother bending with compassion over the grown body of the son who lies in her lap. Some readers perhaps, like Anna, will require the insistence of a Mother Sugar to articulate the name of this icon, but few will not recognize in Anna's projection the archetype embodied in Michelangelo's Pietà, the archetype of the "Great Mother" in our Western cultural tradition.

"I was thinking how extraordinary that an act of kindness, of pity, could be such a betrayal," Anna remembers, describing her feelings just before she succumbed to her desire to cradle her lover in her arms. The recognition of the archetype evoked in the scene poses a similar problem for the reader: how can the adoption by Anna and Saul of the roles of the Virgin Mother and her dead Son be a matter of "mutual shame and humiliation"; how can Anna's Madonna pose and tenderness be considered a betrayal, and a betrayal of what; why does Anna look down with horror and Saul look up with hate when they have surrendered themselves to the archetypal relationship? Before attempting to answer these questions,[4] it will be best to consider the way in which Lessing prepares us for the shock of recognition which the encounter generates, since the questions the episode raises concerning the nature of the archetype embodied in the Pietà are such that we may be inclined to mask our reluctance to face them by denying that it is this archetype that is evoked at all.

Milt, the "real" lover who comes to Anna's flat, is a young man "with close young brown hair, like healthy fur, a lean intelligent face, bespectacled . . . the shrewd, competent, intelligent American" (p. 654). After giving him a Hebraic name, Anna exchanges his healthy physique for a diminished sickly one, ironically contrasting the image he thus presents with that which she says one would expect of an American: "He is not tall, though I keep thinking of him as tall, and then checking again and seeing he was not. . . . One would expect him to be that fair, rather stocky, broad-shouldered American type . . ." (p. 550); "Earlier I had kept looking at him, uneasy, because of how I was expecting to see something different from what he was, and seeing the thin bony man in loose hanging clothes" (p. 553). The

---

[4] Before Lessing, D.H. Lawrence raised—and answered—these same questions in his portrait of the crippled Clifford Chatterley in the arms of the Magna Mater, Mrs. Bolton. We have discussed the implications of Lawrence's use of the Pietà in *Lady Chatterley's Lover* in another essay on the nature of the archetype informing Michelangelo's statue.

definitive characteristics of Anna's transformation, however, are Saul
Green's "unhealthy whiteness," the "deadly coldness" of his body, and
his filial responses toward her.

Anna comes to Saul's room one evening and finds him asleep,
"in a tight curve under neat bedclothes." When he does not answer her
call, she touches him, and his "absolute stillness" frightens her with
the thought that "he was dead." She becomes even more terrified when
she attempts to turn him over and feels "the cold heavy quality of his
flesh." But at this point Saul awakes, and Anna observes: "He simultaneously put his arms up around my neck, in a frightened child's
gesture." "You sleep very heavily," Anna says to him (pp. 555-56).

The operative words and gestures are emphasized when a little
later in the narrative Anna describes a similar bedside encounter. She
awakes to find Saul lying on his back against her, "a weight of inert
dense cold flesh" (p. 562). She looks at him as he sleeps and notices
that "he was locked in fear, and he began to whimper, like a child
afraid." With a feeling of love and compassion she begins to rub his
body, explaining, "Towards morning he gets very cold, the cold was
coming out of him, with the smell of being afraid. When he was
warmed, I put myself back to sleep. . . . When I woke, Saul was again
cold in my arms, a weight of cold" (p. 563).

The third time Anna keeps her ghastly vigil the positions assumed
by the lovers in their final encounter are anticipated and the name of
the Savior is specifically introduced. Saul lies sleeping and Anna lies
beside him; she attempts to fit herself to "the curve of his back," and
when despite the contact he does not move: "I tightened my hold on
him, and he turned, abrupt, his arm up to ward off a blow, and saw
me. His face was dead white, the bones of his face sticking out through
thin skin, his eyes a sick lustreless grey. He flung his head on to my
breasts and I held him" (p. 594). Saul then goes back to sleep and
Anna lies once more "with the cold weight of this man." She tries to
warm him: "But his cold crept into me, so I gently shoved and pushed
him under the blankets and we lay under warm fibres and slowly the
cold went away and his flesh warmed against mine" (p. 594). During
this "Cold Pastoral!" as we would say with Keats in his "Ode on a
Grecian Urn," Anna dreams a consummation between herself and
Saul, but a consummation celebrating destruction. In the morning the
consummation is physically enacted, and the lovemaking is concluded
and punctuated when Saul sits up and says, "Jesus, what time is it. . . .
Christ, I can't sleep my life away like this" (p. 595). Our first im-

pression may be to pass off the presence of the divine names as typical male expletives. But Milt, the "real" lover, never uses these words; his typical expletive is "Gee!" And if in turn we note that "Gee" is a slang synonym for "Jesus," we are left attempting to account for why Anna should prefer the "original."

Thus the blasphemous expletives similarly function as directives when Anna programs Saul's future for him in response to his question, "What's going to happen to me, Anna?"; "You'll become a very gentle, wise, kind man who people will come to when they need to be told that—they're crazy in a good cause"; "Jesus, Anna," is Saul's reply (p. 626). The blasphemies continue as Anna then begins to attack this image of Saul as the serene comforter as a disguise for his emotional cannibalism and goes on to define the sacrificial victim as a defeated cannibal. She tells Saul that people will view him as the epitome of spiritual fortitude; but every now and then, she warns, "one of the corpses" will utter "a small self-pitying bleat." He replies that the "corpses" are all on his side. She retaliates that the willingness of the victims does not remedy the situation; he argues that he is good for people. "Nonsense," she says; "The people who are oh so willing to be victims are those who've given up being cannibals themselves. . . . They know they've given up. What they are really saying is: *I've* given up, but I'll be happy to contribute my flesh and blood to you." Saul concludes the conversation with the words, "Crunch, crunch, crunch," and Anna repeats the refrain (p. 627). On a lighter note is Anna's ridicule of Saul as a "pedagogue" when according to her narrative, one afternoon, after "walking through the streets, walking through the chaos of his imagination, clutching at ideas or sets of words to save him," he returns to find her laughing, and to his questioning of the reason for her hilarity, she replies: "Because you've been rushing about a crazy city, making sets of moral axioms to save us both with, like mottoes out of Christmas crackers" (p. 638).

The conclusive instance of the Pietà roles into which Anna casts herself and her lover, however, is to be found in the doubly mad and ironic passage in which she assaults her own creation of the Madonna-oriented Son: "Like all Americans you've got mother-trouble," she shouts at him; "You've fixed on me for your mother." She stops her hysterical screaming for a minute to observe that his face "was the face of a child who has been smacked," and then goes on: "Why aren't you angry? You ought to be—I'm naming you, Saul Green, and I'm naming you on such a low level that you ought to be angry. You should be ashamed, at the age of thirty-three, to be sitting there taking this kind of banal over-simplification from me" (p. 581).

To appreciate the archetypal thrust of Anna's "over-simplification" one need only notice two things. First, Milt, the man who comes to Anna's flat, is thirty, the age of Christ before he left his private life for his public one—the turning point being his surrender to his Mother's wishes at the Wedding Feast at Cana. Saul is the same age as the Savior when he died—the culmination of the public career into which his mother urged him. The difference between Milt and Saul Green is thus not merely three years but the difference between Jesus before and after he gave in to his mother's wishes. This implication is confirmed by the second difference between Milt and Saul that is highlighted here. Anna accuses Saul of having a mother-fixation; one of the first things that Milt tells Anna about his background has to do with a friend of his: "If you very naturally want to know what his relation to me was, he was my father-figure" (pp. 655-56).

Finally, by way of this conclusive evidence of the Christian prototype inherent in Anna's image of Saul Green, we are prepared to appreciate the passage in which the two senses in which their encounter represents an ultimate low are related—the sexual and the psychological or archetypal. The relationship is established through a play on the phrase "getting laid" and in the manner of the seventeenth-century pun on the phrase "to die." Saul, according to Anna, has been speaking of a friend who has become tired of having affairs, and she asks him whether this friend intends "to give up *getting laid*." The emphasis is hers and by way of accounting for the irritability it reveals she explains, "Whenever you talk about sex or love you say: he got laid, I got laid or they got laid (male)." Saul does not get her point, so she continues, "Always in the passive." Saul still does not comprehend, so she explains, "It gives me the most extraordinary uneasy feeling, listening to you—surely *I* get laid, *she* gets laid, they (female) get laid, but surely you, as a man, don't get laid, you lay" (p. 559).

The "uneasy feeling" may very well arise from Anna's awareness of the other meaning of the operative phrase, for men do "get laid"— when they are dead, as we remember from the gospel descriptions of the burial of Christ: "And when Joseph had taken the body, he wrapped it in a clean linen cloth. And laid it in his own new tomb, which he had hewn out in the rock" (Matt. 27: 59-60); "And he bought fine linen, and took him down, and wrapped him in the linen, and laid him in a sepulchre which was hewn out of a rock, and rolled a stone unto the door of the sepulchre. And Mary Magdalene and Mary the mother of Jesus beheld where he was laid" (Mark 15: 46-47); "And he took it down and wrapped it in linen, and laid it in a sepulchre that was hewn in stone, wherein never man before was laid. . . . And the women also, which came with him from Galilee, followed after, and beheld the sepulchre, and how his body was laid" (Luke 23: 53-55); "Now in the place where he was crucified there was a garden; and in the garden a new sepulchre, wherein was never man yet laid. There laid they Jesus" (John 19: 41-42). The prototypic example of the passive male, the man who was "laid," then, is the dead Christ, the Son of the Virgin Mother, in whose lap his body was laid, as depicted in the Pietà icon. In her madness then, not only has Anna Wulf transformed Milt into Saul Green, she has also shrouded him in the image of the dead Christ.The question why her unconscious should project itself in this form leads us into a discussion of the factors precipitating her madness.

Anna Freeman became a "Wulf" by reason of her marriage to a man she did not love, a man she had lived with for three years in a spirit of brother-sister friendship and sexual incompatibility, a man by whom she has had a child as a result of a last ditch attempt to put some meaning into her life, and a man whom she married for the sake of the child and whom she divorced immediately following its birth. During this period Anna also experienced one totally fulfilling sexual encounter: "I have never, in all my life, been so desperately and wildly and painfully happy as I was then," she recalls (p. 150). The encounter took place against a background of violence, and as Anna remembers it was the juxtaposition of the ugly and the beautiful that profoundly impressed her. The man's name was Paul, and it was this man who idolized Anna as "beautiful Anna, absurd Anna, mad Anna, our consolation in this wilderness"—a chant that Anna describes as having been "a kind of revelation" (p. 120). But Paul died—the day before he was about to leave the "wilderness." "His last evening," as Anna records it, was spent at a party, drinking with the other members of the "Colony." The following morning, "as the sun was coming up," Paul went to say goodbye to his friends at the camp, and there occurred his death and his transfiguration: "He was standing on the air-strip . . . the rising sun in his eyes—though of course, being Paul, he would not have shown the state he was in. A plane came in to land, and stopped a few paces away. Paul turned, his eyes dazzling with the sunrise, and walked straight into the propeller, which must have been an almost

invisible sheen of light. His legs were cut off just below the crutch and
he died at once" (p. 78).

For five years during her career as a "free" woman following this
affair and her divorce from Max Wulf, Anna has lived with a man
named Michael. "This affair had broken up three years ago, against
her will," we learn in the opening chapter of *The Golden Notebook*.
(For three years then, Anna has been separated from her lover, as
for three years the Virgin was distanced from her Son by reason of his
public duties.) A month prior to the date on which the work begins,
Michael has returned for a casual and brief visit to his former mistress.
Anna's first words at the beginning of the novel are: "The point is . . .
the point is, that as far as I can see, everything's cracking up" (p. 3);
her final words at the conclusion of the first chapter center upon her
confession to her friend Molly: "Because when I really face it I don't
think I've ever really got over Michael" (p. 53)—a fact which is
symbolized first, by the flat she returns to as she leaves her friend, a
flat too large for her private needs but one which she had rented to
accommodate her lover and one which she continues to rent in antici-
pation of his return; and second, by the notebooks which record Anna's
attempt to come to terms from a multitude of angles with the nature
of Michael's betrayal. The central rationalization she clings to is that
Michael was jealous of the attention Anna paid to her daughter and
unable to appreciate her motherly responsibilities.

Compounding Anna's inability to get over her lost lover are the
other men with whom she has and continues to come into contact:
these generally fall into two types, the homosexuals who revolt her with
their parody of male-female relationships and who as female imper-
sonators reflect too sharply the pathos of the "kept" woman, and the
boy-men who ascribe their impotence to the fault of the female and
who force the woman to compensate for their inadequacies by building
them into the image of "real men." A final contributing factor to
Anna's madness is the attempted suicide of the son of Anna's liberated
friend, an attempt Anna feels was precipitated by his reading of her
notebooks, and one which culminates in an affair between the son and
the present wife of his father, another betrayed woman, Marion.

The factors impelling Anna toward chaos, then, range from a
sense of betrayal by real men to the sense of guilt for the psychosexual
and physical crippling of a son, with a fear of the perversity and
hostility of the woman-ridden half-men in the middle. Anna's controlling and persistent defense against the threatening chaos is her
image of herself as the good mother—the all-loving, all-giving, creative

woman, the principle of all life and goodness. Whenever madness threatens, whenever she must check an irrational mood, whenever her feelings become violent and aggressive, she is able to sustain her sanity by composing herself into the role of Janet's mother. In turn, as we have seen in her rationalization of Michael's desertion, Janet, her daughter, is the excuse she uses to deny her personal responsibility for the condition of her affairs, and the activities associated with motherhood are the means she uses to prevent herself from facing the nature of her role as a woman.

Hence the stage for Anna's mad encounter is set when Janet leaves the flat for boarding school and the curtain is rung up with the entrance of Milt. Stripped of her defenses, Anna must come face to face with the selves she had cloaked within the mantle of maternity, and disrobed of her excuses she must put the strength of her power as a woman to the test. "In a month Janet will be home and this Anna will cease to exist," she tells herself at one point in the agony; "If I know I can switch off this helpless sufferer because it is necessary for Janet, then I can do it now. Why don't I?" There are two answers: "Because I don't want to, that's why" and "Something has to be played out, some pattern has to be worked through . . ." (p. 583). What is played out is the other side of the role of the Great Mother—the death-dealing, revengeful, castrating female.

Anna has been betrayed by death on the one hand and by sexuality on the other; Paul died and Michael refused her love. And with Max Wulf she was frigid, cold. In her relationship with Saul Green, Anna takes vengeance on all three. To lay the ghost of Paul, Anna resurrects him as the pale and preachy Saul (an inversion, incidentally, of the prototypic Christian conversion experience) and then destroys him by attacking her image of him as "the original puritan, Saul Galahad to the defence" (p. 559). Similarly, the emotional frigidity which Anna experienced with the intellectual Max is avenged in her transference of this quality to the physical condition of her lover's body: Saul's flesh is cold and inert. But it is upon Michael who betrayed her love that Anna takes her choicest revenge.

We have observed the manner in which Anna transforms the healthy Milt into the sickly Saul; at the same time that she does this, however, she also creates the image of Saul as the epitome of virile sexuality: "sexy, he-man, all balls and strenuous erection. He stood lounging, his thumbs hitched through his belt, fingers loose, but pointing as it were to his genitals. . . . It was unconscious but it was directed at me, and it was so crude I began to be annoyed" (p. 553). Her revenge is first to castrate him, which she does by evoking his other face: "I asked why he wore his clothes so big and he looked startled, as if he were surprised I had noticed it, and then evasive, and said he had lost a lot of weight, he was normally a couple of stones heavier" (p. 550; do readers perhaps need to be informed that stone is a measure of weight as well as a synonym for testicle?). In similar fashion she describes how she "took off the Armstrong, and put on his music, cool and cerebral, the detached music for men who refuse the madness and the passion, and for a moment he stopped, then sat, as if the muscles of his thighs had been cut" (p. 629).

Anna, as we have noticed, has made Janet the excuse for her failure to respond to and retain Michael. She introduces this explanation similarly as she prepares for Saul's imminent departure: "If I had had a son, you'd have stayed. You'd have identified with him. . . . But since I've got a girl you'll go because you'll see us as . . . two enemies. . . . But it was chance I had a girl and not a boy. Just pure chance. So it's chance you'll leave" (p. 622). There is, however, one way to eliminate this chance—namely, to turn the lover into a son, and it is precisely this transformation that Anna effects and that is reflected in that lowest of encounters with which the Saul Green episode is concluded.

The consciousness of the Western cultural tradition has been shaped by the image of the Great Mother as the good mother; the unconsciousness apparently recognizes another face.[5] But the horror of this situation does not lie in the disjunction of the two aspects but in the denial of the reality of the "other face," a denial which results in perversion and insanity. The horror does not arise from the "negative" reality but from the perversions that result from its denial. It was Anna's single-minded devotion to her role as good mother to Janet that ultimately occasioned her madness by forcing her to suppress the feelings that could not be accommodated to this image, just as it was Tommy's exposure to two husbandless mothers who scorned materialistic concerns and urged him toward idealistic goals that turned him into a sightless cripple with an oedipal fixation.

---

[5] Numerous psychological studies have explored this aspect, but for the literary scholar, Rudolf Otto's *The Idea of the Holy: An Inquiry into the Non-rational Factor in the Idea of the Divine and Its Relation to the Rational*, trans. John H. Harvey (New York: Oxford Univ. Press, 1969), and Robert Graves' *The White Goddess: A Historical Grammar of Poetic Myth*, amended and enlarged edition (New York: Noonday, 1969) provide the most impressive investigations of the subject.

A correlative of our Western culture's worship of the Great Mother as the *good* mother and refusal to admit the destructive aspect of the archetype is our commitment to rationality and rejection of the irrational on the one hand and our emphasis upon individuality and belief in the historical uniqueness of the individual on the other. Anna Wulf epitomizes the mentality when she ridicules her psychoanalyst's interpretations of her dilemma as a "writer's block" and her insistence that she "name," that is recognize, the archetypal nature of her situation and her dreams.

"Mother Sugar," the name that Anna and Molly have devised to express their antagonism to the cosmic balm that the psychoanalyst applies to their personal wounds, is in theory a descendant of the post-Freudian Otto Rank and Carl Jung. She is introduced in the opening chapter of *The Golden Notebook* when in reply to Molly's assertion that she and Anna are "free" women and thus represent "a completely new type of woman," Anna quotes with an attempt at a German accent, "There's nothing new under the sun" (p. 4). This motto of Mrs. Marks, the real name of the psychoanalyst, is quite obviously the ancient version of Jung's (*pace* Solomon and Schopenhauer) theory of archetypes and their origin in the collective unconscious.

According to Jung the self is a composite of the individual and the collective psyche, the particularized consciousness and the primordial unconsciousness;[6] according to Mother Sugar, "All self-knowledge is knowing, on deeper and deeper levels, what one knew before" (p. 238). We recognize immediately that this theory provides the rationale for Lessing's technique in *The Golden Notebook*; Anna can write what is to happen in advance of the happening because everything that happens has happened before and psychological progress is essentially a matter of discovering who one is and consequently what it is that one is going to do. Anna, of course, is antagonistic to this idea, and herein lies her central problem; she is antagonistic because the collective conclusion to her tale—the other face of her motherly love—is one she does not want to admit; she is antagonistic because of the threat which the archetypes pose to her ego and her Western worship of individuality.

A further point of contact between Jung and *The Golden Note-*

---

[6] See "Aion: Contributions to the Symbolism of the Self," in *Psyche and Symbol: A Selection from the Writings of C.G. Jung*, ed. Violet A. de Laszlo (New York: Doubleday, 1958), pp. 1-60. Jung's theory of the "anima" and "animus" is also theoretically central to and explanatory of the psychomachian nature of the Saul Green section.

book is the emphasis placed by him and by Mrs. Marks on the necessity of dreaming and the nature of projection. Anna takes the tough
realist position that dreams are an escape from reality and scorns Mrs.
Marks's emphasis upon writing as the cure for her "illness" and upon
her insistence that it is her "writer's block" that is at once a symptom
and a cause of her psychological problems. What *The Golden Notebook* illustrates, however, is that Anna's escape has been into her
conscious role and that it is in the concealed notebooks that the truth
of her situation and character is to be found; that only after she has
faced this other half of the world and given it form and projected her
subjective in archetypal images is she "free." The "name game" Mrs.
Marks plays is a method of connecting the autotypic experience with
the prototypic image, in Anna's case a matter of connecting the men
she has "lost" with the dead Christ in the Pietà icon, of connecting her
role in their destruction with the Virgin who cradles the corpse.

The point toward which Mrs. Marks continually attempts to lead
Anna is a recognition of the creative and positive value of destructive
forces, personal as well as collective. In this respect she is closely
allied with Otto Rank in his insistence upon the positive and life-
productive nature of the irrational. The irrational, as he sees it, is the
basis of human behavior, and neurosis arises from the attempts to deny
its vital existence by way of asserting the rational as the natural and
the irrational as the unnatural. The truth, on the contrary, he argues,
is that the rational is a necessary but a life-denying force and that the
function of the irrational is to prevent the cultural suicide that civilization impels us towards: "We still have to learn, it seems, that life, in
order to maintain itself, must revolt every so often against man's cease-
less attempts to master its irrational forces with his mind."[7] As the
outcome of *The Golden Notebook* demonstrates, Anna Wulf's surrender to the irrational has been her salvation; her experience with
Saul Green has been a cathartic and therapeutic one as best indicated
by the fact that she is able to say to Milt "I want you to stay" and when
he rightly interprets her words as a notice of his dismissal and asks
why he should have to go, to reply, "Because I want you to stay."
Similarly, we discover that when Janet arrives Anna is "in the process
of finding another, smaller flat" (p. 664), in short, of facing the fact
that Michael will not be coming back. The irrational forces operative
in the Saul Green section, then, are creative and conducive to life and

---

[7] Otto Rank, *Beyond Psychology* (New York: Dover, 1958), p. 18. This
work of Rank's is incomplete and was first published posthumously in 1941.

psychic health. But the irrational in this instance projected itself in terms of one of the central icons of our culture and took the form of a destruction of the totally positive face we traditionally read in the statue. The issue that *The Golden Notebook* therefore raises is a cultural as well as an aesthetic one; namely, does the Virgin of our culture have a darker face which only madness is able to recognize, and is this darker face the creative one and the stoic serenity of the good face a life-denying one? Is the shock we experience when we discover Anna's "joy in destruction" projecting itself in terms of the archetype embodied in the Pietà a shock of recognition or a shock of outrage—and if the latter is it because of the recognition?

"It was that damned art all over the place," Anna says to Molly in the opening chapter of *The Golden Notebook*, recollecting her "last" meeting with Mother Sugar; "I remember that afternoon, knowing I'd never go back" (p. 5). Anna's determination not to return arises from her fear of recognizing her own features in the representations in the psychoanalyst's room, and the thematic result of her decision is her psychic collapse. But during her period of madness, Anna does "go back"; she descends to the lowest and most primal reaches of the collective unconscious, and this ultimate point in her regression is symbolized by her projection of herself as the Great Mother of the Western and Judaeo-Christian tradition, the Virgin Mother depicted in Michelangelo's Pietà. The icon, the episode thus generally seems to suggest, is the artistic representation which most directly reflects the imagistic content of the unconscious, and the Pietà is the icon which best embodies the most basic archetypes of the Western mentality. The nature of the iconographic scene, however, does not endorse the traditional interpretation of the Great Mother as the good mother, but rather emphasizes the darker face of the resigned Madonna and the destructive nature of maternal love, and thereby evokes the true archetype of the Magna Mater. Hence an examination of the Pietà as icon in *The Golden Notebook* is not only essential for our understanding of the work itself, but it also leads us to a better appreciation of, first, the role of iconography in literature; second, the importance of iconology in archetypal criticism; and third, the relationship between a culture's icons and its psychic health.

Alienation of the Woman Writer in *The Golden Notebook*

Ellen Morgan

In her interview at Stony Brook (1969), Doris Lessing said, "I'm impatient with people who emphasize sexual revolution. I say we should all go to bed, shut up about sexual liberation, and go on with the important matters."[1] But looking at the text of *The Golden Notebook*, which is, after all, about the female-male relationship in the middle of the twentieth century and about the meaning of femaleness in contemporary Western culture, one cannot help being being aware of the tension that exists between Lessing's sensitive observations of the malaise between the sexes and such denials of the importance of discomfort with the sexual status quo.

In the course of *The Golden Notebook*, Lessing writes in the persona of Anna: "the quality a novel should have to make it a novel [is] the quality of philosophy. . . . Yet I am incapable of writing the only kind of novel which interests me: a book powered with an intellectual or moral passion strong enough to create order, to create a new way of looking at life."[2] This statement is a good entrance into *The Golden Notebook*, for the novel contains all the perceptions neces-

---

[1] Jonah Raskin, "Doris Lessing at Stony Brook: An Interview," *New American Review 8* (New York: New American Library, 1969), p. 175.

[2] Doris Lessing, *The Golden Notebook* (New York: Ballantine Books, 1962), p. 61. All subsequent references in the text are to this edition.

sary to create a radical transforming and ordering vision of the relationship between women and men. These perceptions, however, are
not gathered into the philosophical form proper to and inherent in
them. Reading *The Golden Notebook* carefully forces one to realize
how women writers can be, and have been, alienated from their own
authentic, sensitive, and accurate perceptions of sexual politics because nowhere in their culture, in eras in which feminism is kept
quiescent and latent, do they see such perceptions corroborated rather
than made targets of antifeminist criticism, ridicule, and disparage-
ment.

The world of *The Golden Notebook* consists, in addition to its
artistic, racial, and other political dimensions, of Anna Wulf's closely
rendered experiences with a number of acquaintances and lovers,
sometimes told through Ella, her alter-ego and literary creation. But
more significantly, the book consists of Anna-Ella's interpretations of
these experiences, her judgments and evaluations of them and of herself. Repeatedly, as I shall attempt to show, her judgments belittle,
deny, or distort her experiences and censor her spontaneous responses
to them. The difference between Ella's actual attitudes and responses
and those she does not permit herself is the measure of her alienation
from her own perceptions and, I believe, the extent of Lessing's failure to come to terms with female authenticity.

Ella and her friend Julia quite obviously feel, on the one hand,
an instinctive human need to respect themselves as people, and, on
the other, a conditioned contempt for themselves as women. Spontaneously they trust one another and are very close, but they *judge*
this trust to be less valuable than they *feel* it to be, less valuable than
their far less trusting relationships with men. As Anna says of herself
and Molly, no matter how close they are on the basis of shared understanding, experience, and life style, their "real loyalties are always to
men, and not to women" (p. 48). Anna-Ella feels strongly inclined
to discuss with Molly-Julia her problems with men, but she judges
that all the "complaints and the reproaches and the betrayals" (p. 48)
ought not to be voiced. These judgments, which undermine the solidarity between the two women, are the result of their conviction that
men are superior to women and that their own self-interest lies not in
relationships with women but in those with men, however damaging
individual female-male relationships may be. The two women share a
minority-group psychological orientation which compels them to de-
preciate their femaleness and their friendship and seek approval from

and identification with men. This fact becomes clear when Ella describes the contempt she feels for the magazine for which she works (p. 178) and even for the stories she writes because they are "feminine" (p. 170). The two women also reveal this self-deprecatory orientation by blaming only themselves for troubles to which men have contributed, as Julia wryly recognizes (p. 458).

Ella judges that the future without a man is unimaginable. But she hates the parties she has to go to in order to meet men because the parties make her aware of the fact that she is "on the market again" (p. 171). Neither Ella nor Julia, however, thinks that there is any use indulging in complaint over this fact. Julia says, "It's no good taking that attitude—that's how everything is run, isn't it?" (p. 171). The two women thus dismiss their feelings, convinced that they have no legitimate grounds for complaint and that complaining would only be self-pity.

The pattern of opposition between feelings and judgment is shown in particularly high relief when Dr. West, Ella's employer, tries to start an affair with her while his wife is away. When she refuses, he turns to the other women in his office and finally to the eldest, who is grateful and flattered. Ella's spontaneous reaction is to become "angry on behalf of her sex," but she quickly turns away this feeling, telling herself that the emotion really is "rooted in a resentment that has nothing to do with Dr. West" (p. 450), a resentment which she sees as shameful. Ella retreats from sympathizing with the older woman for fear of "cutting off some possibility for herself" (p. 203). She feels a natural bond with other women but judges solidarity with them dangerous because it is to men that women, she believes, must turn for any advantages which they may gain.

"Sometimes," says Julia, "I think we're all in a sort of sexual mad house" (p. 458). But Ella tries to quash this rebellious reaction in her friend and in herself: "My dear Julia, we've chosen to be free women, and this is the price we pay, that's all" (p. 458). Neither woman considers actually fighting back; there is no visible solidarity among women which would sanction and support such rebellion. Moreover, their analysis of the situation is fundamentally apolitical. For example, Ella says that unlike men, women cannot obtain sexual satisfaction without love, and that therefore the inequality in sexual relations is inherent. Neither woman sees that the vulnerability she feels may be caused not by some kind of fixed biological or psychological difference between the sexes, but by the fact that in a culture in which sex is still apt to be viewed as a kind of conquest for the man, the psychologically healthy woman cannot afford to experience sexual relations without asking love in return to even the bargain. Ella and Julia know that the kind of sex offered them is a threat to their dignity and self-respect. They cannot act directly while holding the apolitical view they do of female-male relations, but neither is willing simply to capitulate—hence their bickering and criticism of men and Ella's inability to function sexually unless she is in love.

Most of Ella's keenest observations are followed by turnings away, efforts to escape the essentially political consequences of their logic. She is very much afraid that her perceptions, because feminist, are illegitimate and inconsistent with the broader humanism to which she is committed. But the woman who has permitted herself to consider the real extent of her oppression as a woman, and has stopped being ashamed of her anger and bitterness before asking of herself the humanism to view men as co-victims of the cultural web of power patterns, is one phenomenon. Quite another is the Lessing woman, who consistently tells herself that her oppression is her own fault or an unchangeable condition to which one must gracefully resign oneself. She refuses to face and deal with the anger always just under the surface and forces herself not only to regard men as co-victims, but to sympathize with them against the healthy interests of her own sex.

It is only in the vignettes Ella writes that she shows the willingness to describe, albeit indirectly, the reality of female-male relations as she has experienced them. The vignettes are about Ella's openness to men as persons, her desire to communicate with them as people both sexually and emotionally, and their refusal to relate on this personal basis to her and to love. Ella grasps the fact that this refusal in the men to connect sex and love (and thus integrate the emotional and sexual components of personality) is a sickness. But she fails to make the connection between the fact that society teaches men not to allow themselves to be fully trusting, open, and involved emotionally with women and her observation that men ask women for refuge, strength, commitment, and loyal support while withholding these things from them. Neither of the women in *The Golden Notebook* connects this male fear of reciprocity to prevailing concepts of masculinity. Neither does either woman see that healthy men may retreat from women rather than try to fill the emptiness and assuage the self-contempt women often feel because, having internalized the prevailing social estimate of femaleness, they feel incomplete and inferior as persons.

Ella's relationship with Paul gives the reader even more convincing proof that the pattern of her psychic life is withdrawal from and censorship of her perceptions, of failure to live an authentic existence. Believing that female-male relationships are inherently unequal and therefore not susceptible to transformation, she seeks to justify the inequalities so that she may convince herself to accept them without the resentment and rebellion she constantly feels.

She senses and resents, for instance, Paul's will to dominate her. But Ella, like the other women in this book who are confronted with the choice of taking a man on terms which are less than egalitarian or of turning away from him to uphold her own terms, chooses the man on his own terms. When a sexual relationship is offered, she is unable to refuse because the terms available are the only ones imaginable to her. She does not make any attempt to change the basis of relating from exploitation to genuine egalitarian friendship and love. The idea that she could refuse to deal with men in the style suggested by their behavior does not occur to her. Rebellion and self-assertion are present in her propensities for condemning men with Julia and for feeling mistreated and hurt, but she tries to hide from herself the kinds of thoughts which encourage these propensities. Thus Ella perceives that part of Paul's personality is rakish, corrupting, and detrimental to her dignity, but she refuses to connect this part of him with the rest, which she calls his true self. His rakishness, she tells herself, "was on a level that not only had nothing to do with the simplicity and ease of their being together; but betrayed it so completely that she had no alternative but to ignore it. Otherwise she would have had to break with him" (p. 197). She is happy only when she does not think about the ugly aspects of their relationship. Anna writes of her, "she drifted along on a soft tide of not-thinking" (p. 199). At one point Paul's behavior makes her envision his paying her money as if she were a prostitute: "It was somewhere implicit in his attitude." But Ella pushes the thought away: "What's that got to do with all these hours we've been together, when every look and move he's made told me he loved me?" (p. 202).

After five years as Paul's mistress, Ella begins to be disturbed by thoughts about his wife and not only stops feeling triumph over her for having captured her husband, but envies her. Ella builds up a picture of the other woman as a "serene, calm, unjealous, unenvious, undemanding woman, full of resources of happiness inside herself, self-sufficient, yet always ready to give happiness when it is asked for" (p. 207). She realizes that this picture is not derived from what Paul says about his wife, but that this is the kind of woman she herself would like to be, especially since she has grown aware and afraid of the extent of her dependence upon Paul. It is interesting to note that Ella's idea of a defense against her own dependency is selflessness, the old ideal of the woman as giver who does not require gifts for herself. She is incapable of thinking of less self-damaging ways than self-abnegation to reduce her vulnerability. Significantly it is not because Ella wishes to respect herself more for being a complete, self-sufficient, self-motivated person that she admires and envies this figure; it is because she envisions such a woman as relatively invulnerable to being hurt by people like Paul. The attraction to the figure has a negative motive, as all of Ella's emotional life is negative, because she does not allow her spontaneous reactions to her experience to govern her behavior and shape her values.

When Paul finally leaves Ella, she is devastated. She feels "as if a skin had been peeled off her" (p. 312) and realizes that the relationship was not free for her, as she had thought, simply because she had remained unmarried; nor was it really a love relationship, since it pulled her out of herself, unbalanced and diminished her, and proved altogether a destructive experience with regard to her self-respect and firmness of identity. Openly she admits, "I am unhappy because I have lost some kind of independence, some freedom," and she acknowledges that her attitude toward Paul has been "dishonest" (p. 314). But then Ella turns away from this realization. She concludes that it is not Paul, or society's sexual mores and views, but she herself who is to blame for the failure she feels.

Ella's life is a long series of encounters with the unhappy dislocation between the sexes, the implications of which neither Ella nor her creator Anna can face. The extraordinary amount of energy Ella expends in interpreting her relationships with men and compartmentalizing, disapproving of, and suppressing her feelings is a good indication of the seriousness of the discrepancy between what Ella is capable of perceiving and what she can afford to admit to herself, and therefore of her alienation from her perceptions and distance from personal authenticity.

The pattern of alienation, of withdrawal from authenticity, is also apparent in the Anna-Molly spectrum of *The Golden Notebook*. The two women allow Molly's ex-husband and son to bully them despite the fact that they are aware that the two men are hurting them. They extend friendship to other men who also mistreat them, such as

Nelson, de Silva, Willi, George, and Paul, who are sadists and misogynists. In connection with one of these relationships Anna comments, "Sometimes I dislike women, I dislike us all, because of our capacity for not-thinking when it suits us; we choose not to think when we are reaching out for happiness" (p. 485). Again one sees Anna turning the anger she feels at being ill-used against herself and other women and refusing to curtail relationships with men which damage her. One could interpret her responses to these men as humanistic in the profoundest sense—as evidence of a mature ability to see that no human being is all good or bad, that most have something to offer which redeems at least in part that which is ugly in them. But such a view misses the crucial point here, which is that Anna and Molly have legitimate cause for anger, and that they feel the anger but believe it to be an illegitimate reaction to their experiences. Their behavior is inconsistent with their real self-interest and shows them once again to be alienated from themselves.

With her two rabidly antiwoman homosexual tenants, Anna permits some of her anger to surface and links their attitudes toward women with those of men in general. "The mockery," she says, "the defence of the homosexual, was nothing more than the polite overgallantry of a 'real' man, the 'normal' man who intends to set bounds to his relationship with a woman, consciously or not." She continues, "It was the same cold, evasive emotion, taken a step further; there was a difference in degree but not in kind" (p. 393). But Anna, true to form, then criticizes herself for her anger and feels unfree to oust the tenants simply because they are so disagreeable to her. Finally she also rejects her perception of the connection between the tenants' attitudes toward women and those of men in general. Deciding to throw one tenant out so her daughter will not be damaged by his misogyny, she declares that her daughter is someday to have a "real" man, implying that the attitudes toward women of "real" men are not, after all, classifiable as damaging as she had spontaneously remarked.

The discrepancy between Anna's spontaneous perceptions and superimposed judgments is even clearer with regard to two men at a further remove from her: one who follows her out of the subway and another who exposes himself to her. Her immediate reaction to both is, naturally, fright. On second thought she tells herself that something is abnormal about her. "This happens every day, this is living in the city," she says (p. 390), refusing to indict a society in which such treatment of women is to be expected.

The discrepancy is most obvious, however, in Anna's major relationships with men. With Michael, she is periodically happy and resentful. She resents his inability to accept her as a writer and a responsible mother and his refusal to give her the kind of unmeasured love and support he asks of her. She also resents the fact that because he is a man, the petty details of his life are taken care of for him by women, whereas because she is a woman, her life is composed largely of seeing to the details of others' needs. Anna calls this resentment the "housewife's disease" (p. 333). But instead of facing squarely the fact that she resents Michael because he is a holder of the privileges which accrue to males in a patriarchal society and is taking advantage of this fact and of her, she turns her anger away, depersonalizing and depoliticizing it. She tells herself the anger has nothing to do with Michael. It is "impersonal," the disease "of women in our time" which is evident in their faces and voices, a protest against injustice, but nevertheless a protest which should be fought down and not on any account turned against men (p. 333). The idea is that one must adjust rather than act in one's own self-interest to change the system.

With Saul the relationship is more complex because he alternates communicating with Anna on a very high level with misogynistic, hostile withdrawal from her. But the pattern still holds. For example, at one point she gets angry enough to explode at him for referring to women and sex in demeaning terms. But predictably there follows the retraction, the denial of legitimacy of her own spontaneous emotion. She feels "ridiculous" (p. 560) and softens toward Saul. As with Michael, Anna is ambivalent, but she only accepts her positive feelings for him.

Anna sees that any relationship structured along the lines of the heterosexual model of our culture, as are the female-male relationships in *The Golden Notebook*, pits the interests of women and men against each other, women being driven to need and grasp for security and protection and men resisting being drawn into the restrictive role of provider: "I am the position of women in our time" (p. 579). But although she is aware of this separation of interests, and also of the rhythm of alternating love and hate in her relationships with men, she never connects these two phenomena. And because she does not make this connection, the sexual pain which she experiences never is recognized as a problem susceptible of solution, a problem calling for remedial action. Thus when Saul vents hatred upon her, Anna does not *act* to alter the situation. Instead she follows her preestablished pattern, turning her anger and frustration in upon herself. Instead of defending herself from his attacks, she disparages herself for the very strength with which she meets them. "I longed," she writes, "to be free of my own ordering, commenting memory" (p. 585). Her stomach clenches and her back hurts, but she does not connect these details with the fact that her refusal to act in her own self-interest hurts her and is making her lose her sense of personal worth and identity. She relates the physical ills rather to Saul's hostility. The solution to the pain is thus made to lie with him and not with herself; she adopts the posture of a helpless victim instead of acting to bring herself relief.

Anna is aware that what is wrong between her and Saul is a problem common to women. She wonders to herself what it is that women need and are not getting from men and senses that perhaps this unfulfilled need is the cause of the note of betrayal that women strike in this era. But predictably, instead of permitting herself to conclude that this "note" is legitimate, she disparages women by describing it as self-pity, a "hateful emotion" which is "solemn" and "wet" (p. 597). She never really stands up for herself as a woman and never opts out of the self-damaging collusion of tolerating and playing a role in the submission-dominance syndrome which is the leitmotiv of female-male relations in patriarchal societies. The only approach to the problem which she feels legitimate is described in her dream about Saul as a tiger. The tiger claws her and she sympathizes with it instead of with herself; she then concretizes this approach in the image of flying above the tiger's cage: it is legitimate to try to "rise above" the situation, but not to change it.

As she views the imaginary movie composed of scenes from her past life, Anna realizes that the meaning with which she has endowed each scene has been "all false" (p. 620). She finds that the judgments she has been making have ordered the material "to fit what I knew" (p. 620) rather than emerging in a direct response to her experience. But she never escapes her pattern of self-punishment and alienation. The novel ends with Molly getting married although she knows "the exact dimensions of the bed" (p. 666) and with Anna entering marriage counseling work and the teaching of delinquent children. There is a "small silence" as the two women together contemplate their capitulation, their integration "with British life at its roots" (p. 666).

The Golden Notebook, therefore, reveals the peculiar problem of the woman writer working in a climate of assumptions and sympathies about women and sex roles which do not support female authenticity. The woman writer in this situation is unlikely to conceive of the relative status of women and men in political terms; prevailing opinion convinces her that the condition of women in society is rooted in biological and psychological immutables. She may, nevertheless, be acutely sensitive to and resentful of the power dynamics which characterize female-male relations, aware to a large extent of what we have come to call sexual politics. If so, she finds herself on the horns of a dilemma: she cannot completely deny her awareness, but, unencouraged by any cultural sanction for those of her perceptions which are, at the deepest level, feminist and potentially political, she doubts these perceptions and feels they are indicative of some aberration or defect in herself. It is not necessary to assume that this book is autobiographical to arrive at the idea that Lessing, and not simply her characters Anna and Ella, is confronting this dilemma. Lessing has so conceived the book that nowhere within it are Anna's and Ella's judgments of their experiences implied to be anything but unavoidable.

The overriding weakness of *The Golden Notebook* is alienation from the authentic female perspective, a perspective which repeatedly is clearly sketched in and then smeared by the censor in Lessing. The discrepancy between the perceptions and the alien standards which are imposed upon them seriously flaws the novel. But at the same time, the tension produced by this discrepancy makes the book a superb rendering of that state of alienation from themselves, from authentic selfhood, to which women, like blacks and members of other minority groups, are subjected until they find solidarity and begin to confirm and legitimize their experience. In addition, Lessing's study of the malaise and dislocation between the sexes in Western society does set a very important precedent in literature because it examines the relationship between women and men so humanistically and analytically, in such great detail and variety, and with a good faith which never permits a descent into vituperation or abuse.

The Grass Is Singing:
A Little Novel
About the Emotions

Michele Wender Zak

In Doris Lessing's *The Golden Notebook*, during an early discussion of Anna Wulf's struggle with her writer's block, Molly accords Anna the "correct" party-line approval, defining her not as "someone who writes little novels about the emotions" but rather as someone who "writes about what's real." Anna's retort provides a key to the aesthetic that informs the entire Lessing canon: "If Marxism means anything, it means that a little novel about the emotions should reflect 'what's real' since the emotions are a function and a product of a society. . . ."[1] Lessing's first novel, *The Grass Is Singing*, is such a "little novel about the emotions" seen through that Marxist lens. It eschews the endless cataloging of apparently self-perpetuating dislocations—psychological and social—that serves as substance for much of what has come to be called modernist literature. Seldom in that literature is there so much as a nod in the direction of the material causes that must at least contribute to the dislocations in question. And Lessing, even in this, her first and in many ways slightest, effort, rejects the world view of the modernists, preferring instead to portray the dialectical relationship that Marxism insists always exists between the individual circumstances of one's life and the material nature of the social and economic system within which one lives. To the extent that modernists abandon that dialectic, or what in another context existential psychia-

---

[1] Doris Lessing, *The Golden Notebook* (New York: Ballantine, 1962), p. 23.

trist R. D. Laing terms "vital contact with the world,"[2] their literature is impoverished, just as impoverishment of the self results from the schizophrenic's withdrawal from reality. Mary Turner, the female protagonist of *The Grass Is Singing*, suffers that schizophrenic impoverishment, but the novel itself keeps before us, in consistent and exacting detail, the nature of the world from which Mary is compelled to withdraw. Her descent into madness and a self-willed death is as complete a documentation of psychological disintegration as might occur in any modern novel of sensibility. But in this case, that regrettable disintegration also serves as a focus for a keen-edged analysis of the state and quality of women's lives in a colonial society.

The novel opens with a brief newspaper account of the murder of Mary Turner by her houseboy and then moves to a description of the sham inquiry into her murder by neighbors and by colonial officials. Since her husband has been rendered incurably mad by the shock of the murder, we are left to judge the community's response through the perceptions of the single resident on the Turner property, Tony Marston. A young man recently over from England who had been preparing to assume management of the Turner farm and is still very much an outsider in his adopted country, Marston wonders incredulously at that response. He understands, finally, the gentlemen's agreement that prevents inquiry into the motive for the murder, rife as it is with implications of forbidden human—perhaps even sexual—contact between the victim and her suspected assailant. Marston's astonished groping after a clearer vision of what is "customary in this country" furnishes us with a contextual account of the narrow and oppressive world in which Mary Turner was born, went slowly and undramatically mad, and violently died.

Mary's death, like her life, is shaped by the profound hatred, contempt, fear, and grudgingly acknowledged economic need of the black upon which white African society is predicated. And Lessing insists upon the equivalent effect on Mary's life and death of the similar complex of attitudes the white male Afrikaner reserves for women, a point of view barely disguised by his familiar posture of fierce protectiveness toward white women. Certainly he did not like "niggers murdering white women."[3] On the other hand, an easy, shared con-

---

[2] R. D. Laing, *The Divided Self* (Middlesex, England: Penguin, 1965). My use in this article of such terms as "ontological" and "existential" will refer to definitions assigned them by Laing.

[3] Doris Lessing, *The Grass Is Singing* (Middlesex, England: Penguin, 1969), p. 23. Further parenthetical references in the text will be preceded by *GS*.

tempt for women perhaps alone provides a point of understanding between black men and white. As they stand over Mary's body, Charlie
Slatter, the Turners' closest neighbor, and Sergeant Wenham agree
that " 'Needs a man to deal with niggers. . . . Niggers don't understand
women giving them orders. They keep their own women in the right
place.' He laughed. The sergeant laughed. They turned toward each
other, even including Tony, in an unmistakable relief. The tension
had broken; the danger was past" (*GS*, p. 24). Abruptly, then, their
dialogue ends with an eye to the heat and a consequent decision to
move the body. "And that brutally matter-of-fact remark, Tony
realized afterwards, was the only time poor Mary Turner was referred
to directly!" (*GS*, p. 25).

Having roughly defined for us the world in which Mary lived by
its reception of her death, the narrative undertakes to describe "the
sort of woman . . . Mary Turner had been before she came to this farm
and had been driven slowly off balance by heat and loneliness and
poverty" (*GS*, p. 29). Growing up the only surviving child of a father
who nightly drank himself into sodden cheerfulness and a mother
whose bearing was always one of a hardened, even a self-satisfied,
despair and an unrelieved attitude of contempt toward her husband,
Mary remembers as the "happiest time in her childhood" the period
following the deaths of her older brother and sister. For then her
parents were friends in sorrow a little while, and her mother, while
she wept, had lost "that terrible hard indifference" (*GS*, p. 35). The
scathing poignancy of that memory stands in revealing contrast to the
habit of emotional detachment that marks Mary's adult life. Having
abandoned the farm for one of "those sleepy little towns scattered like
raisins in a dry cake over the body of South Africa" and comfortably
employed as a stenographer, she is happy in the "friendly impersonality" of her job and in its unvarying routine. Mary "liked things to
happen safely, one after another in a pattern" (*GS*, p. 36). Like
Camus' Meursault, she is unmoved except by relief when her parents
die, her father long after she had abandoned all ties to him.

Pretty in a childlike way as a girl, Mary continues to dress and to
live as an ingenue well into her thirties. She prefers to maintain resi-
dence in the girls' club that was her first home in town. Her social life
—which indeed is her life—is entirely dependent on men. But in spite
of her many male companions, she lives pointedly without sex and
without emotional ties of any kind. Clearly, the indifference that so
dismayed the child Mary in her mother comes to be the defining quality
of the adult Mary. And at last, Mary's life assumes the exact propor-

tions of her mother's poor existence. On her wedding night, her first night on Dick Turner's farm, she is gradually possessed by the feeling "that it was not in this house she was sitting, with her husband, but back with her mother, watching her endlessly contrive and patch and mend—till suddenly she got to her feet with an awkward scrambling movement, unable to bear it; possessed with the thought that her father, from his grave, had sent out his will and forced her back into the kind of life he had made her mother live" (*GS*, p. 57).

The repeated suggestion heretofore in the novel that Mary somehow regards men, her social dependence on them notwithstanding, as the embodied threat to her identity, to her independent life, is here made explicit. Her grasp on who she is is tenuous at best; she suffers the effects of what Laing has termed "ontological insecurity." The ontologically insecure person, Laing explains, possesses no sense of a healthy or vital self, and he draws for his examples upon two modernist writers—Kafka and Samuel Beckett. Modernist literature[4] is, of course, rife with ontological insecurities, commonly referred to as "identity crises." Primarily, such crises involve male characters, ranging from adolescents like Holden Caulfield to middle-aged lost souls like Herzog. Occasionally there appears a novel in which the crisis is suffered by a female protagonist, like Plath's Esther Greenwood, or Joan Didion's Maria in *Play It as It Lays*. Regardless of the sex of the protagonist or the author, however, it is only on rare occasions that fictional explorations of ontological insecurity reveal the material roots of the problem. Those works that fail even to prod in the direction of causality stand in tacit denial of that reverberating insistence of Marx and Engels that "Life is not determined by consciousness, but consciousness by life."[5] *The Grass Is Singing* is one of those rare works of fiction which acknowledges that basic truth of Marxian analysis. And as a consequence of the acknowledgement, we have thrust upon us the bitter details of Mary's childhood and adolescence—the hot, barren countryside, the irresponsibility of her economically defeated father, her enlistment as bewildered confidante by her profoundly disappointed mother. Then, temporarily, our consciousness of her unhappy past recedes as Mary enters into the superficially con-

---

[4] For an interesting discussion of some effects of modernism in literature, see Lillian S. Robinson and Lise Vogel, "Modernism and History," *Images of Women in Fiction: Feminist Perspectives* (Bowling Green: Bowling Green Univ. Popular Press, 1972), pp. 278-305.

[5] Karl Marx and Frederick Engels, *The German Ideology* (New York: International Publishers, 1947), p. 15.

tented existence of a single young woman in one of South Africa's "larger" towns. But the suggestion of permanent psychological dislocation as a result of that dismal childhood implicitly continues. For in her new life, the tenuous nature of Mary's grasp on her identity, on her "being," reveals itself both in her unconscious insistence on continuing to seem the "Mary of sixteen" in appearance and life style and in her determination to fend off any intrusions on that existential position. She lives at the girls' club and serves "her girls" as a benign confessor, but she offers no confidences of her own in return. Rather, she remains determinedly aloof, although sociable, toward both men and women. In fact, as the narrative points out, Mary really had no troubles of her own. As long as she was able to maintain her "false self," she was safe from emotional distress. And crucial to her defense against, to borrow again from Laing, "engulfment"—that process so feared by the schizophrenic in which one's identity is overwhelmed by a relationship with another person who is perceived, at least, as the stronger—is the maintenance of a "small core of contempt for them [men], of which she was quite unconscious, and which had protected her from sex as surely as if she had been hideous . . ." (*GS*, p. 43).

Mary's protective stance is supported in part, we are told, by the "arid feminism" she had inherited from her mother. In this pejorative reference to a femininist sensibility, we find the first clue to what we come to recognize in later works of Lessing as a revulsion against that facile feminism whose proponents see their sufferings in isolation from the broader themes of human oppression. Thus, Mary, who feels deeply her mother's suffering, cannot see that her father might, too, have suffered. " 'About what?' she would have retorted, had anyone suggested it. 'He's a man, isn't he? He can do as he likes' " (*GS*, p. 36). Lessing's insistence on a full comprehension of "what's real" pillories the easy and uninformed judgments of a girl who, in her relatively unencumbered life as a single woman in South Africa, "had no measuring rod to assess herself" (*GS*, p. 36). At any rate, the "arid feminism" and its corollary, the contempt for men unconsciously nurtured by Mary, ultimately fail to protect her from encroaching attacks on her "false" existential position. Her protective stance collapses when she is forced to see herself according to the standards of the world through which she had so far naively moved. Having unavoidably overheard unflattering comments about her age, her manner of dress, and her unmarried state, Mary fixes on one line from the unwelcome gossip that refers to her failure to marry: "She just isn't like that, isn't like that at all. Something missing somewhere" (*GS*, p. 43). With no clear idea of the meaning of the comment, Mary nonetheless undertakes to remodel herself into a socially acceptable image of a marriageable thirty-year-old woman.

There follows her pathetic attempt to find a "real" self to replace the "existentially true" one that had at least allowed her to preserve a certain independence and freedom in an extraordinarily oppressive society. "It is terrible," the narrator editorializes, "to destroy a person's picture of himself in the interests of truth or some other abstraction. How can one know he will be able to create another to enable him to go on living. Mary's idea of herself was destroyed and she was not fitted to recreate herself" (*GS*, p. 45). Sexually vulnerable for the first time, she undergoes a period of vacillation between painful personal experiences and ever-multiplying trips to the "pictures" where, typically, she seeks connections between "the distorted mirror of the screen and her own life." But she fails even there to find a way to "fit together what she wanted for herself, and what she was offered" (*GS*, p. 46). For the first time in her life, Mary begins to feel uncomfortable with men. That "small core of contempt" on which she unconsciously depends to stave off her fear of marriage and consequent dependence on a man like her father is diminished.

Accepting finally "what she was offered," she marries weak, ineffectual Dick Turner who, revealingly, had sought her out after having been engaged by the absorbed and softened image of her he had discerned in a darkened theater. She accepts Dick because his worship restores "her feeling of superiority to men, which was really, at bottom, what she had been living from all these years" (*GS*, p. 46). Nor is she disappointed in that. Even their wedding night is tolerable to Mary because of Dick's "timid adoration which was the only touch she could have borne" (*GS*, p. 57). But her husband's continuing veneration, his respect, and even his nervous wonder at her efficiency, her energy, and her intelligence fail to save her from her mother's fate. Mary's destiny thus determined, the remainder of the novel is a predictable, almost mechanical rendering of her helpless confrontation with "woman's lot" in a society whose capacity for oppression is remarkably unsated by its treatment of blacks.

Understandably disappointed and depressed by the ugly and primitive farmhouse that seems to hold back so temporarily the threatening bush, Mary nonetheless brings to bear on these inhospitable new surroundings the virtues of her former life. As long as possible she busies herself sewing curtains and furniture covers, embroidering her clothing, and otherwise adding to the meager comfort of the bare, unceilinged house. At last, of course, there is nothing more to do, and she must surrender herself to the smothering heat and the oppresive loneliness of a farmer's wife. Still without an operational sense of self, she withdraws increasingly from normal intercourse with the surrounding farm families, for isolation provides at once her only safety from threat of engulfment and her ultimate destruction. Eventually her only social expression becomes her overweening hatred for the blacks whom she treats with exaggerated cruelty and impersonalness because they threaten her not only as men, but as usurpers of her only useful, though hated, function on the farm—housekeeping.

With the passage of time, certain outlets for her energy and intelligence present themselves. Most significant is her long-repressed recognition of why Dick's farming has so consistently failed and her own opportunity to help him to material success. But after some disappointing efforts, she withdraws from that opportunity, in part, the narrator explains, because demonstration of her superior ability would provoke Dick to destructive defensiveness and in part because she shrinks from real involvement with the hated farm:

And the third reason, though she was not aware of it, was the strongest. She needed to think of Dick, the man to whom she was irrevocably married, as a person on his own account, a success from his own efforts. When she saw him weak and goalless, and pitiful, she hated him, and the hate turned in on herself. She needed a man stronger than herself, and she was trying to create one out of Dick. (*GS*, p. 134)

Mary had earlier grasped at Dick's love and respect for her as support for the only position available to her at that time in her life—a personal conviction of superiority to men. At the same time, however, she needed, and continued to need in ever greater measure, a man stronger than she who could assume responsibility for shaping both their lives.

At about this time, Mary attempts, abortively, a return to her old life. She leaves Dick and visits both her old employer and the girls' club where she had lived. Greeted on the one hand by shocked pity at her changed appearance and on the other by curious stares of strangers, she withdraws in defeat. At great expense to whatever vestiges of positive feelings that still remain to her, she returns to the farm and to a final spasmodic effort to make of Dick the only thing she really wants him by now to be—a material success. Again she fails, and the process of deterioration that began in the months before her marriage accelerates. But before engaging us in that final and inexorable destruction of Mary Turner, the narrative pauses to elaborate on a concern with those opposing life principles that will figure so crucially in the struggles of Martha Quest and Anna Wulf, and which help, in conjunction with the reference to "arid feminism," to explain the essential lack of sympathy we sense Lessing has for Mary. At work here, as in the later novels, are assumptions about the existence of a "feminine principle" that moves toward a wholeness of vision and of a "masculine principle" that accepts division of intellect and feeling and a rigid limitation of vision. Usually, in the Lessing novels, it is the women who strive after unity, or at least a sense of it, that the masculine world determines they will fail to achieve. But Mary Turner's "divided self" includes no vestige of the feminine principle so defined, while her husband's participation in it contributes to the poignancy of his failure:

She was looking at the farm from the outside, as a machine for making money: that was how she regarded it. She was critical entirely from this angle. But she left so much out of account. She gave him no credit for the way he looked after his soil, for that hundred acres of trees. And he could not look at the farm as she did. He loved it and was part of it. He liked the slow movement of the seasons, and the complicated rhythm of the "little crops" that she kept describing with contempt as useless. (*GS*, p. 129)

After the last hope for material success has failed, and after she is denied her lingering desire for a baby that "would give her something to do," Mary gives way. Simultaneously, Moses, the black whom Mary had struck with a whip some years before, appears and is hired by Dick to be the new houseboy. What follows for Mary is a period of change culminating in a self-aware destruction reminiscent of the "recognition" phase of Aristotelian tragedy. The final chapters are heavy with implied sexuality as Mary moves from fearfully surreptitious glances at Moses' powerful body to the final days in which she sits passively while he dresses and undresses her. By then Mary's relinquishment of self is almost complete. During that period she moves from obsessive fear of Moses whom she sees as "her father, menacing and horrible, who touched her in desire" (*GS*, p. 174) to submission to him whom she comes to regard, with unconscious irony, as the strong and secure man she had ambivalently wanted Dick to be. It is a period of profound illness for her, a period when she is forced to confront her worst fears and to acknowledge her sexual desire and her attraction to a strong and demanding man. The release from those fears, when at last it comes, is in part a sexual one, although it is never clear whether Moses and Mary actually consummate the relationship. Nor does that seem in the end really important, for the easy interpretation here is not the valid one. Lessing is not depending on that worn conception of the superior sexuality of the black male, nor is she implying that Mary's mental health required only that she be sexually overpowered by a dominating male—black or white. When Tony Marston stumbles upon Mary being dressed by Moses and, in his confusion, questions her, she mutters, "They said I was not like that, not like that, not like that." And in answer to Tony's bewildered "Not like what?" she simply repeats the phrase in a tone "furtive, sly, yet triumphant" (*GS*, p. 198). Her repetition of that well-remembered phrase indicates that Mary has at last begun to reckon honestly with her sexual desire and has exposed her "true self" to a relationship with another person without, as she had always feared, suffering "engulfment."

Ignorant of the implications of Mary's sexual and existential search, Tony is horrified by her behaving "simply as if she lives in a world of her own, where other people's standards don't count" (*GS*, p. 198). In his bewildered anger, Tony sends Moses away and Mary acquiesces reflexively to that enforcement of "other people's standards." But that acquiescence is a betrayal of her emerging self, and, as Mary realizes in the last moments before her death, of "him, to whom she had been disloyal, and at the bidding of the Englishman" (*GS*, p. 216).

In the end, Mary dies in terror-striken willingness at the hands of Moses, who had helped her. As she moves feverishly through her last hours, knowing Moses will kill her, she resists her impulse to seek help from her husband who was always "there, a torturing reminder of what she had to forget in order to remain herself" (*GS*, p. 202), or from Tony Marston because looking at him she remembers how she long ago had turned to Dick, and how "It had seemed to her that she would be saved from herself by marrying him." And she understands at last "That was the lesson she had to learn. If she had learned it long ago, she would not be standing here now, having been betrayed for the second time by her weak reliance on a human being [Marston] who should not be expected to take the responsibility for her" (*GS*, p. 212).

As Mary seeks no escape from Moses' vengeance, he seeks none from that of the Afrikaner community he has outraged. If there is any triumph of vision in this novel, it resides in these two acts of courageous surrender, in which both victims accept the consequences of their self-betraying submission to a dehumanizing world. The triumph is slight, however, overshadowed by the novel's insistence on the deterministic principles that shape lives and that thereby shape consciousness in the unhappy world of colonial South Africa. There is no tragic catharsis in the self-knowledge painfully achieved by Mary Turner before her death. One rather wishes, in fact, that Mary had been able to sustain the "false self" that preceded the accidentally overheard conversation. For, as Laing repeatedly points out, a "false" existential position, even unto madness, may be somehow sane and true in a world whose sanity is itself questionable.

Disorderly Company:
From *The Golden Notebook*
to *The Four-Gated City*

Dagmar Barnouw

So it must be said that if a man starts
thinking a bit he gets into what one
might call pretty disorderly company.
—Robert Musil,
The Man Without Qualities[1]

The Golden Notebook, thought by most critics to be Doris Lessing's
best novel so far,[2] has been praised for its formal control. Lessing herself, in a 1969 interview at Stony Brook,[3] said she was "very proud"
of the novel's form, describing, in contrast, the form of *The Four-
Gated City* as "shot to hell." There is indeed a marked change in atti-

---

[1] Robert Musil, *The Man without Qualities*, trans. Eithne Wilkins and Ernst
Kaiser (London: Secker & Warburg, 1960-61), 3 vols., I, 130.

[2] "Form" does not refer to careful organization of small structural units,
for instance, the sentence; many of her admirers admit Lessing's verbosity, her
tendency to overwrite. "Form" refers here to the larger structures, for instance,
the arrangement of the material by means of the four notebooks and the "frame"
"Free Women," 1-5. See Florence Howe, "Narrative, History and Prophecy,"
Nation, 209 (Aug. 11, 1969), 116; with slight reservations: Irving Howe,
"Neither Compromise nor Happiness," *The New Republic,* 148 (Dec. 15, 1962),
19; Frederick R. Karl, "Doris Lessing in the Sixties: The New Anatomy of
Melancholy," *Contemporary Literature,* 13, No. 1 (Winter 1972), 15. See fur-
ther Dorothy Brewster, *Doris Lessing* (New York: Twayne, 1965), pp. 139ff.;
Selma R. Burkom, " 'Only Connect': Form and Content in the Works of Doris
Lessing," *Critique,* 11 (1968-69), 54ff.; Joseph E. Brewer, "The Anti-Hero in
Contemporary Literature," *Iowa English Yearbook,* 12 (1967), 58.

[3] Jonah Raskin, "Doris Lessing at Stony Brook: An Interview," *New American Review,* 8 (1970), 170.

tude toward the organization of the narrative as well as toward the protagonist; yet, the narrative anarchy and the insistence on the potential dimension in the development of the protagonist's consciousness, new in Lessing's work, deserve serious consideration. The new, much more open narrative structures may be seen as thoroughly functional: "shot to hell," after all, points to the central concern of the novel, the descent into the self which is partly hell. Assuming, as a working hypothesis, that the indeed surprising differences between *The Golden Notebook* and *The Four-Gated City* are indicative of changes in Lessing's concept of the function and responsibility of the novelist, I should like to explore these differences in some detail, starting with a reexamination of the function of the organizational devices and their influence on intellectual decisions in *The Golden Notebook*.

Attempting to bridge the gap between experience and self-knowledge, but aware of the probably insurmountable difficulties, Anna acknowledges the division of the self by keeping four notebooks: "a black notebook, which is to do with Anna Wulf the writer; a red notebook, concerned with politics; a yellow notebook, in which I make stories of my experience; and a blue notebook which tries to be a diary."[4] After the publication of one successful novel, Anna is afraid of the premature, static quality of form that excludes truth; she works to develop a sufficiently flexible—as it turns out, elaborately sophisticated—system of cross-commentaries that is meant to restrain, but in fact exploits, irony and a skeptical ambiguity. Tommy, talking to Anna in her room before he attempts suicide, is derisive about the four notebooks, accuses her of avoiding truth for fear of being chaotic, of irresponsibility, even dishonesty (*GN*, p. 233). This accusation, so obviously well-founded, ought to be shattering for Anna. It is not, however, because she knows her failure. Tommy, having said the things that have to be said to Anna, goes and shoots himself blind; protected by his blindness that claims all his resources of intellect and will, he will then settle for the life of a progressive businessman, a life of ambiguities and compromises. Anna, holding at a distance the memory of her descent into disintegration of the self after the "disastrous" affair with Saul Green,[5] settles for social work and the established Progressive

---

[4] Doris Lessing, *The Golden Notebook* (New York: Simon and Schuster, 1962), p. 406. Parenthetical page references in the text will be preceded by *GN*.

[5] Irving Howe, p. 18. The relationship to Saul Green is generally seen as merely destructive; Anna's part in the failure is not recognized. See also Karl, p. 27; Brewster, p. 147.

Party. Molly marries money with the obligatory progressive business-man, adjusting to her own and her son's compromises. She is, however, still afraid of whatever emotional and intellectual energy is left in Anna:

> Annoyed with herself, Molly's hands made an irritated gesture, and she grimaced and said: "You're a bad influence on me, Anna. I was per-fectly resigned to it all until you came in. Actually I think we'll get on very well."
> "I don't see why not," said Anna.
> A small silence. "It's all very odd, isn't it Anna?"
> "Very." (*GN*, p. 568)

Lessing's narrative tact does not permit these lines to be the very last ones; yet, the novel does end on the "safe tone" (*GN*, p. 51)[6] of that "odd, isn't it?"—the safety of exhaustion which has just enough strength left for ironical ambivalence. It is true that Anna is aware of using that "safe tone"; she also speaks to Molly of "that awful moral exhaustion" (*GN*, p. 43) which she dreads, yet accepts as inevitable. In the conclusion—"The two women kissed and separated"—Anna is as much defeated as Molly, and her keener awareness of the defeat is only turned back on herself.[7]

A distinctly hostile irony is projected by the sentence that closes the golden notebook, that unsuccessful attempt at recording truthfully whatever is Anna's share of chaos: "This short novel was later pub-lished and did rather well." Of course it would, written by Saul Green who has put "a curse" (*GN*, p. 523) on Anna's most honest, most desperate attempt to understand the division. Anna's gift to Saul, to whom she owes a new depth of descent she cannot bear, much less, give form to,[8] is the first sentence of his novel; it will exploit and be exploited by a literary market, as was Anna's *Frontiers of War*. Both this fact and the abstract of Saul's novel, available to the reader (*GN*, pp. 549f.), are a condemnation of ambivalence and a recognition of its power.

---

[6] See also pp. 135f.

[7] Florence Howe sees the ending of *The Golden Notebook* much too posi-tively in terms of the intellectual's—Anna's—function as "boulder pusher, that is, a teacher of the humane principles . . ." (p. 177).

[8] See pp. 523ff. for the description of the frightening "new state of being, one foreign to me"; I cannot agree with Florence Howe's view of "ordered chaos made possible" (p. 116) in *The Golden Notebook*.

Ultimately, this recognition is what *The Golden Notebook* is all about. The novel offers a courageous, formally interesting, absorbing analysis of what it means to be an intelligent woman in our times; but it does not go beyond the first stage. As women have to define themselves against men—that implies an enormous advantage for the creators of male protagonists in the battles of consciousness—Anna projects herself and her creation Ella into one relationship after the other. The fact that almost all of those relationships are nothing but "affairs" is in itself information of analytical value; it ought not to be taken as literally, however, as it is in this novel. The only meaningful relationships Anna is permitted are with Michael, of whom we know not much more than that he is loved by Anna, and with Saul, of whose illness we get some glimpses but not enough to form a picture sufficiently clear to be of help in understanding what he needs from Anna. Saul is too much of a caricature anyway. Irving Howe rightly criticizes Lessing for writing "about Americans with the astigmatism peculiar to certain English leftists: she has no ear for American speech nor eye for American manners."[9] His diary entries, read by Anna, are comical rather than "ruthless," and it is difficult to see how Anna could be hurt by them (*GN*, pp. 488 ff.). Michael presumably leaves Anna in spite —or because—of his love for her; Anna makes Saul go when she realizes how extraordinarily she is going to suffer from that relationship. What has happened to the men, what will happen to them, we are not told. They are, by decree of their creator, in a much better position to combat despair than the women whom they unfailingly exploit; they also seem to be much more in control in situations of emotional crisis: Michael runs but remains calm and cool (*GN*, pp. 313 f.); Saul wants to stay quite desperately (*GN*, pp. 547 ff.) but leaves, ready for another try at exploitation of women, certain of survival: "I could see standing beside the small, thin, fair man, with his soft brush of blond hair, his sick yellow face, a strong sturdy brown-fleshed man, like a shadow that would absorb the body that cast it" (*GN*, p. 548).

The world contained in *The Golden Notebook* is too exclusively a woman's world. Irving Howe, in his very positive review of the novel, points out that "the feminine element in *The Golden Notebook* does not become a self-contained universe of being, as in some of Virginia Woolf's novels. . . ."[10] I would agree with him, especially in view of

---

[9] Irving Howe, p. 20
[10] *Ibid.*, p. 17.

Anna's experience with the Communist Party. Here her despair appears credible and legitimate to a high degree because the reader can himself supply knowledge of the cruel ironies, and because Lessing-Anna has clarified the obvious, but powerfully destructive, absurdities to the point where they can be presented fully and concisely. The nightmare about the execution squad with the interchangeable prisoner is a good case in point (*GN*, p. 295). But it is precisely this more comprehensive exact presentation of a human dilemma that draws attention to the unbalanced concept of the man-woman relationship. Howe himself admits to a researcher's eagerness in reference to the "other" on both sides—man's and woman's—which implies an extraordinary distance between them: "My own curiosity, as a masculine outsider, was enormous, for here, I felt, was the way intellectual women really talk to one another when they feel free and unobserved"; "For both women remain interested in men with a curiosity that is almost archeological: as if there were so few good ones left that it is necessary to hunt for them amid the ruins."[11] Howe seems to accept that fact quite calmly.

In this sense the novel's intimacy is confining and overprotective. Anna's white room, with its black and red surfaces a space bravely outlined against chaos,[12] has this quality as much as, for instance, her cooking for Michael, or, even more distinctly so, her taking care of her daughter Janet, a curiously conventional, bright little girl who seems to need as little protection as Matty's daughter Caroline. It is significant that Matty-turned-Martha will feel responsible for Caroline's polish of conventionality, recognizing it as the child's need to protect herself as a consequence to Matty's "mad" act of "setting her free" (*FGC*, p. 66).

Anna's fear of letting in chaos, "becoming that chaos" (*GN*, p. 313) is interrelated to her need to make fictitiously whole beings out of her child and the men she comes into contact with. These other selves can then be used by her to patch up, if only temporarily, the imperfections of her self. The central ambiguity of the novel is founded in the reader's inability to decide whether Anna is judged guilty of a

---

[11] *Ibid.*, p. 18.

[12] Cf. here Jack's room in *The Four-Gated City* (New York: Knopf, 1969), p. 42, and Bill's room in "Dialogue," *A Man and Two Women* (New York: Simon & Schuster, 1963), p. 237: "It was large, high, had airy white walls, a clear black carpet, the dark red settee, his machinelike chair, more books." Further parenthetical page references to *A Man and Two Women* and *The Four-Gated City* will be preceded by *MTW* and *FGC*.

fragmented vision by her author, or whether such judgment is rejected as meaningless, because fragmentation is inevitable. Significantly, the sexual basis of the woman's dilemma is dealt with in detail—realistically and very intelligently—in the most distancing form Anna is capable of: her fragmentary novel about Ella and Julia.

Ella, sharing Anna's needs and desires, also her particular vulnerability, is allowed to define her incompleteness more narrowly than Anna would permit herself to do. After Paul has left Ella, she "suffers sex desire in a vacuum. She is acutely humiliated, thinking that this means she is dependent on men for 'having sex,' for 'being serviced,' for 'being satisfied.' She uses this kind of savage phrase to humiliate herself" (*GN*, p. 390). Anna writes this into her yellow notebook, waiting, as it were, for Ella's next move. Ella, trying to counter the humiliation, concentrates on reminding herself how entirely personal sex had been with Paul, remembering their life together, how she had been stirred only by him, had been free of desire when he was absent. So she is able to explain to herself, make herself believe "that her present raging sexual hunger was not for sex, but was fed by all the emotional hungers of her life. That when she loved a man again, she would return to normal: a woman, that is, whose sexuality would ebb and flow in response to his. A woman's sexuality is, so to speak, contained by a man, if he is a real man; she is, in a sense, put to sleep by him, she does not think about sex" (*GN*, p. 390). This "knowledge," however, is immediately disclosed by herself (and her author) as "a set of words, the phrases of a kind of knowledge" (*GN*, p. 390). Yet, it is never made clear whether she realizes that she is caught in a vicious circle. She relies on this "set of words" to come to life, once life comes back to her, and, also, to sustain her hope that life will indeed come back to her. The self-critical comment she is allowed by her author is an elusive "But how strange that one should hold on to a set of sentences, and have faith in them" (*GN*, p. 390).

Anna shares this faith; mocking Ella gently, even granting her self-mockery, leaving her puzzled like this, leads straight back to the "safe tone" of "it is odd, isn't it?" to which Anna, after all is said, also retreats. The self-projection into Ella does not help to clarify the division; it muddles it. Anna herself repeatedly uses the abstraction "real man" (*GN*, pp. 414, 479) though she would not otherwise permit herself such escape from the obligation to define a problem clearly; Ella, allowed a lesser degree of rigor, turns into a liability.

Caught between her four notebooks, Anna cannot do without the protection of abstractions and generalizations about the "other."

She is both waiting for the "real man" to come down like a *deus ex machina*, impossibly perfect, closing her wounds without getting himself infected by them, and ready to form such a man herself, forgetting for the time her own limitations as well as those of her materials. Irving Howe implicitly accuses Anna, though he explicitly accepts her on her own terms: "She wants in her men both intimacy and power, closeness and self-sufficiency, hereness and thereness. Modernist in sensibility, she is traditionalist in her desires."[13] With this, the central problem of the novel is summed up so neatly that it does not seem a problem anymore.

Michael—one of the very few times he is allowed to speak— says to Anna at the end of their "great love affair":

"Ah, Anna, you make up stories about life and tell them to yourself, and you don't know what is true and what isn't." "And so we haven't had a great love affair?" This was breathless and pleading; though I had not meant it. I felt a terrible dismay and coldness at his words, as if he were denying my existence. He said, whimsically: "If you say we have, then we have. And if you say not, then not." "So what you feel doesn't count?" "Me? But Anna, why should I count?" (This was bitter, mocking, but affectionate.) (*GN*, p. 283)

Anna is made to misunderstand Michael's words as withdrawal. Consequently, in her diary entry, attempting to write "as truthfully as I can," she again outlines a story about Michael and her relationship with him. It is very early morning; Anna watches Michael in his sleep, projecting past and future for him, but she is unable to see his present. What she says about their relationship, a temporary bulwark against death, is true and moving, but she still does not understand how his "why should I count?" interacts with her need to make stories out of her attachments to men. The scene is very subtly developed, and I may very well have overinterpreted it in terms of an intended criticism of Anna by her creator; yet, the change in the relationships between men and women in *The Four-Gated City* could be discovered here in an embryonic stage.

Anna's story-making is, of course, one of the few defenses she has against the men who resent her using the relationship for her own desperate needs instead of understanding that need. Threatened in the very substance of her self by the exposure and rejection inflicted on her, she feels, by the man, she has to turn to that part of herself "which

---

[13] Irving Howe, p. 19.

Michael dislikes most; the critical and thinking Anna" (*GN*, p. 283),
trying to write the truth and unable to do so because this split of her
self is too crude, a destruction from the outside.

Anna wants the impossible; she is not told so by her author with
sufficient clarity. The scene I described is the only instance of a very
tentative approach toward such clarity. Apart from that Anna is
occasionally allowed to be aware of her potentially dangerous procrus-
tean measuring of men (*GN*, p. 410), but she is made to refer it to a
past Anna, when, in fact, her relationships continue to be informed by
her exclusive self-projection. Most importantly, the narrative device
of the four notebooks, accommodating the "crack up" too neatly (*GN*,
p. 43), obscures the aspect of wastefulness implicit in such Utopian
arrest of her search for the self. I cannot, therefore, agree with Frederick R. Karl's interpretation of the problem:

When Mrs. Lessing foresees that her imperfect female characters will always select an inadequate man to make themselves miserable, she is insist-
ing that hell is within—a visceral time bomb—and it will not be simply
exorcised by anything the external world can offer. With this, we have
placed Mrs. Lessing with the nineteenth-century novelists whose protagonists are themselves piecing together fragments of experience and attempting to derive some unity; she is not with the later novelists who have taken
patterns of fragmentation for granted.[14]

The Golden Notebook neither denies nor accepts the existence of
fragmentation; it halfheartedly flirts with some of its patterns. Hell is
indeed within, but not limited to a "visceral time bomb." It is both a
much more destructive and much more promising potential of human
existence; and, in order to avoid such degree of destruction and realize
the promise, it has to be explored. Anna will have to be made to face
chaos, though *The Golden Notebook* stops short of that.

The "small personal voice" which Lessing defended in her 1957
statement in *Declaration*[15]—the author's as well as the protagonist's
—has contributed greatly to the success of her novels and stories. It
has been a precise, nuanced, intelligent voice; but in its best perform-
ance, in *The Golden Notebook*, it disclosed most clearly its limitations.
In the interview given in 1969 at Stony Brook Lessing said:

---

[14] Karl, p. 19. Karl's study is one of the most interesting essays on Lessing;
I shall therefore spell out my disagreements with him in detail.

[15] *Declaration*, ed. Tom Maschler (London: MacGibbon and Kee, 1959),
p. 27.

Since writing *The Golden Notebook* I've become less personal. I've floated away from the personal. I've stopped saying, "This is *mine*, this is *my* experience." . . . Now, when I start writing, the first thing I ask is, "Who is thinking the same thought? Where are the other people who are like me?" I don't believe anymore that I have a thought. There is a thought around.[16]

This means, as Lessing herself points out, different narrative structures—the form of *The Four-Gated City* "shot to hell"[17]—and a different attitude to her protagonist. It also means a different concept of what ought to be important in the relationship between a man and a woman. Quoted out of context, Lessing's Stony Brook statement, "I'm impatient with people who emphasize sexual revolution. I say we should all go to bed, shut up about sexual liberation, and go on with the important matters,"[18] is indeed startling after the four volumes of the *Children of Violence* and *The Golden Notebook*. In its context, the apocalyptic threat of "the bomb," it expresses a logical development. "The bomb," obviously, is much more than the physical power to destroy—though the physical effects produced approach the metaphysical; it is the mental operations and manipulations sustaining it, a mental state of frenzied exclusion that has to be opposed by restructuring human relationships. In *The Four-Gated City* Lessing has accepted this responsibility.

Karl's misunderstanding of Lessing's development is so radical as to be helpful. He is shocked by the statement I quoted above:

Her turn upon herself is curious, for this conflict between collective politics and personal matters had been the crux of her work of the last two decades. Anna's psychiatrist, in fact, suggested that her political activity was an avoidance of personal blockage. The conflict was real. Now, the conflict has been "resolved." The incredibly difficult question of man-woman relationships becomes "going to bed," and sexual liberation seems an act of conscious choice, whereas before the very question of liberation raised all the familiar problems of identity and will.[19]

Neither Lessing's statement in the Stony Brook interview nor the development of relationships in *The Four-Gated City* suggests in any way that the conflict is considered "resolved"; on the contrary, it has

---

[16] Raskin, p. 173.
[17] *Ibid.*, p. 170.
[18] *Ibid.*, p. 175.
[19] Karl, p. 30.

become much more painful. It is only suggested that the locus of the conflict has shifted. Relationships between a man and a woman remain "incredibly difficult"; it is, however, no longer enough to state that fact, no matter how intelligently and lucidly. Variations of "It's all very odd, isn't it?" are not acceptable anymore because they place too much importance on premature safety (*GN*, pp. 51, 135 f.). Sexual liberation is possible only if it includes the "other,"[20] the man who was so obviously not included in *The Golden Notebook*; it will have to begin again—from the beginning—as the process of contemplation of the "familiar problem of identity and will." Liberation as a conscious choice proved to be impossible in *The Golden Notebook* because the conflicts the women were caught in were kept too static. Now, though still only a potential, its very potentiality is recognized as an indispensable reality in the fight against a domineering destructive technology and the mental and physical acts that made this particular form of domination possible.

The Four-Gated City, as Doris Lessing points out with calm defiance, is a *Bildungsroman*, and as such its structure is informed by Utopia. All the protagonists of *Bildungsromane*, especially in the German tradition from Wolfram's quester hero Parsifal to Musil's Ulrich, the man without qualities, are moving toward the possibility of a conscious choice. In the nineteenth century the process of consciousness usually ended with the protagonist making a meaningful choice—though Utopia ended right there, if the choice (the author controlling it) was honest. In the twentieth century the protagonist has usually been shown unable to make any such decision. Honesty in this context meant renunciation in the nineteenth century; in the twentieth it has meant a fusion of hope and despair, accepting Utopia as a structural principle informing the barely begun process of the self rather than as a defined goal.

The first four volumes of the *Children of Violence* are not *Bildungsromane* in the strict sense of the concept.[21] Matty is neither moving toward a choice, a determining decision she will make at one time or the other, nor is the fact that she is incapable of such a choice

---

[20] "All attachments are symbiotic," Karl points out (p. 27). This is, of course, the single most important problem *The Four-Gated City* is dealing with; yet, in the context of his reading of the novel, Karl sees it negatively.

[21] It follows from Karl's misunderstanding of the intentions of *The Four-Gated City* that he would see Matty as the protagonist of a *Bildungsroman* in the first four volumes of the *Children of Violence*, but not Martha in *The Four-Gated City* (pp. 31ff.).

integrated into the substance and structure of her development. The
first three volumes offer an absorbing examination of the tragicomedy
of socio-political manners a young, intelligent woman finds herself
caught in, especially illuminating because of the clearly outlined mechanism of the colonial setting. They are, however, already "dated" to
a degree, belonging to that majority of novels that Anna describes in
her black notebook as "a function of the fragmented society, the
fragmented consciousness. Human beings are so divided, are becoming
more and more divided, *and more subdivided in themselves,* reflecting
the world, that they reach out desperately, not knowing that they do it,
for information about other groups inside their own country, let alone
groups in other countries" (*GN,* p. 59). Such "novel-reports" are
continuously superseded by new information about, for instance, the
political-social consciousness in the colonies, the consciousness of
women. Lessing-Anna realizes that very well. The sheer expanse of
the *Children of Violence,* the inexorably detailed account of Martha's
political education, is mainly justified as sustaining and making credible—in different ways—the concentration in *The Golden Notebook*
and *The Four-Gated City.* The 1965 *Landlocked,* however, anticipates, if only by implication, certain aspects of the new Martha who,
on the whole, seems to have been born during that sea voyage, separating Africa from England, and *The Four-Gated City* from the rest
of the *Children of Violence.*

Walking through London at night in the beginning of *The Four-
Gated City,* Martha acknowledges precisely those dimensions of experience that Anna found overwhelming and turned away from.
Though it did not expose Matty to a new stage of the self, *Landlocked*
prepared her to an extent to become Martha. In this fourth volume,
individuals and the relations between them are suddenly, if infre-
quently, penetrated by an understanding that has to be founded on an
attitude toward psychological and narrative control different from
that in the other three volumes as well as in *The Golden Notebook.*
Matty-Martha's relationships with her mother and with Thomas Stern
—both of great importance in her process of consciousness in *The
Four-Gated City*—assume an illuminating immediacy, detached from
any distinct perspective, even Matty-Martha's. In Mrs. Quest's dream
about her own mother, which is interwoven in her daydreaming and
preparations connected with the Victory Parade,[22] her relationship to
Martha can suddenly be understood. This dream also provides insight

[22] Doris Lessing, *Landlocked* (New York: New American Library, 1970),
pp. 60ff. Parenthetical page references in the text will be preceded by *L.*

into Martha's need to explore the passionate pity and fear tying her to her mother, leading her toward madness in *The Four-Gated City*.

Matty-Martha's relationship with Thomas, "sucking her into an intensity of feeling" unknown to her before (*L*, p. 81), would have been unimaginable for Anna and Michael: they never achieve such degree of mutuality. If it is almost too much for Martha to bear this intensity of openness to the "other," it is explicitly so for Thomas. He is as vulnerable as she is, and as he tries to understand her needs, she tries to understand his. Thomas' peculiar desire for women can then be accepted by Martha as arising out of his individual need; it is not "the man" who inflicts pain on the woman merely by virtue of being a man. Neither can Thomas fail her in the role of the "real man," because Martha understands the unreality of such roles. If one chooses to speak of failure at all in this context, one would have to say that they both fail their own potentiality.

Martha may be stronger and more intelligent than Thomas— Lessing's women usually are, being part of their creator[23]—but he is ahead of her on the way toward the self, having admitted chaos. Sensing this dimly from the documents of madness he leaves behind, she alone understands them as "messages" (*L*, p. 272), copying them, trying to make "sense" the way she will much later try to keep some control over her own descents into the self,[24] mapping the route of his search. She takes Thomas' crumbling papers with her into her new life. Only much later will she come to understand the full meaning of his search outlined in one of the "stories" Thomas made up for himself: " 'Once there was a man who travelled to a distant country. When he got there, the enemy he had fled from was waiting for him. Although he had proved the usefulness of travelling, he went to yet another country. No, his enemy was *not* there.' (Surprised, are you! said the red pencil.) 'So he killed himself' " (*L*, p. 270). She will have to recover her past.[25]

Martha, setting out on the search herself, having cast off Matty

[23] See the strangely abstracted, very much oversimplified man-woman model in "Dialogue": Bill, meant to present an extreme, yet admirable position, appears almost a caricature; so does Saul; middle-aged Mark, generous, understanding, still loves his wife Lynda in a way which is destructive for her and judged almost grotesquely immature by Martha (*FGC*, pp. 351ff.).

[24] See, for instance, *The Four-Gated City*, pp. 507ff., 522ff.

[25] See *The Four-Gated City*, pp. 206ff., in which Martha prepares herself for her mother's visit.

entirely for that purpose, is a strikingly different person, certain pre-
paratory similarities in *Landlocked* notwithstanding. The change is
clearly indicated by the author-narrator's attitude toward her. As
narrator Lessing withdraws from the tone of omniscience, from explanations, comparisons, encouragements, and patient irony that had
pervaded the first three volumes of the *Children of Violence*, the author-narrator now tries to preserve a high degree of immediacy, which
is extended also to the relationships that Martha forms. Martha is
given time and space for confusion, eventually even chaos. Lessing is
much less protective of her than she is of any other female protagonist.
Anna and the Matty of the *Children of Violence* are eminently more
vulnerable, judging from their author's possessive attitude toward
them alone. The degree of vulnerability seems to be connected with
the insistence on "*my* experience" Lessing referred to in her Stony
Brook interview. This very personal relationship between the author
and the protagonist before *The Four-Gated City* is clearly reflected in
Anna's creation of Ella for her yellow notebook, resembling her in
mental and physical make-up, fascinating her by her state of being
besieged: "She wore her hair tied back with a black bow. I was struck
by her eyes, extraordinarily watchful and defensive. They were windows in a fortress" (*GN*, p. 393). Ella is a metaphor for Anna, including even Anna's absorbed interest in exact chemical measurements
(*GN*, pp. 393 ff.), the elements in the experiment being members of a
social group. Parts of the metaphor are then used independently, for
instance Ella in the act of tying back her hair, fighting back chaos
(*GN*, p. 394). In its mimetic simplicity this personal intimate gesture
seems to defy abstraction; and the success of *The Golden Notebook* is
partly based on this illusion. In reality, the abstraction and oversimpli-
fication inherent in the structural use of such metaphors—the four
notebooks, the Anna-Ella projection as a whole and in details—have
not been avoided. Attempting "to create order, to create a new way
of looking at life" (*GN*, p. 59), Doris Lessing-Anna superimposes
structures of order on chaos in a way that precludes mediation.

The structure of *The Golden Notebook*, then, hinders the process
of self-knowledge. Neither the four notebooks, meant to guarantee
flexibility, nor the stories, meant to guarantee multiperspectivity (*GN*,
pp. 455 ff.), fulfill their purpose; they yield only prematurely arrested
analyses of relationships, closing off precariously for a time what will
destroy them anyway in the end. The enemy is intensely feared but
not known. In this the novel's ambivalence, really a structural problem, is essentially different from the ambivalent endings of *The Four-*

Gated City or *Briefing for a Descent into Hell*, where the concept of knowledge of the self as process is consistently supported by narrative means.

Walking toward Jack's house by night, Martha is suspended between two protective enclosures that she does not want or need: Baxter's cozily shabby self-evident upper-middle-class security and Jack's starkly outlined, threatened "pure" space, determined to shut out a chaotic outside. Martha already has a very different relationship to rooms, enclosures, than Matty or Anna. Anna's room (*GN*, p. 52) resembles Jack's (*GN*, p. 43) and Bill's in colors and the feeling of lines creating space; these are all rooms of defiance, in the center of which is a desperate need for protection from unexplored chaos and unexplored fear of chaos. Martha is ready for the room in Mark's house, which is open, unthreatened, admitting the presence of thoughts distilled from past inhabitants; the sycamore tree defines the room from the outside, suggesting shifts of space in the temporal flux rather than protective static space against time (*FGC*, pp. 100 ff.).

Walking, Martha is "nothing but a soft dark receptive intelligence," open to the "invasions" of people and places she has experienced (*GN*, p. 36). She is given by her creator the freedom of "narrated monologue"[26] to a degree which has no precedent in the *Children of Violence* or *The Golden Notebook*. Seeing Jack and calling Phoebe on the telephone are like two blocks in the swiftly moving sequence of pictures and sounds. The recognizable elements of her experience seem to be changing their meaning, oscillating between fear and "a state of quiet" which, however, she is losing fast. At the telephone box where she will arrange for an appointment that will end her "aimless" open wandering through London, she feels she has lost already what she had just found: "Yes, but remember the space you discovered today. It was gone, gone quite, not even a memory, and she sunk down out of reach of the place where words, bits of music, juggled and jangled and informed. And even the calm place below (beside?) was going, it was a memory, a memory that was going" (*FGC*, p. 39). Martha's "education" in *The Four-Gated City* is toward the conscious recovery of that space with its pictures and voices that she received here by chance, made sensitive, receptive by her "aimless" walking,

---

[26] I borrow this translation for the German expression "erlebte Rede," that is, "the rendering of a character's thoughts in his own idiom, while maintaining the third-person form of narration," from Dorrit Cohn's essay, "Narrated Monologue: Definition of a Fictional Style," *Comparative Literature*, 18 (1966), 98.

talking, listening. Much later, when Martha is on her first willed, and now controlled, reconnaissance descent into the self, she will remember, when she reaches that space, that she had been there and forgotten:

If she sat quite still, or walked steadily up and down, the space in her head remained steady, or lightening and darkening in a pulse, like the irregular pulse of the sea. She had known this lightness and clarity before—yes, walking through London, long ago. And then too, it had been the reward of not-eating, not-sleeping, using her body as an engine to get her out of the small dim prison of every day. (*FGC*, p. 472)

It takes Martha almost fifteen years and 450 pages closely packed with people, acts, and ideas to get back to where she had once been, prepared now to chart this landscape of the self in order to be able to use it. Repeatedly pointing out the extraordinary power of conformity to certain dimensions of experience, reinforced through centuries of standard education, to the explosive impulse contained in social ridicule,[27] Lessing moves Martha very slowly and cautiously to the point where she thinks it possible to claim credibility for the "disorderly company" she will have to ask the reader to join.[28] Martha has proved herself a very shrewd, capable, skeptical woman, living in Mark's house, coping with very different but always difficult human situations, showing a great deal of common sense. Yet, social developments, on a personal and general level, make it imperative for her to pursue her search for identity through a descent into the unexplored self.

The richly detailed story of a group of men and women living through the fifties and sixties, participating, resisting, changing, and

---

[27] After her first descent, Martha starts gathering information on the greatest possible variety of aspects of the occult. She begins with Jimmy Wood's "potted library representing everything rejected by official culture and scholarship" (*FGC*, p. 486)—these books, of course, feed Jimmy's mind, triggering ideas for his machines which are perfectly acceptable to and exploitable by "official culture." Martha asserts her distaste for the "dottiness," "eccentricity," "shadiness" of most of the occult, but she is also aware of her conditioned response (*FGC*, pp. 488f.); see also Francis writing to Amanda about the powerful concept "superstition" (*FGC*, p. 584).

[28] Some reviewers have not responded very generously to that invitation: see D. J. Enright in *The New York Review of Books,* July 31, 1969, pp. 22-24, and Mary Ellmann in the *New York Times Book Review,* May 18, 1969, pp. 4-5.

watching themselves change, discourages the reader from more than occasional identification with the protagonist. Martha does not emerge clearly enough from the symbiotic relationships she is drawn into, formed by and forming herself during those fifteen years in Mark's house. Shedding Matty, she has overcome the need to define herself against the "other," man: now she traces the process of self-definition within the group Martha-Mark-Lynda, the permanent center around which changing constellations of young and old people, lovers, friends, and enemies revolve. This center group, however, is itself constantly changing—an important element in Martha's preparation for the descent. Martha fully understands the meaning of this fluidity in their relationship during one of the peace marches where she sees variations of Lynda-Mark-Martha, Mark-Martha-Lynda pass by in the long line of the marchers: she realizes that the only promise of permanence is in change (*FGC*, pp. 397, 518).

In this context Martha's position as secretary to Mark is of significance. She is not an independent intellectual like the writer Anna whose independence is, very importantly, extended to the economical aspect of her existence. She "serves" Mark in the archetypical role of the exploited female, the secretary. Yet, because of the individual situation in Mark's house and because of her essential participation in his work, the conception, birth, and precarious development of the four-gated city in the desert,[29] she gains moments of true independence which were inaccessible to Anna because they are essentially informed by mutuality.

The plea for mutuality, potentially dangerous because it can be perverted so easily into liberal rhetoric, gains strength and substance from the detailed accounts in *The Four-Gated City* of men and women trying to achieve it through politics, through personal relationships, failing mostly, achieving it in rare vulnerable moments. In spite of its sprawling character, the novel moves fairly fast through those fifteen years of political change and changing attitudes toward politics. Martha, having gone through her communist phase when she meets Mark, seemingly has an advantage over him, as she knows what is going to come next from remembering herself moving through the different stages of passionate involvement and disillusion. And Mark does in-

---

[29] Especially important is the part she plays in drawing Mark into the social dimension of experience: she anticipates much more realistic threats of destruction for the archetypical city; informed by her experience of the past she can insist on responsibility to the reality of the future (*FGC*, p. 134).

deed follow those stages, but he is also granted his own rhythm of change. Lynda, beyond politics from the very beginning (*FGC*, p. 165), is not judged right or wrong. Lessing refrains from making her even sympathetic; the victim is by no means idealized. Lynda may know more than Martha, who has lived through all those stages as a healthy intelligent young woman; she also may not. For all of them, knowledge is a process they are engaged in; the movement of the process differs from person to person; it is open-ended for all of them.

The greatest strength of Lessing's argument for the possibility of truly mutual relationships lies in the manner in which these three people, Martha, Lynda, and Mark, are shown to move along together for some time so that they can part without bitterness. There is none of the brilliant bitterness of *The Golden Notebook* in *The Four-Gated City*: Mark, emotionally more immature than the two women, is a very cautious intellectual whose main virtue is to resist prematurely brilliant sentences on life; Martha is above all shrewd and common-sensical, patiently intelligent about herself and other people; Lynda, badly hurt and repressed in her specific talents, is largely inarticulate. The only certainty they have reached in middle age is their trust in the help they can give each other by understanding more and more clearly their own unresolved problems. Martha, for instance, fighting furiously with the various shapes of the self-hater (*FGC*, pp. 507 ff.) imposed on her by insufficient recovery of her past, understands now the particular form of defeat in Lynda; she also understands why Mark, too possessively "in love" with Lynda, is still unable to explore her defeat and needs to close himself off to that particular part of the search, though he accepts the responsibility for the partial results of Lynda's search and Martha's: tracing, charting on the "outside," on the walls of his study (*FGC*, pp. 282, 414) what their "working" (*FGC*, pp. 354 ff.) their way down into the self will make them see.

One could say, then, that it is not Martha who is the protagonist of the *Bildungsroman, The Four-Gated City*, but Martha, Mark, and Lynda together. This is underscored by the failure of Martha's relationship with Jack. Walking toward his house in the beginning of the novel, she knows that Jack is the only one in London who would allow her "to go on living as she was now, rootless, untied, free," which is, as far as she knows, the condition of reaching the inner space with pictures and voices:

And she understood just why he lived as he did. She had "understood" it before; but she understood it differently now that she was in that area of the human mind that Jack also inhabited. Yes. But in that case, why did she shy so strongly away from Jack, from what he stood for—or at least, she did with a good part of herself. That part whose name was Self-preservation. She knew that. *He was paying too high a price* for what he got. (*FGC*, p. 38)

Jack at this point knows more than Martha; making love, he has discovered that "hatred is a sort of wavelength you can tune into. After all, it's always there, hatred is simply part of the world, like one of the colours of the rainbow. You can go into it, as if it were a *place*" (*FGC*, p. 57). But Jack cannot sustain that knowledge; when Martha sees him again years later, he has "become stupid"; once "all a subtle physical intelligence," his body has been taken over by hatred, by a degraded mind that needs to possess the other completely by degrading her morally (*FGC*, p. 386). This development is implicit in his relationship with women when Martha first makes love to him: his end is the body; the silences between her and him are not filled, contented (*FGC*, p. 62). The comfort he offers her (the acceptance, in her body, of the passing of time and death) isolates her further, as he makes even that acceptance part of his taking possession of her and, at the same time, frees himself from the changes that time works on his own body (*FGC*, pp. 54, 63, 381). The relationship with Jack is a step between Anna's love that did not reach such depth of intimacy through the body and Martha's attachment to Mark which goes beyond it (*FGC*, pp. 227 ff.).

The second part of *The Four-Gated City*, in which Martha really begins her life with Mark and Lynda, is introduced by a long quote from Robert Musil's *Man without Qualities*. It is taken from a chapter entitled "A chapter that can be skipped by anyone who has no very high opinion of thinking as an occupation"[30] in which Ulrich, the man without qualities, Musil's mathematician-protagonist, is straying in his thoughts from the research paper he is working on. He has just

---

[30] Chapter 28: "Ein Kapitel, das jeder überschlagen kann, der von der Beschäftigung mit Gedanken keine besondere Meinung hat." Robert Musil, *Der Mann ohne Eigenschaften*, ed. Adolf Frisé (Hamburg: Rowohlt, 1970). Wilkins/ Kaiser's translation is not very accurate and misses the irony; a more accurate reading is as follows: "A chapter that can be skipped by anyone who does not think very highly of getting involved with thoughts." A large posthumously published part of *The Man without Qualities* is still not available in English, nor are Musil's socio-philosophical essays and his extensive diary commentaries; the translations used here are mine.

written down an equation of the state of water, and so he starts thinking about water. Musil, like any writer working with the *Bildungsroman*, concentrates on the development of his protagonist's consciousness. Ulrich, his creation and his friend, is speculative by temperament
and shares with his author a discipline of mind and imagination
that makes it difficult for him to accept the solid established reality
of dailiness as real. His many abilities and qualities, highly favored by
the twentieth century, have only been used to a very small degree in
his scientific work that rewarded him with a promising academic
career. When he realizes this, he breaks off his career, taking "a year's
leave from his life"[31] to test his abilities by applying them to the
(assumed) reality of his time. He understands immediately that this
reality is at least one hundred years behind what is being thought, behind its potential, in other words,[32] and that anyone who consistently
confronts reality with modern thought processes will get involved in
recreating reality, that is, will have to admit chaos. Musil developed
specific verbal forms to present these thought processes; he uses the
term "essayistic" to define them, and this definition has been used by
critics to praise or blame the novel. But "essayistic" means much more
for Musil than the assumption that the novelist is entitled to ask the
reader to put up with occasional reflective passages—as the one
Lessing quoted from, for instance. It means for Musil: to integrate the
adventure of reason into the novel, to accept the responsibility for a
verbal precision that is usually limited—to mention only examples
from the German language—to philosophers of language like Ludwig
Wittgenstein, Karl Kraus, or the eighteenth-century mathematician
Georg Christoph Lichtenberg. Essayistic is synonymous with Utopian
for Musil; that is, Utopian understood as a structural principle, informing the direction of the process of consciousness, but refraining
from the imposition of a goal, which would, by definition, negate the
single most important element in man's understanding and projecting
reality, potentiality. The basis of Ulrich's intellectual (verbal) discipline is his "sense of possibility," his *Möglichkeitssinn*.

   To return to the passage that evidently interested Lessing: Ulrich,
thinking about water, follows religious, scientific, and just daily, "normal" associations connected with that concept and, as usual, is stopped
by the problem of communication:

---

[31] *Man without Qualities*, I, 49; *Mann ohne Eigenschaften*, p. 47.

[32] "dass die Wirklichkeit um mindestens 100 Jahre zurück ist hinter dem,
was gedacht wird." Robert Musil, *Tagebücher, Aphorismen, Essays und Reden*,
ed. Adolf Frisé (Hamburg: Rowohlt, 1955), p. 786.

Ultimately the whole thing dissolved into systems of formulae that were all somehow connected with each other, and in the whole wide world there were only a few dozen people who thought alike about even as simple a thing as water; all the rest talked about it in languages that were at home somewhere between today and several thousands of years ago. So it must be said that if a man just starts thinking a bit he gets into what one might call pretty disorderly company.[33]

Admitting this "disorderly company" into the decisions defining the main structures of the novel, Musil and Lessing share essential assumptions about the novelist's function and responsibility. They are both basically unconcerned about the fate of the novel as form, declaring their quite extraordinary confidence that the novelist is indeed responsible for the whole potential stratum of an aware intelligent person's experience. It is true that Ulrich's is an exceptional mind; Mark and Martha have neither the trained mental discipline nor the dedication to epistemological problems that Ulrich has. His thought processes, immersing and dissolving the mimetic surfaces of the story he is part of, his need to shape and reshape each sentence until it is a sentence on reality, a judgment of the split between knowledge and experience, put the novel on an intellectual level which is very different from that of *The Four-Gated City*. Musil, a mathematician and behavioral psychologist—he wrote his dissertation on Ernst Mach and did considerable research in the field—deeply influenced by the Viennese School, spent three decades writing and rewriting the huge torso of his *Man without Qualities*; his idea of verbal precision and verbal discipline is, obviously, quite different from Lessing's. Yet, his primary concern as a novelist, to pursue the interrelationships between the potential and the real, is also Lessing's in her last two novels.

Musil sets the (intellectual) action of the novel in the years immediately before the First World War, 1912 to 1914; the novel, never "completed," was meant to end with Ulrich's mobilization, the apocalyptic disaster of the Great War. The First World War, as the first total war, had an effect on the imagination probably stronger than the explosion of "the bomb"; at least, the effect was intellectually more

---

[33] *Man without Qualities*, I, 130. "Schließlich löst sich das Ganze in Systeme von Formeln auf, die untereinander irgendwie zusammenhängen, und es gibt in der weiten Welt nur einige Dutzend Menschen, die selbst von einem so einfachen Ding, wie es Wasser ist, das gleiche denken; alle anderen reden davon in Sprachen, die zwischen heute und einigen tausend Jahren früher irgendwo zu Hause sind. Man muß also sagen, daß ein Mensch, wenn er nur ein bißchen nachdenkt, gewissermaßen in recht unordentliche Gesellschaft gerät!" (*Mann ohne Eigenschaften*, p. 113)

confusing and destructive. Musil always claimed that he was not writing a historical novel at all, as he was interested in the typical. The intellectual confusion he describes so brilliantly in his novel and in many socio-philosophical essays[34] is indeed rather postwar; his analysis is meant to show that the intellectual problems that led to the disaster of the First World War could not be resolved by it, but were intensified, and led straight into the Second World War and—had he lived to know of "the bomb"—into the Third (Atomic) World War. The split between experience and knowledge has become too wide; the caricature of knowledge, scientific technological specialization, carries a great potential of destruction. The evil is by no means science *per se* for Musil—on the contrary, it has contributed greatly to the adventure of reason—but its openness to exploitation by the stupidity of power which is made possible by extreme unmediated specialization.

Whole areas of the human mind, continents of human potential, have not been explored, and their existence is denied precisely by those who, by virtue of their intellectual training and discipline, ought to be most interested in them, but who see their intellect too much as a highly sophisticated machine, defining problems in terms of instrumental rationality. Scientific decisions are determined by the question of means rather than of ends; they are "value-free." What to do with the moon after we landed on it is a layman's question, as well as what to do with "the bomb" after it has been developed. Most of these questions will be answered by the Department of Defense, another specialist. Science, dependent on a more and more complicated technology, has changed from being man's adventure of coping with nature into an instrument of domination that constantly defeats its own purpose, as it neglects the open rational structure of coping. The concept of coping is a concept of mediation, dependent on feedback from many sources; modern science has limited the number of those sources to one, the specialist. The seemingly extreme case of the inventor Jimmy Wood, writer of science fiction and consumer of old occult documents, is really a good case in point—though Musil would probably have

---

[34] See, for instance, the essays "Mathematical Man" (1913)—"Der mathematische Mensch"; the Rathenau review, "Notes on a Metaphysics" (1914)— "Anmerkung zu einer Metaphysik"; "Helpless Europe" (1922)— "Das hilflose Europa"; the Spengler review, "Mind and Experience. Notes for Readers Who Have Come Through the Decline of the West" (1921)—"Geist und Erfahrung. Anmerkungen für Leser, welche dem Untergang des Abendlandes entronnen sind"; "On Stupidity" (1937)— "Über die Dummheit." All these essays are collected in *Tagebücher*.

found him too much of a caricature. But then, technology itself has become much more of a caricature since the Second World War. Not only is Jimmy completely oblivious to human values, but his real genius consists in extending instrumental reason a step into the barely charted areas and destroying them before they can be charted properly (*FGC*, pp. 504 ff.).

In his 1921 essay, "Helpless Europe," Musil formulated the problem: "It is not that we have too much reason and too little soul, rather, we don't apply enough reason in problems concerning the soul."[35] Ulrich moves in a direction informed by this mediation. After a great deal of brilliantly detailed socio-psychological satire which has some parallels in the shrewd observations on the intellectual-political life in the fifties and sixties Lessing offers in *The Four-Gated City*, Ulrich decides that he has to go further. So far he has been quite invulnerable, being so irresistibly right in his sentences on a society that is constantly one step behind some phantom "Zeitgeist," instead of controlling it intelligently. He is watching, observing, commenting—somewhat like Martha and Mark. When he begins the next stage of his experiment of "exact living," that is, of attempting to mediate between reason and feeling, which will take him toward the inner space Martha and Lynda are experimenting with—Musil calls the exploration of that space "der andere Zustand" ["the other state"]—he will be much more vulnerable. Taking the responsibility of this mediation so very seriously, Musil-Ulrich never found his way out of this particular stage of the experiment. He had intended to lead the protagonist back to a more obviously social involvement; but the further he advanced on his exploration, the more difficult the problems became, the smaller the steps he was able to define. As he understood psychological problems above all as epistemological questions, he could not abandon himself or Ulrich to the descent into the self the way Lessing can make Martha or Charles Watkins abandon themselves. Martha, it is true, retains control, even a degree of common sense on her descent (*FGC*, pp. 507 ff.; 522 ff.), but by no means the precisely articulated control Ulrich cannot do without: rejecting what he calls "pedantic precision," he searches for a "fantastic precision."[36]

Ulrich is always afraid of drowning in the wrong kind of mysticism;[37] he abhors intellectual sloppiness, which Martha will accept if

---

[35] "Wir haben nicht zuviel Verstand und zuwenig Seele, sondern wir haben zuwenig Verstand in den Fragen der Seele." (*Tagebücher*, p. 638)

[36] See *Man without Qualities*, I, 294; *Mann ohne Eigenschaften*, p. 247.

[37] Musil's expression "Schleudermystik" (*Mann ohne Eigenschaften*, p.

she thinks it necessary; he, however, cannot, in this way, project the end separated, if only temporarily so, from the means. Attempting to mediate between mathematics and mysticism, pursuing a "taghelle Mystik," a mysticism as clear as plain daylight,[38] Ulrich will never stop doubting what he experiences in his love for his sister Agathe, his "self-love,"[39] completing him to the perfection of "the other state," the Millennium[40] of that unexplored space within. Ulrich will always maintain the distance of irony while courting most seriously the "disorderly company" he meets on his exploration of the self. It is, however, a specific kind of irony:

This is irony: to present a clergyman in such a way that a Bolshevik is hit too. To present an oaf such that the author suddenly feels: that's what I am too in part. This sort of irony—constructive irony—is more or less unknown in Germany today. It must emerge naked from the total connection of things.[41]

This "constructive irony," as Musil further points out, has nothing to do with ridicule or condescension; it is rather a structural principle to include the reader into the protagonist's process of consciousness. It is easier to follow Ulrich than to follow Martha or Watkins because we will always be given the means to question, to doubt and to reject the "disorderly company" we have been invited to join. This, however, ought not to be misunderstood as a negative judgment of Lessing's attempts to push further into the inner space: as her fear is more urgent, more immediate than Musil's was, her means to document it have to be more drastic, and her prescriptions for hope both more striking and more vulnerable.[42] *The Four-Gated City* is a courageous

---

1088) is untranslatable, combining the associations "centrifugal," "hurling," "selling out below cost-price."

[38] *Mann ohne Eigenschaften*, p. 1088.

[39] Ulrich says to his sister: "Du bist meine Eigenliebe!" *Mann ohne Eigenschaften*, p. 899; *Man without Qualities*, III, 274.

[40] *Man without Qualities*, III, 431; *Mann ohne Eigenschaften*, p. 1029.

[41] "Ironie ist: einen Klerikalen so darstellen, daß neben ihm auch ein Bolschewik getroffen ist. Einen Trottel so darstellen, daß der Autor plötzlich fühlt: das bin ich ja zum Teil selbst. Diese Art von Ironie—die konstruktive Ironie—ist im heutigen Deutschland ziemlich unbekannt. Es ist der Zusammenhang der Dinge, aus dem sie nackt hervorgeht." (*Mann ohne Eigenschaften*, p. 1603)

[42] See Martha's letter to Francis (*The Four-Gated City*, pp. 596ff.). Her description of "the new children" (p. 608), tentative as it is, is still too much of a good thing.

and a necessary piece of work; Enright's negative review of it in *The New York Review of Books* in fact illuminates the justification of Lessing's development from *The Golden Notebook* to *The Four-Gated City*: "That Mrs. Lessing is so shrewd about things as they are makes me resent the more sharply her uneasy excursions into things to come."[43] Uneasy these excursions may be; they are now the indispensable basis for her precise observation of things as they are.

---

[43] Enright, p. 23. See, however, Roger Sale in his review of *Briefing for a Descent into Hell, The New York Review of Books,* May 6, 1971, p. 15.

Feeling and Reason
in Doris Lessing's Fiction

Lynn Sukenick

Of all the clichés about women, the belief that they are creatures of feeling—and men creatures of reason—is one of the most ancient and persuasive. The extent of this belief has ranged from a mistrust of woman's irrationality to an ardent faith in the saving power of her emotional nature. As nonreflective *bios*, woman has been seen as the root, the source, and the touchstone; she gives the surety of the natural. In her function as lifegiver woman is supposedly simple and whole; her power to give birth defies and makes unnecessary the complexities of self-consciousness.

The division between emotion and reason has been apportioned not only to men and women but among kinds of women. Jane Austen —whose freedom from inner conflicts about gender perhaps helped to supply that beautifully unruffled prose whose ironies we find so comforting—posed the terms in her novel *Sense and Sensibility*. Although there could indeed be a Man of Feeling, as Mackenzie showed in his novel of that name, it was primarily the women who enacted the iconography of tears and fainting as it appeared in novels of sensibility in the eighteenth and early nineteenth centuries. Such women were the target of Mary Wollstonecraft's *A Vindication of the Rights of Woman*, and living proof, for her, that women had to be educated out of the propensity toward exaggerated emotion which idleness encouraged. Women of sensibility were the object, too, of Austen's indicting wit in *Sense and Sensibility* and *Northanger Abbey*. To Marianne's fit of nostalgia in the former book, Elinor, the sister of good

98

sense, comments dryly, "It is not everyone who has your passion for dead leaves."[1]

The satire of the first great female novelist did not, however, kill off the novel of sensibility; refined away from the eighteenth-century potboilers of empathy, it has emerged full-blown and serious in our century in the sensitive and lyrical fiction of writers like James, Proust, Woolf, and Mansfield. In spite of the influence of male writers (and Proust was homosexual and James sexually ambiguous), the novel of sensibility has been associated insistently with the feminine. Whether it is correct or not, Diana Trilling's statement is fairly typical: "In our own century certainly, from the time of Dorothy Richardson right down to our present-day women writers for *The New Yorker*, the female self has been the locus of all the sensibility presumed to have been left us by modern life."[2] Women, although without perhaps the silliness of Austen's heroines or of Wollstonecraft's subjects, have maintained themselves as the caretakers of sensibility in this century as well.

Doris Lessing, whose position as one of the major women writers of the twentieth century would now seem assured, stands quite apart from the feminine tradition of sensibility. Her fiction is tough, clumsy, rational, concerned with social roles, collective action and conscience, and unconcerned with niceties of style and subtlety of feeling for its own sake. She is, nevertheless, fully aware of the bifurcation between sense and sensibility and the meaning it presents to women, and it is with an awareness of the terms that she makes her choice. In the preface to *African Stories* she writes, "*The Pig* and *The Trinket Box* are two of my earliest. I see them as two forks of a road. The second— intense, careful, self-conscious, mannered—could have led to a kind of writing usually described as 'feminine.' The style of *The Pig* is straight, broad, direct; is much less beguiling, but is the highway to the kind of writing that has the freedom to develop as it likes."[3] The latter part of this statement is ambiguous enough; suffice it to mean that Lessing finds her freedom in a realm apart from the traditional feminine resource of sensibility.[4]

---

[1] Jane Austen, *Sense and Sensibility* (New York: Harper, 1961), p. 53.

[2] Diana Trilling, "The Image of Women in Contemporary Literature," in *The Woman in America*, ed. Robert J. Lifton (Boston: Beacon, 1964), p. 66.

[3] Doris Lessing, *African Stories* (London: Michael Joseph, 1964), p. 9.

[4] Even her characters are averse to the kind of work customarily expected of women. Ella "had written half a dozen short stories which she herself de-

Sensibility comes in for mockery and worse in Lessing's work. In *In Pursuit of the English,* an Orwellian memoir, one of her first encounters is with an Australian lady:

She was a woman of inveterate sensibility. Her name was Brenda. . . . She wore artistic clothes. She had been crying, and was still damp. Almost the first thing she said was, "I do hope your child is sensitive. My Daphne is very sensitive. A highly strung child." I knew then that the whole thing was doomed. . . . Then she said everything was too much for her, and so I went out and bought the rations and had some keys cut. While I did this, I reflected on the value of helplessness.[5]

Lessing indulges her grudge against sensibility elsewhere as well. In *The Golden Notebook* she engages her heroine in a literary practical joke against a sensitive homosexual editor. Collaborating with a cynical young writer, she invents a journal supposedly "written by a lady author of early middle-age, who had spent some years in an African colony, and was afflicted with sensibility" (*GN,* p. 437). The "lady" writes of a conversation at a cocktail party:

He suggested I should do a play . . . which should take no sides but emphasise the essential tragedy of the colonial situation, the tragedy of the whites. It is true, of course . . . what is poverty, what are hunger, malnutrition, homelessness, the *pedestrian* degradations (his word—how sensitive, how full of *true* sensibility are a certain type of Englishman, far more intuitive than any woman!) compared to the reality, the human reality of the white dilemma? . . . I went home, nearer to reality I think than ever in my life . . . to my fresh narrow bed. (*GN,* p. 438)

Heavy-handed as the irony is in this passage, it points to a reason for the rejection of sensibility which is on Lessing's part not casual and temperamental but rather an aversion based on her commitment to something larger than private consciousness, or more precisely, a commitment to link private consciousness with historical event. She believes, in George Eliot's words, that there is no private life that has not been conditioned by a larger public life, and she is galled by those whose decorum or inclination excludes the troublingly unattractive by

---

scribed as 'sensitive and feminine,' and which both she and Julia said were the kind of stories they most disliked." *The Golden Notebook* (New York: Ballantine Books, 1968), p. 170. Parenthetical page references in the text, preceded by *GN,* are to this edition.

[5] Doris Lessing, *In Pursuit of the English* (New York: Ballantine Books, 1966), p. 37.

proclaiming it unworthy of attention. In a statement made in 1957 she chided Colin Wilson for finding starvation and illiteracy uninteresting and urged that "he and people like him should at least try and understand it exists and what a great and creative force it is, one which will affect us all."[6] Discussing *Children of Violence*, which she had planned in 1952, she said it is

a study of the individual conscience in its relations with the collective. The fact that no critic has seen this does not, of course, surprise me. As long as critics are as "sensitive," subjective, and uncommitted to anything but their own private sensibilities, there will be no body of criticism worth taking seriously in this country. At the moment our critics remind me a lot of Victorian ladies making out their library lists. . . .[7]

Victorian ladies, lady authors of early middle age—the reversion to the image of a certain kind of lady as the repository of foolishness or hysteria is an instinctive cartooning which the contemporary, rigidly ideological feminist would check. Yet this sort of lady (to use the word "woman" would be inaccurate) is very much apparent in Lessing's fiction and serves as a key to the development of the women of the generation after her, those "free women" whom Lessing describes so well.

The most fully portrayed middle-aged woman in Lessing's fiction is Mrs. Quest, mother of the central figure of *Children of Violence*. It is against her mother's vapidity that Martha Quest forms her character; her self-respect is fashioned out of her sense of difference from the woman who hovers uselessly in the margins of her life. Although it is Martha's nature to behave sensibly, her common sense is reinforced by her desire to avoid the manipulative histrionics, the mindless tabulations of inconsequential matters, the cruel helplessness, which seem to inform repeatedly the older woman's behavior.

Both Martha and her friends wage a battle against the pressing image of the older, lifeless, unfulfilled women around them. The lives of these women are suggestive, possibly prophetic, and the younger women bank their character building on their ability to outwit the future. Many succumb: in *Landlocked*, Marjorie, ashamed of her tears and her tension, says, "If I don't watch out I'll be having a nervous breakdown—imagine, I always used to despise women like

---

[6] Doris Lessing, "The Small Personal Voice," in *Declaration,* ed. Tom Maschler (London: MacGibbon and Kee, 1959), p. 25.

[7] *Ibid.,* p. 22.

me."[8] Although there are modern variations on the older women's powerlessness, still, the women, who at thirty-five are divorced, neurotic, alcoholic, are, Lessing takes pains to point out, those "who are at twenty the liveliest, the most intelligent, the most promising" (*L*, p. 205). It is women, not men, who are the enemy, and in defense against any alliance with the women who fail, who give in, Martha ranges herself with the men. Working against an admission of female resemblance is the mistrust of female irrationality, an irrationality which crops up in Lessing's fiction not only as eccentricity, or paralyzing neurosis, but, as in *The Grass Is Singing*, a foaming craziness.

Lessing's hostility to the literary attitude of sensibility is based upon her commitment to large issues and to the political. Martha Quest's avoidance of the emotions is in large part a result of her matrophobia. Both Martha and the heroine of *The Golden Notebook*, Anna Wulf, resist so powerfully the claims of emotion while at the same time deploring the numbness of the society around them that we are forced to regard this not as an inadvertent or supportive theme but as a dominant subject. Let us examine the kind of attention Lessing brings to emotion in *The Golden Notebook*, *Children of Violence*, and one or two shorter works.

It is necessary to be wary, but not too wary, of amalgamating the heroines in a study of Lessing's works. Just as some critics have confused Lessing with her heroines, to the author's just annoyance, so one may accidentally combine the traits of Martha and Anna, similar in many respects, into one prototype. There is, in fact, a good deal of genuine overlapping among Lessing's characters, occurring in part from the fact that she is less interested in producing a fine, shapely, and unforgettable character than in conveying the angles and stresses of responsible consciousness, the roughened confrontations of conscience and culture, the attraction to certain ideas and the changes of mind that occur when an individual thinks, as a way of moving through life and plot. In the case of Martha, moreover, there is a complete transformation by the fifth volume of Lessing's "continuous novel"; as history becomes increasingly the protagonist, Martha loses most of the personality that has earmarked her as Martha and dissolves into the lives of those around her like some sort of intellectual Mary Worth.

What strikes us first about Martha Quest, whom we meet initially as an adolescent, is her watchfulness, her care to perceive the world

---

[8] Doris Lessing, *Landlocked* (New York: New American Library, 1970), p. 273. Parenthetical page references in the text will be preceded by *L*.

accurately and without the intervention of sentiment. One of the pivotal and most rewarding pasages in *Martha Quest* is Martha's experience of what she calls "the moment," which is something like the sort of "moment" that appears in the fiction of Virginia Woolf, or for that matter in the poetry of Wordsworth. This moment is, for Martha, an experience which can be repeated but not willed, one where she feels "a slow integration" with the world around her in which "everything became one, shuddering together in a dissolution of dancing atoms," and in which "her flesh was the earth . . . and her eyes stared, fixed like the eye of the sun."[9] This moment of immersive trance soon becomes intolerable, but once out of it she tries to possess it by recollecting it. The memory changes, however, as the effort is being made, and "it was with nostalgia that she longed to 'try again.' " Martha watches herself, tempted to transform a moment of process into a keepsake of well-being, and becomes irritable: "the wave of nostalgia made her angry. She knew it to be a falsity; for it was a longing for something that had never existed, an 'ecstasy,' in short. There had been no ecstasy, only a difficult knowledge. It was as if a beetle had sung. There should be a new word for *illumination*" (*MQ*, p. 53). The emblem of her transport, then, is the dry rasp of a Rhodesian beetle rather than, say, the liquid notes of the nightingale that accompany a Keatsian moment, and the texture of value in the experience is not the unleashing of spiralling emotion that is ecstasy, but a "difficult knowledge," a "message," the access of spiritual information.

Martha is as critical of her own emotions and of potentially false feeling in the later books of the *Violence* series; often the sentiment she has not freed herself from is a bait she dangles in front of her condemning intellect. In *A Ripple from the Storm* Lessing writes of her:

Martha watched in herself the growth of an extraordinarily unpleasant and upsetting emotion, a self-mockery, a self-parody, as if she both allowed herself an emotion she did not approve of, allowed it and enjoyed it, but at the same time cancelled it out by mockery. ". . . It's as if somewhere inside me there was a big sack of greasy tears and if a pin were stuck into me they'd spill out. . . ."[10]

---

[9] Doris Lessing, *Martha Quest* (New York: New American Library, 1970), p. 52. Parenthetical page references in the text will be preceded by *MQ*.

[10] Doris Lessing, *A Ripple from the Storm* (New York: New American Library, 1970), p. 226. Parenthetical page references in the text will be preceded by *RS*.

Hysteria is as unwelcome as sentiment. In *The Four-Gated City* a more extreme Martha Quest yields to hysteria as she educates herself in the psychic lore of insanity, and the same inner division occurs: "Martha was crying out—sobbing, grovelling; she was being wracked by emotion. Then one of the voices detached itself and came close into her inner ear: it was loud, or it was soft; it was jaunty, or it was intimately jeering, but its abiding quality was an antagonism, a dislike of Martha."[11] This particular detachment from self is a demonized and externalized version of the rigors of watchfulness which Martha Quest puts herself through. Helped perhaps by the didactic Party meetings in which mutual criticism and self-criticism are part of the program (and whose organ is *The Watchdog*), Martha also has a talent for chastising herself into a self-dislike and self-punishment which might sit well on a Charlotte Brontë heroine but which in a twentieth-century character gives the impression of a pulverizing masochism.[12]

For many of Martha's emotions, and for Anna's as well, there is a countering intelligence, not always so devilish and punishing as this but one that insures detachment and a split between thinking and feeling. Habitually, Martha's intellect mocks her feelings. But in the deeper recesses of mental disturbance, the priority of the intellect is abolished: "She would discover herself uttering sloganlike phrases, or feeling emotions, which were the opposite of what she, the sane and rational Martha, believed. For instance, she would find herself using the languages of anti-Semitism. . . . She floundered about in a total loss of her own personality . . ." (*FGC*, p. 538). Rationality is personality; for Lessing it is intelligence that gives one a sense of self and preserves some approximation of integration in the face of invading irrationalities. Anna Wulf sees it quite clearly: "She could . . . feel that intelligence there at work, defensive and efficient—a machine. And she thought: this intelligence, it's the only barrier between me and . . . cracking up" (*GN*, p. 395). Martha, too, in *Landlocked,* "was holding herself together—like everybody else. She was a lighthouse of watchfulness; she was a being totally on the defensive" (*L*, p. 14).

Lessing invokes the intellect as sanity's guardian, and emotion is an inimical and threatening suitor to both Martha and Anna. The

---

[11] Doris Lessing, *The Four-Gated City* (New York: Bantam Books, 1970), p. 518. Parenthetical page references in the text will be preceded by *FGC*.

[12] The narrator of *The Golden Notebook* says to herself: "I see I am falling into the self-punishing, cynical tone again. Yet how comforting this tone is, like a sort of poultice on a wound" (*GN*, p. 90).

former thinks, in *A Ripple from the Storm*:

> Now she wanted to cry. But she would not allow herself tears. Just as tenderness, moments of real emotion with William left her exposed . . . so did tears, even brief tears, open her to a feeling of deep, impersonal pain that seemed to be lying in wait for her moments of weakness like an enemy whose name she did not know. . . . (*RS*, p. 25)

In the same book, the only older woman of any stature, Mrs. Van (who, in her gentleness, sacrifice, and equilibrium, resembles Woolf's Mrs. Ramsay) decides early in her marriage that "it was emotion . . . she must ban from her life. Emotion was dangerous. It could destroy her" (*RS*, p. 194). And Martha, in a later volume, still refuses to weep: "Anguish, the enemy, appeared: but no, she was not going to weep, feel pain, suffer" (*L*, p. 76). Anguish is the enemy, as is any other emotion that sets off an uncontrollable chain of feeling; any emotion has the power eventually to topple the lighthouse of watchfulness.

For Lessing's heroines, emotions disrupt the self as if they, the emotions, are outside of the self. As a Puritan might be habitually militant against evil, the figures in Lessing's novels scan the landscape for the approach of the irrational. In *Landlocked*, Martha has a "lit space on to which, unless she was careful . . . emotions would walk like actors and begin to speak without (apparently) any prompting from her" (*L*, p. 28). Later, she thinks again of "the stage on to which might walk, at any time, the disembodied emotions she could not give soil and roots to within herself" (*L*, p. 113). When emotion has rooted in the self, Lessing's heroines try to expel the organ traditionally responsible for it. Martha, in *The Four-Gated City*, tells her heart "to be quiet. . . . Her heart as it were came to heel; and after that, the current of her ordinary thought switched off. Her body was a machine, reliable and safe for walking . . ." (*FGC*, p. 37). Lessing has, in fact, a whole story about the dislodgement of that troublesome organ. In "How I Finally Lost My Heart," a short, fanciful piece, the heroine explains, "It would be easy to say that I picked up a knife, slit open my side, took my heart out, and threw it away; but unfortunately it wasn't as easy as that. Not that I, like everyone else, had not often wanted to do it."[13] After carrying her heart, "largish, lightish," around for awhile, the heroine passes it on to a mad young woman in the Underground

---

[13] Doris Lessing, *A Man and Two Women* (New York: Simon and Schuster, 1963), p. 83. Parenthetical page references in the text will be preceded by *M*.

as a reward for her suffering and a replacement for lost emotion. "No heart," she concludes, "no heart at all. What bliss. What freedom" (*M*, p. 95).

The resistance to emotion which appears so frequently in *Children of Violence* and *The Golden Notebook* is in part, of course, a resistance to pain. Yet it is not the avoidance of pain and pleasure, of the kind that numbs Tommy in *The Golden Notebook*; rather, what characterizes the emotional life of Lessing's heroines is a resistance to loss of personal will and consequent loss of freedom. Emotions, for them, are a swiftly flowing stream that can put a woman up the creek in no time at all. In *The Four-Gated City*, "Martha felt as if she were being swept fast over an edge, and by her own emotions; for the first time since she came to London, she was unfree" (*FGC*, p. 93). It is not only "sensibility" that incurs helplessness, then, but emotion itself.

Overwhelmed by or even touched by emotion, one is vulnerable, in Lessing's view, not only to the allurements of sentiment (and the attendant punishments by the intellect), or to a dangerous resemblance to the emotional women of the older generation, but to love, the resulting betrayals by men, and the trappings (and traps) of domesticity. Anna explains, in *The Golden Notebook*, "Being so young . . . I suffered, like so many 'emancipated' girls, from a terror of being trapped and tamed by domesticity" (*GN*, p. 128). Older, Anna is wry about her freedom (and would like to marry) but determinedly aware of her need to maintain it. It is no longer the image of failed older women or the temptation to convention that has to be fought against, but the yearning to fall in love, or stay in love, at the price of loss of self and a relinquishing of identity and will to a usurping male.

Lessing has little vindictiveness toward men, and her caution about men is no greater, and often far less great, than the traditional cautions of men about women. She is enormously sensitive to the ways men do not value women and to the adjustments women make in order to increase or preserve their portion of praise, love, and comfort. It is, in fact, because her heroines like men so much, and because they make such good Galateas of themselves, that they must be so careful. It is woman's vulnerability rather than man's culpability that is stressed; both sexes are caught in a labyrinth of expectation and motivation which, although it is often of their own making, has ample precedent.[14]

---

[14] Examples of this vulnerability and ready obedience abound in Lessing's fiction, beginning with *Martha Quest*: "Martha walked beside Binkie with the same gentle, submissive gesture that had until five minutes before been Dono-

The Golden Notebook is an anatomy of woman's independence and the impediments to it, and it is in this novel that Lessing brilliantly dissects the nature of that freedom which is, paradoxically, incomplete without love, yet almost invariably undermined by it. There is, for example, the heroine of the novel-within-the-novel, Ella, and her husband George, who is a sort of Lovelace-Grandcourt-Osmond in his manipulative perversity: "The last few weeks with George were a nightmare of self-contempt and hysteria, until at last she left his house, to put an end to it, to put a distance between herself and the man who suffocated her, imprisoned her, apparently took away her will" (*GN*, p. 181). Anna later has Ella fall in love with Paul, and "from the moment Ella . . . uses the word love, there is the birth of naivety. . . . Again and again he put her intelligence to sleep" (*GN*, p. 211). Such a state is, in a sense, a condition of faith, yet it is a faith that is invariably to be broken by the man, and Anna, the author-within-the-author, says of herself, "I would be incapable now of such trust" (*GN*, p. 212).

For Lessing, intelligence is at the heart of liberation, and a fall from intelligence is, for her heroines, a cause for self-denigration. Intelligence, however, is precarious and beset by an irrational attraction to happiness. When Anna Wulf, for example, trespasses on that common enough property, obtuseness, she chastises herself severely:

> As soon as I entered their flat I realised how much I had not been using my imagination, how stupid I had chosen to be. Sometimes I dislike women, I dislike us all, because of our capacity for not-thinking when it suits us; we choose not to think when we are reaching out for happiness. . . . I knew I had chosen not to think, and I was ashamed and humiliated. (*GN*, p. 485)

Far better then not to feel rather than not to think, since the first not only keeps one out of a stultifying dependency and consequent humiliation but better matches the capacities of men as Lessing describes them. For if there are only a few thinking women, there are even fewer "feeling" men. Each relationship in *The Golden Notebook*, whether part of the real novel or the novel within it, demonstrates the thinness of emotion on the man's part and the fuller feeling—and resulting demands—on the woman's. Ella thinks, "for the hundredth time that in their emotional life all these intelligent men use a level so

---

van's due; the mere fact that he had asked her to dine with him was as if her emotions had been gathered up, twisted together, by him" (*MQ*, p. 151).

much lower than anything they use for their work, that they might be different creatures" (*GN*, p. 457). This disparity creates a sense of loss, disappointment, and loneliness for the women, and antagonism and fearful evasiveness in the men.

The closely watched relationships in *The Golden Notebook* are not, however, designed to demonstrate a Lawrentian polarity and fundamental opposition of the sexes, but rather to show the difficulties of emotional life for both men and women. The difficulties are enhanced, moreover, when the woman is a "free" woman, that is, an intelligent woman who supports herself, whose ideas are definite, reasoned, and earned, whose activity in the world is accomplished without the assistance or intervention of a man, and who, peripherally perhaps, but not insignificantly, is not too coy to excel at the art of the retort.

Anna is well aware of "the difficulties of being my kind of woman"; she regards her condition as one without much historical precedent or present company (*GN*, p. 406). She also recognizes, with some irony, that free women are both saved and burdened by their intelligence. Having undergone a scene with her lover, his casualness making their coming separation more painful, Anna remarks in her diary, "Afterwards I fought with a feeling that always takes hold of me after one of these exchanges: unreality, as if the substance of my self were thinning and dissolving. And then I thought how ironical it was that in order to recover myself I had to use precisely that Anna which Michael dislikes most: the critical and thinking Anna" (*GN*, p. 331). The new woman is both more and less vulnerable: less so because, in her victory over sexual apartheid, she has her work to resort to; more so because her intelligence is a threatening element in her relations with men and its full expression gives them a reason to abandon her.[15] Anna thinks to herself that in this new condition "is a fearful trap for women, but I don't yet understand what it is. For there is no doubt of the new note women strike, the note of being betrayed. It's in the books they write, in how they speak, everywhere, all the time" (*GN*, p. 596).

The betrayal Anna speaks of is in part the sexual betrayal, the

---

[15] Martha, too, is made aware of the awkwardness a woman's intelligence can create: "She began talking to him, rather awkwardly, about a book she had just read. He answered reluctantly. When she persisted, he gave a public sigh. . . . Then he indicated Martha with an outstretched thumb, and said, 'She's intelligent. This baby's got brains.' And he laughed and rolled up his eyes . . ." (*MQ*, p. 150).

lack of loyalty, she describes in *The Golden Notebook* and even more single-mindedly in *Play with a Tiger*—but it is also the betrayal of the intelligent woman by the man who refuses to honor her claims to thinking. In a memorable episode in *A Ripple from the Storm*, Mr. Van goes up to his new wife, who is waiting in bed for her husband while he has been sitting up late to prepare a case, and finds her "reading Ingersoll. He had already taken her into his arms when he saw the title of the book lying beside her pillow. At this he had withdrawn his arms and turned away, remarking in his humorously dry voice, 'I see you have better company than me, my dear. Sleep well' " (*RS*, pp. 193-94). In a situation not parallel but of the same bolt of cloth, the psychiatrist in *The Four-Gated City* tells Martha, knowing it will anger her, "I think you are proud of your knowing—you are proud of that more than anything. It's your intelligence you are proud of. You are still fighting your mother with that—the masculine intelligence" (*FGC*, p. 241). The essential truth of this is overshadowed by the objectionable or questionable use of the word "masculine." Aside from insulting Martha with its obvious prejudice against the likelihood of feminine intelligence, it severs her from the heart of her identity by assuming that it belongs to another gender and threatens the female intellectual at the point where she is weakest—the question of her femininity. In her attempt to get help as an individual Martha is betrayed by a generality.

Of what is commonly thought to be "feminine intelligence"—intuition—both Martha and Anna have little, and deliberately so. Anna confesses, "It frightens me that when I'm writing I seem to have some awful second sight, or something like it, an intuition of some kind; a kind of intelligence is at work that is much too painful to use in ordinary life; one couldn't live at all if one used it for living" (*GN*, p. 572). And the heroine of *Play with a Tiger*, also called Anna, says with indignant irritation, "Intuition!" at the suggestion that she might be engaging in a fit of this capacity.

In spite of, or perhaps because of, their vulnerability, both Martha and Anna err on the side of rigor rather than of laxity. Mrs. Van sees Martha as "too hard—almost," and Anna is described by others as "cold-brained," "too intelligent," and by herself as "over-critical and defensive." Martha, unable to respond to her father's illness with the expected emotions "thought miserably of her own lack of feeling. She only felt resentful that her father was ill. . . . She felt resentful that at any moment it might be used as an emotional argument against her" (*MQ*, p. 123). Anna, on a first visit to her psychiatrist, explains that she has come "because I've had experiences that should have touched me and they haven't" (*GN*, p. 232). Looking at her daughter she thinks, "that's my child, my flesh and blood. But I couldn't feel it" (*GN*, p. 233). And an older and improbably different Martha visits the psychiatrist in *The Four-Gated City* and is "emotionless. She had had no emotions since she had sat there last, two days before" (*FGC*, p. 236).

It is when feeling, that guest which has so often been turned away, fails to call altogether, that both Martha and Anna feel the need to invite it back. Moving from I-won't-feel to I-can't-feel, they proceed from the luxury of caution to the crucial battle for a part of themselves that is lost. Martha's essentially elitist rebellion against the mawkish feeling of an older generation begins to resemble the general numbness of the current generation. Anna, unwilling to be caught up in the decade's paralysis, sees a psychiatrist and battles her emotional indifference as if she is fighting for her conscience. Sustained perhaps by vestiges of socialist optimism, she is unwilling to buckle under to the everlasting nay which has begun to cover the culture like a deep smog:

> But it isn't only the terror everywhere, and the fear of being conscious of it, that freezes people. It's more than that. People know they are in a society dead or dying. They are refusing emotion because at the end of every emotion are property, money, power. They work and despise their work, and so freeze themselves. They love but know that it's a half-love or a twisted love, and so they freeze themselves. (*GN*, p. 545)

For Lessing's heroines the refusal of emotion becomes worth considering and worth opposing when it becomes a general condition, for it is then that emotion becomes attached to meaning; the absence of tears or of the completeness of loving comes to signify a configuration, a situation, higher than itself, more abstract, more susceptible to rationalization, and therefore more likely to be appreciated and understood.

It is through the rationalizations of psychoanalysis rather than through the emotional surprises of a personal relationship that Anna manages to regain her feelings. "You have taught me how to cry," she tells her analyst, typically "not without dryness" (*GN*, p. 252). Yet in spite of the extrapolation of her personal cure into a scheme of values ("if what we feel is pain, then we must feel it, acknowledging that the alternative is death. Better anything than the shrewd, the calculated, the non-committal, the refusal of giving for fear of the consequences . . ." [*GN*, p. 546]), the narrative ripples with caution. The message is feeling; the medium is reason. Not dispassionate, for it is concerned, yet full of a care to understand and not to relinquish an issue or situation before it is understood, the style and point of view of *The Golden Notebook* exemplify a tenacious, if fragmented, consciousness. Feeling is one of the subjects of the book, but it does not infuse the narrative.

Lessing's own predisposition, as it emerges from her statements in interviews, parallels the inclination of her heroines towards rationality. In a recent interview she describes herself as once "aggressively rational."[16] In a conversation conducted seven years ago she declared her annoyance with readers of *The Golden Notebook* in the following way:

When *The Golden Notebook* came out, I was astonished that people got so emotional about that book, one way or another. They didn't bother to see, even to look at, how it was shaped. . . . What I'm trying to say is that it was a detached book. It was a failure, of course, for if it had been a success, then people wouldn't get so damned emotional when I didn't want them to be. . . .[17]

Lessing's meaning here is not clear. For although *The Golden Notebook* is experimental in shape, it is realistic and conventional in texture, syntax, and incident, and plays on the same responses a realistic novel might elicit. Lessing is no Joyce, detaching her work into a perfection of style, a distillation of language, a floating and self-sufficient condition. Furthermore, if one concentrates on the formal satisfactions of *The Golden Notebook*, as she would like, to the exclusion of those large themes that are scrutinized through domestic relationships, or to the exclusion of interest in the relationships themselves, then one will find Lessing bulky, inconsistent, and disappointing, and be convinced that she has mistaken her gifts.

It is clear, in any case, that the response Lessing wished for was not an emotional one. In another and earlier interview, when asked for her favorite story in her collection, *A Man and Two Women*, she responded, "I like . . . 'One Off the Short List' because it's so extremely cold and detached—that one's a toughy."[18] Again her preference is for

---

[16] Jonah Raskin, "Doris Lessing at Stony Brook: An Interview," *New American Review*, 8 (Jan. 1970), 172.

[17] Florence Howe, "A Talk With Doris Lessing," *Nation*, March 6, 1967, p. 312.

[18] In *Counterpoint*, ed. Roy Newquist (Chicago: Rand McNally, 1964), p. 420.

the unemotional and the detached. Writing about an incorrigible Romeo in the story mentioned, she is perhaps proud of her detachment not so much as a feat of form as of point of view; she triumphs over the obvious pitfalls of self-pity, bitter bias, and shrillness, and manages to write in a way that no one will pigeonhole as feminine.

In a recent piece of fiction, Lessing demonstrates a mistrust of emotion that reaches exaggerated proportions. "Not a Very Nice Story" is not a very good story, yet it is worthy of notice in that it marks her extremest statement of resistance to emotion. The tone of the omniscient narrator is surprisingly, and persuasively, cynical:

because of all this they had enjoyed a decade of profoundly emotional experience. In joy or in pain, they could not complain about flatness, or absence of sensation. And after all, emotion is the thing, we can none of us get enough of it.

The point was not the periods of making love . . . but . . . the spilling of emotion afterward, the anguish, the guilt. Emotion was the point. Great emotion had been felt, had been suffered.

And since none of us feel as much as we have been trained to believe that we ought to feel in order to prove ourselves profound and sincere people, then luckily here is the television where we can see other people feeling for us. So tell me, madam, what did you *feel* while you stood there believing that you were going to be burned to death? Meanwhile, the viewers will be chanting our creed: we feel, therefore we are.[19]

In a writer of Lessing's stature, the oily, accusatory tone of the excerpts is startling. One wonders why feeling should take the blame for media greed or for the desire of people to lead lives made more interesting by intensity. The bleating objections in this story are, paradoxically, out of control and of far less value than her wry criticism of sensibility in *In Pursuit of the English*. One thing is clear, however: her criteria for acceptable and unevasive emotions are insistently, perhaps impossibly, high.

Between Lessing's aversion to the attitudinizing of "sensibility" and her caution about feeling in general, there is not much contradiction. When one turns to *Briefing for a Descent into Hell*, however, and the light it sheds on preceding novels, one has to make room for a change of direction which would seem to mark an absolute inversion of the attitudes described above. For *Briefing*, published in 1971, is a

---

[19] In *Ms.*, August 1972, pp. 80, 81, 118.

defense of insanity which follows closely the lines and at times the style laid down by R. D. Laing in *Politics of Experience*.[20] Writing in an abstract and aqueous style, Lessing takes her hero on a journey away from the customary responsibilities of his social role and into schizophrenia. Foreshadowed by the dull-but-combustible Martha's experiment with madness in *The Four-Gated City*, and by Thomas' journals in *Landlocked*, Lessing's novel makes her position clear, at least for the moment: it is not only the sane who are mad, as Thomas says (*L*, p. 116), but the mad who are sane.

A study of madness in Lessing's work—beginning with colonial eccentricity and ending with her ideological apprenticeship to Laing —deserves a book of its own. It is necessary to treat briefly, however, the question of Lessing's conversion to irrationalism, if only because an emphatic case has been made for her rationality. Although she is hardly the first to regard suffering, melancholy, and derangement as perquisites to enlightenment, she is one of the few anti-Romantics to do so. Rationalists—Dr. Johnson, for example—have been as afflicted with mental infirmity as Romantics but usually lack the condoling belief that it is a step into a higher state. Lessing's handling of irrationality, moreover, is, as is her attitude toward dreams, typically practical, rational, and even mechanical, in spite of her respect for the subconscious. For Lessing, "dreaming," as Brewster says, "seems to be something of a discipline,"[21] and Lessing confirms this in an interview:

Dreams have always been important to me. The hidden domain of our mind communicates with us through dreams. I dream a great deal and I scrutinize my dreams. The more I scrutinize the more I dream. When I'm stuck in a book I deliberately dream. I knew a mathematician once who supplied his brain with information and worked it like a computer. I operate in a similar way. I fill my brain with the material for a new book, go to sleep, and I usually come up with a dream which resolves the dilemma.[22]

This deliberateness in dreaming, this encouragement of the unconscious to serve conscious, problematic purpose rather than to remain an alternative to the purposeful, is a model for Lessing's approach to madness, as Martha's pursuit of meaning in insanity testifies.

In *The Four-Gated City*, the commonsensical, rational Martha experiences a reversal of personality: "I've been turned inside out like

---

[20] (New York: Pantheon, 1967).

[21] Dorothy Brewster, *Doris Lessing* (New York: Twayne, 1965), p. 30.

[22] Raskin, p. 172.

a glove or a dress. I've been like the negative of a photograph. Or a mirror image. I've seen the underneath of myself" (*FGC*, p. 553). The obverse of rationality is irrationality, and in either case the root term for describing consciousness is rationality: rationality is either absent or present but never negligible. In this last of the *Children of Violence* series, outer violence moves in on the human personality, destroying once and for all the barrier intelligence has provided. Apocalypse and cataclysm replace skepticism, as if the implicit prophecy of doom that lurks within every act of caution has burst the watchful bonds of reason.

Yet Martha *invites* madness and *wants* her watchfulness to be wrecked on the jaggedness of insanity. Lessing is not writing a tale of tragic naturalism like *The Grass Is Singing*, in which the environment presses the heroine toward madness, but rather a *Bildungsroman* in which the climax of education is insanity. Martha, down to the last grain of vision, battles received assumptions about reality. She works hard at it. Madness is a task, and she toils through it toward a higher condition of integrity, a deeper version of self. If that version is disastrous, it is because the world is, in Lessing's eyes, a disaster; Martha's new vision gains access, with great clarity and no intervening sentiment, to that terrible knowledge. Most important, madness is moralized into a condition of responsible consciousness—the extremes of emotion it involves are significant because they teach, not for the release they afford; emotions are a means, not an end.

Insanity has Lessing's sympathy and interest for reasons continuous with her past concerns. She engages madness as a subject not because its chaos may allow her to taste the rich peripheries of rationality but because it is "part of the mainstream"[23] at the center of contemporary life. Essentially a realist, she travels parallel to the culture and keeps her eye on its movements. Madness has, moreover, a political dimension and a radical one. Lessing is concerned with the poor treatment afforded the mentally ill, whose dissenting perceptions make them powerless, but her aim is not only liberal reform or social amelioration. She wants, rather, an abolition of the traditional hierarchy of the sane and insane, and a recognition of the revolutionary nature of madness. "People who are classified as sick are becoming more and more important in England, the U.S.A., and in socialist countries too," she notes: "People who are called mentally ill are often those who say to the society, 'I'm not going to live according to your

---

[23] *Ibid.*, p. 173.

rules. I'm not going to conform.' Madness can be a form of rebellion."[24]
Finally, and curiously, the madness Lessing describes seems to
circumvent the personal, an area of experience about which she has
always been ambivalent. In the cool futurism of *Briefing*, Lessing is
light years away from her nostalgia for the human warmth of the
nineteenth-century novel expressed in "The Small Personal Voice," a
lengthy statement of literary values written in 1957.[25] And although
she mocks the doctrinal impersonality of socialist writing from time to
time, her own "habit of mind," she tells us, is to see "socially, not
personally."[26] Although she says in one interview that *The Golden
Notebook* "is a social novel,"[27] in a later conversation she explains:

Since writing *The Golden Notebook* I've become less personal. I've floated
away from the personal. I've stopped saying, "This is *mine*, this is *my* experience." Ever since I started writing I've wondered why the artist himself
has become a mirror of society. The first novelists didn't write about themselves, but now almost every novelist writes about himself. . . . Now, when
I start writing, the first thing I ask is, "Who is thinking the same thought?
Where are the other people who are like me?" I don't believe anymore that
I have a thought. There is a thought around.[28]

The personal is, by definition, a private possession and may represent
for the former communist a form of selfishness, a capitalist hoarding
of emotional territory.
The quality of emotion expressed in the condition of madness
that Lessing describes is unlike the emotions woven through our daily
lives at the level of the ordinary which Lessing's earlier novels describe.
It is not only much more violent and aberrant, but, most significantly,
it is collective and impersonal, like the "thought" that is "around."
Mark, husband of the mad Lynda in *The Four-Gated City*, says:
"Sometimes it's as if . . . I don't know how to explain it . . . it's as if
. . . not that *she* is mad, but there's madness. A kind of wavelength of
madness—and she hooks into it and out, when she wants. I could hook
into it just as easily. Or it could hook into me—it's in the air" (*FGC*,
p. 398). Martha herself eventually becomes a vessel, a channel, for all
the emotions seething around her, dissolving into their madness and

---

[24] *Ibid.*
[25] In *Declaration*, ed. Maschler.
[26] Brewster, p. 145. Quoted from an interview conducted by Robert Rubens
in *The Queen*, August 21, 1962.
[27] *Ibid.*
[28] Raskin, p. 173.

participating in the collective psyche much as an earlier Martha had participated in the collective conscience of communism.

The appreciation and understanding which Lessing extends to insanity takes madness from the realm of the clinical, where it is domesticated and judged, confined, as it were, to an institutional attic, into the realm of the cosmic. As a new plane of perception, a coming sixth sense, it is made metaphysical, impersonal. In *Briefing*, one of the characters asserts that Charles, the protagonist, "doesn't even pay lip service to ordinary feelings," and adds, "perhaps they aren't as important as we think."[29] Another character complains that he is "above every normal human emotion" (*B*, p. 232). Charles himself mentions his "new mode of feeling," and the "sympathetic knowledge" he experiences is not with other individuals but with the world itself, fused into a rhapsodic and egalitarian whole.

For Lessing to choose a male protagonist is not unusual, and *Briefing* may feature a man's consciousness simply as a preference of imagination. One suspects, however, that a man was chosen in order to give madness its fullest due and its deepest persuasion: the fact that women are more often considered irrational would give a conventional taint to a disordered female and rob madness of the novel authority it possesses in *Briefing*. In both *Briefing for a Descent into Hell* and *The Four-Gated City*, sexuality and gender begin to fade into a transcendent condition and are greatly reduced in stature under pressure of a higher androgynous knowledge. Things in general are too dire and sorrowful for the "sex war" to be important,[30] and women can abandon their caution as their center shifts from men, their reason no longer hostage to the chemistry of attraction. Sex is only one more of those personal elements which are superseded by a greater impersonal force:

Great forces as impersonal as thunder or lightning or sunlight or the movement of the oceans . . . swept through bodies, and now she knew quite well why Mark had come blindly upstairs to the nearest friendly body, being in the grip of this force—or *a* force, one of them. Not sex. Not necessarily. Not unless one chose to make it so. (*FGC*, p. 496)

Lessing is telling us what one of the Sufi tales she is so fond of

<hr />

[29] *Briefing for a Descent into Hell* (New York: Alfred Knopf, 1971), p. 227. Parenthetical page references in the text will be preceded by *B*.

[30] Except for a playful poke in a mythological interlude in *Briefing* in which Minerva is described as "a bit of [sic] blue-stocking; her feeling of justice and fair play . . . usually led her to the question of women's rights, and men's vanity" (*B*, p. 132).

tells us: "If you remain attached to the few things with which you are familiar, it will only make you miserable. . . ."[31] Always pained by narrowed horizons, Lessing gives her novels a broadness of scope which is one of their most striking and enriching features, a feature with which she contradicts the conventional idea that woman's excellence in the novel comes from her habitual acquaintance with the domestic, the ordinary, the small private corners and minor nuances of existence. Like George Eliot, the exception before her who is most often praised with the assertion that "she writes like a man," Lessing writes novels with irreducibly intellectual content, strong moral commitment, thorough social description, and large temporal and geographical range.

Unlike Eliot, and as a result of historical placement, Lessing cannot enjoy the comforts of equivocal feminism. Though she is nowhere nearly so bitter as Olive Schreiner, she possesses an enlightened consciousness that is full of flashing signals and loud warnings about conformity to an image that is often pressed on women like a gift but which, when it does not fit them, is no gift but a burden. Writing out of a context of twentieth-century numbness rather than nineteenth-century enthusiasm, she is chary of those attributes supposedly natural to women but of little value in dealing with the world. "Our strongest emotions are irrelevant to the time we live in," says Ella in *The Golden Notebook* (GN, p. 625). Without the congruence of morality and feeling which George Eliot carved out in her books and which her readers regarded as practical wisdom, intuition and affect seem superfluous and threatening, except when they have diminished to a fatally low level.

In her resistance to writing the feminine novel, in the choice Lessing made of "The Pig" over "The Trinket Box," she sacrifices suppleness and gratuitous beauty; there are few admirers of her work who would defend the careless homeliness of her style, far inferior to the style of George Eliot. Yet Lessing writes novels for grown-up people, to paraphrase Virginia Woolf's remark about *Middlemarch*,[32] and she offers an elusive quality called maturity which is far rarer

---

[31] Idries Shah, *Tales of the Dervishes* (New York: E. P. Dutton, 1969), p. 143.

[32] Virginia Woolf called *Middlemarch* "the magnificent book which with all its imperfections is one of the few English novels written for grown-up people," in "George Eliot," *The Common Reader* (New York: Harcourt, 1925), p. 172.

than the quality of sensibility she so cheerfully ignores. Wary of being typically feminine, she becomes typically contemporary in her suspicion of emotion, and although this does not nourish our optimism, our sense of the real tells us that she is our most powerful interpreter of difficult times—past, present, and future.

The Limits of Consciousness in the Novels of Doris Lessing

Sydney Janet Kaplan

Martha Quest is dead by the end of *The Four-Gated City* (1969). That long series of novels, *Children of Violence*,[1] has come to its end, and with it perhaps, a notion of "feminine consciousness" which has permeated most of Doris Lessing's fiction. It is not really surprising that the direction of her most recent work is away from the concerns of feminism, from the kind of penetration of the female mind which was so remarkable, especially in *The Golden Notebook* (1962).[2] In fact, Doris Lessing has recently remarked that she is annoyed with advocates of sexual liberation, which she now sees as a minor issue compared with the overwhelming possibility of nuclear war.[3] Shifting her focus to the consciousness of a male character in *Briefing for a Descent into Hell*[4] might in itself be a statement of her new position.

---

[1] *Children of Violence* consists of *Martha Quest*, 1952; *A Proper Marriage*, 1954; *A Ripple from the Storm*, 1958; *Landlocked*, 1965 (all rpt. New York: Plume Books, 1970); and *The Four-Gated City* (New York: Alfred A. Knopf, 1969). Parenthetical page references in the text will be preceded by the following abbreviations: *MQ, PM, R, L,* and *FGC. Martha Quest, A Proper Marriage*, and *The Four-Gated City* are copyrighted by Doris Lessing. Excerpts from the first two works are used by permission of Simon & Schuster, Inc.; from the last, by Random House, Inc.

[2] *The Golden Notebook* (New York: Simon & Schuster, 1962). All parenthetical page references, preceded by *GN,* will be to this edition. Copyright © 1962 by Doris Lessing. Used by permission of Simon & Schuster, Inc.

[3] See Doris Lessing's remarks on sexual liberation in Jonah Raskin, "Doris Lessing at Stony Brook: An Interview," *New American Review*, No. 8 (1970), 175.

[4] *Briefing for a Descent into Hell* (New York: Knopf, 1971). Parenthetical page references will be preceded by *B*.

But even though the issue of sexuality seems to have been eliminated in *Briefing* (which moves its characters into worlds close to those of science fiction), it is still the puzzle of human consciousness that confronts us.

Again we seem to plunge deep within the layers of the mind. But we go even further now; we observe the consciousness of a man who has lost his "memory," who is supposed to be "mentally ill." The man himself, Charles Watkins, remains shadowy, incomplete, vague—impersonal. Yet this very impersonality helps one to discover that the entire concept of "personality" has changed. Tendencies, insights, perceptions that are revealed only in bits and pieces in the earlier novels are now carried to their firmest and most logical conclusion. For by now, the feminine consciousness has disintegrated, and the idea of individual consciousness itself has been radically altered.

Actually, if *Children of Violence* is really a *Bildungsroman* (and Doris Lessing defines it as such at the very end), Martha, its heroine, has always differed from the typical focus of that genre—the sensitive youth discovering individuality—in that her search was always associated with larger issues, such as racism, class conflict, and war. It is very clear that Martha was to represent what Doris Lessing defined as "a study of the individual conscience in its relations with the collective."[5] The difference is most easily discerned when one considers an earlier example of the feminine *Bildungsroman*: Dorothy Richardson's even longer series, *Pilgrimage*.[6] Of course, it is more than fifty years since an adolescent Miriam Henderson, in the first novel of that series, *Pointed Roofs* (1915), set out on her journey to Hanover. Miriam, who reveals herself as optimistic, open, and enthusiastic about the possibilities life offers to a young woman seeking independence, would have been incapable of even imagining the fate of her later counterpart. Martha Quest also takes a journey, but hers takes her first to a dying England, and last to a remote island where survivors of an atomic holocaust struggle to maintain life. Yet, the two women began their search for reality in ways not at all dissimilar: reading iconoclastic authors, questioning the beliefs and values of their societies, living alone in the city, experimenting with sexual relationships. But their conclusions reflect the vast differences in their worlds. Miriam's discovery involves an assertion of the superiority of a feminine con-

---

[5] Doris Lessing, "The Small Personal Voice," *Declaration*, ed. Tom Maschler (London: MacGibbon and Kee, 1957), p. 22.

[6] Dorothy M. Richardson, *Pilgrimage*, 4 vols. (London: J. M. Dent, 1967).

sciousness which allows her to accept and enhance essentially mystical and individualistic notions about the self. But Martha reaches the limits of self-concern; she discovers a social world, a political world, and a communal consciousness. Her individualism is tempered by worldwide movements, historical changes, and the coming end of the known civilization. Long before her death, she is aware of her insignificance. And the very struggle for some kind of identity that is specifically female is left far behind.

The basic powerlessness of individuals who are determined by their personal and cultural histories makes the kind of search for "freedom" which characterizes the *Bildungsroman* difficult to achieve indeed. And since Doris Lessing always tried to consider individual consciousness in terms of its connection with the larger system—social, political, or psychological—the picture of human effort which emerges from her novels continually suggests the smallness and weakness of individual human beings. Consequently, the whole subject of consciousness itself needs to be considered within this perspective. The cosmic view of humanity which emerges in *Briefing* complements the descriptions of Africa in the earlier novels, with their abundance of ants, locusts, and other insects. For even here the individual mind is "a pulse in a great darkness" (*GN*, p. 407), and the landscape of the mind itself resembles more the vastness and dryness of Africa than the water-soaked, protected isles of Great Britain. The usual metaphors for consciousness, streams and fountains,[7] may better be replaced by those of plains and vast spaces, and eventually even by the infinitude of space, of wavelengths, distances.

In *The Four-Gated City*, Martha Quest completes her search for reality by envisioning a new race of human beings whose minds have been expanded to fit them for life involved with distances: extrasensory perception which enables them to "tune-in" to a shared consciousness. It is at this point that one becomes aware of the difficulties inherent in containing this level of consciousness within the confines of the conventional novel. The "stream of consciousness" was always an awkward metaphor in relation to Doris Lessing's work, and it is especially inadequate in this context, implying as it does an individual stream, made up of personal associations separated from the "streams" of others. Perhaps Doris Lessing has used Anna Wulf's psychoanalysis

---

[7] Anna uses the conventional image of the well and the source in her own novel-within-the-novel (*GN*, pp. 336-37). Its ineffectiveness there might be a purposeful statement about its limitations as a metaphor.

with a Jungian analyst in *The Golden Notebook* as a tentative reference point along the way. What Jung called the "collective unconscious" might serve as the connection between Anna's own personal experiences and the universal significance of those experiences. Instead of a personal stream, there might be Jung's "ocean of images," accessible to everyone. Charles Watkins' preliminary mental journey over the world's oceans in *Briefing* might be a reflection of it. The difficulty, however, is in ordering this vastness, in joining the "individual" to the "collective," without making a work so esoteric (like Joyce's *Finnegans Wake*) that it cannot communicate to the uninitiated.[8] This is important, since for Doris Lessing the novel must also serve to teach, to be a social instrument (in fact, in these latest novels, to reveal and prophesy as well). *The Four-Gated City*, with its forecast of the destruction of Western civilization and its suggestion that individuals with the capacity for extrasensory perception are the evolutionary forerunners of a race of humans more fit for survival, points out the direction but is better able to depict the dissolution of individual consciousnesses and the society which is made up of them than to *demonstrate* the communal consciousness of the future.

Doris Lessing is more successful in *The Golden Notebook* because its actual structure resembles the condition of its main character's consciousness: fragmented. Anna's consciousness of herself is split up into several notebooks of different colors, and this separation symbolizes her relation to herself, her body, to other people, and to society in general. She remarks that "the novel has become a function of the fragmented society, the fragmented consciousness" (*GN*, p. 59). But to express that new sense of a unity pervading the universe, moving with the forces of light and water and the planets and stars, to express that which is not yet completely understood, since "the main feature of these human beings as at present constituted being their inability to feel, or understand themselves, in any other way except through their own drives or functions" (*B*, p. 141), calls for the development of a kind of novel that does not, as yet, exist. Doris Lessing tries. Some of her desires are realized in *The Four-Gated City*, others in *Briefing*, as she attempts to awaken humans who "have not yet evolved into an understanding of their individual selves as merely parts of a whole, first of all humanity, their own species, let alone achieving a conscious knowledge of humanity as part of Nature; plants, animals, birds,

---

[8] See Anna's discussion with her analyst on why she does not "hold the aristocratic view of art" (*GN*, p. 406).

insects, reptiles, all these making a small chord in the Cosmic Harmony" (*B*, p. 141). Yet somehow both of these novels leave something unsatisfied, especially in readers bound up with the individualistic tradition—probably because there is as yet no new form. *The Four-Gated City* resembles the traditional novel in its structure, and the oddly colorless, if shocking study of the mind in *Briefing* goes very little further in technical innovation. The quest for knowledge of reality which shapes all Doris Lessing's novels is here thwarted by the inadequacies of the novelistic form. This is not to say that these later novels are failures; they provoke, they stimulate, they disturb, even if they do not succeed in unifying form and content.

It may well be that the very medium of fiction is not the right one for the kind of vision Doris Lessing is now trying to communicate. She has often expressed her concern over the limitations of language, especially in regard to its inability to communicate the richness of dreams and other manifestations of deeper levels of consciousness.[9] The final dreams in Anna's golden notebook, for instance, which begin to allow her to envision a merging of people, ideas, and emotions to take the place of the fragmentation implicit in the other notebooks, are connected finally to the suggestion of cinematic form. After struggling to pull her many selves together, a new character enters Anna's dreams, a "projectionist" who takes control of her images and runs them before her eyes. Scene after scene from her life flashes by, image after image caught in close-up:

Then the film went very fast, it flicked fast, like a dream, on faces I've seen once in the street, and have forgotten, on the slow movement of an arm . . . all saying the same thing—the film was now beyond my experience, beyond Ella's, beyond the notebooks, because there was a fusion, and instead of seeing separate scenes, people, faces, movements, glances, they were all together. . . . (*GN*, p. 543)

Throughout the novel there are references to film, and these suggest an artistic evolution which puts Anna's attempts at ordering chaos through writing into a new perspective. The "fusion" which goes beyond her own experience is reminiscent of Eisenstein's comment: "It is only in cinema that are fused into a real unity all those separate elements of the spectacle once inseparable in the dawn of culture."[10]

---

[9] Lessing's comments to Jonah Raskin about her own use of dreams is especially illuminating (pp. 172-73).

[10] Sergei Eisenstein, *Film Form*, ed. and trans. Jay Leyda (New York: Meridian Books, 1957), p. 182.

What is "fused" is "the full embrace of the whole inner world of man
. . . a whole reproduction of the outer world."[11] Aside from its ability
to incorporate everything, film is a powerful medium in that its images
are *shared*, thus taking it beyond the individualism of the novel.

Anna Wulf's sense of self-identity had always been intimately
related to the power of words. The creation of Anna is of a character
accessible through words—her own words. She is never described by
anyone else; no one peers into her consciousness and interprets it.
Since she is supposed to be a writer, she is shown to be concerned with
the expression of self in written words. But when words fail, her "self"
begins to fall apart. Anna's disintegration is tied up with the whole
question of the existence of individual consciousness: what makes up a
"self" and what holds it together. Her attempt at self-definition slowly
collapses, finally, because it hinges on the power of words and she
discovers that words cannot contain a reality too immense for them:

I am increasingly afflicted by vertigo where words mean nothing. Words
mean nothing. They have become, *when I think*, not the form into which
experience is shaped, but a series of meaningless sounds, like nursery talk,
and away to one side of experience. Or like the sound track of a film that
has slipped its connection with the film. *When I am thinking* I have only to
write a phrase like "I walked down the street," or take a phrase from a
newspaper "economic measures which lead to the full use of . . ." and immediately the words dissolve, and my mind starts spawning images which
have nothing to do with the words, so that every word I see or hear seems
like a small raft bobbing about on an enormous sea of images. So I can't
write any longer. Or only when I write fast, without looking back at what
I have written. For if I look back, then the words swim and have no sense
and I am conscious only of me, Anna, as a pulse in a great darkness, and
the words that I, Anna, write down are nothing, or like the secretions of a
caterpillar that are forced out in ribbons to harden in the air.

It occurs to me that what is happening is a breakdown of me, Anna,
and this is how I am becoming aware of it. For words are form, and if I
am at a pitch where shape, form, expression are nothing, then I am nothing, for it has become clear to me, reading the notebooks, that I remain
Anna because of a certain kind of intelligence. This intelligence is dissolving and I am very frightened. (*GN*, pp. 407-8)

Anna is dissolving, and as she dissolves the boundaries between
what she has defined as her own consciousness and the consciousness
of others become blurred. The sensitivity which allowed her to receive

---

[11]*Ibid.*, p. 184.

so many impressions (note that the term "receive" implies that perception is passive) also allows her to receive emotions. Her self-identity
has become so amorphous that what she receives *becomes* part of herself. As a consciousness not totally self-contained, it displays within it
the disorder and confusion of the world outside. But "outside" and
"inside" are losing their meanings.

During her intense affair with Saul Green, Anna begins to absorb
his mental disturbance. It takes great effort on her part to even recognize the merging of emotions: "I was clenched with anxiety, and saying over and over again: This isn't my anxiety state, it isn't mine—
didn't help at all" (*GN*, p. 486). Thus, if one considers *The Golden
Notebook* as Doris Lessing's last attempt to define consciousness as
self-contained, even that definition falters when Anna's attempt to fit
the pieces of her life together fails because consciousness breaks out
of its containers. The shared madness of Anna and Saul provides a
new starting point.

Nonetheless, the very structure of *The Golden Notebook*, with
its innumerable stories within stories, expresses what Doris Lessing
meant by her comment that "the shape of this book should be enclosed
and claustrophobic—so narcissistic that the subject matter must break
through the form."[12] The narcissistic ego which breaks out of the form
as well accompanies a body that desires to take in, to hold on to, and
to be made pregnant. And in keeping with this aim, there is an abundance of organic imagery in *The Golden Notebook* and an emphasis
on the sexual, reproductive capacities of its main character. But all
that is replaced in *The Four-Gated City* by a body that is a "machine"
(*FGC*, p. 35) and a psyche which is "nothing but a soft dark receptive
intelligence" (*FGC*, p. 36). The contained consciousness evolves now
to consciousness as *receiver*.

Anna's absorption of Saul's sickness resembles, if in a more
limited way, Martha's absorption of Lynda's insanity in *The Four-
Gated City*. But Martha's evolution of consciousness goes much further. By now, the interpenetration of consciousnesses no longer may
be considered a weakness but a precious ability which foresees the
future course of human evolution. Martha's rebellion began on the
basis of concepts derived from books; like Anna she also started with
abstractions and grew to break free from them. In the earlier volumes
of *Children of Violence*, the reader is caught up in Martha's progres-

---

[12] Lessing's remarks here come from the dust jacket of the first London
edition. I have quoted them from Paul G. Schlueter, "A Study of the Major
Novels of Doris Lessing," Diss. So. Illinois 1968, pp. 151-52.

sions through various "isms," which are actually opposed to her own mode of consciousness:

She was engaged in examining and repairing those intellectual's bastions of defence behind which she sheltered, that building whose shape had first been sketched so far back in her childhood she could no longer remember how it then looked. . . . It was as if she, Martha, were a variety of soft, shell-less creature whose survival lay in the strength of those walls. Reaching out in all directions from behind it, she clutched at the bricks of arguments, the stones of words, discarding any that might not fit into the building. (*PM*, p. 94)

Hard words protect her. The imagery of intellect is all inanimate and solid, lifeless and rigid, inferring the dogmatism of her stance. Yet Martha herself is described as a "soft, shell-less creature," making her open and *receptive* by nature, even if she is overwhelmed by the chaos that openness must take in.

By the end, Martha is to discover "that somewhere in one's mind was a wavelength, a band where music jigged and niggled, with or without words; it was simply a question of tuning in and listening" (*FGC*, p. 37). But in order to "tune-in" one must have the equipment with which to do so. Martha reflects that "living was simply a process of developing different 'ears,' senses, with which one 'heard,' experienced, what one couldn't before" (*FGC*, p. 225). An evolutionary process is at work, and Doris Lessing quotes from *The Sufis* to explain how "*organs come into being as a result of a need for specific organs. . . . What ordinary people regard as sporadic and occasional bursts of telepathic and prophetic power are seen by the Sufi as nothing less than the first stirrings of these same organs*" (*FGC*, p. 426).

Human beings need these new organs to transcend time and space; thus within this context of mind-expansion, the subject of "words," which had so troubled Anna Wulf when she became frustrated by her failure as a writer to explain her life through language, takes on a new interpretation. Anna had looked upon words as containers of experience, but for Martha in *The Four-Gated City*, words no longer enclose meaning but are used as *initiators* into the search for it. They have become catalysts, or powers which *conduct* meaning. They even retain some of their old use as magic: words which act like the mystic symbols in ancient and occult religions. Consequently, when Martha begins to "overhear" the thoughts of others, she discovers that words in themselves have no inherent meanings: "Was what she picked up words in its original form? Or did some mechanism exist which could pick up an idea, rather than words, . . . and translate it into words—like one of those simultaneous translators at a conference. Or like . . . a kind of computer that changed one language into another" (*FGC*, p. 353). The references to "simultaneous translators" and "computers" serve to intensify an imagery of electronics which becomes increasingly obvious in this novel. It is, of course, all in keeping with the struggle to connect individual and communal consciousness—a process of *communication*: "It is not a question of 'Lynda's mind' or 'Martha's mind'; it is the human mind, or part of it, and Lynda, Martha, can choose to plug in or not" (*FGC*, p. 473).

One might ask then, what is it that one plugs into? The following passage may give at least a partial answer when it sets forth the unbelievable chaos and energy of what is approached when the mind is opened:

It was as if a million radio sets ran simultaneously, and her mind plugged itself in fast to one after another, so that words, phrases, songs, sounds, came into audition and then faded. The jumble and confusion were worse when she allowed the current that pumped through her to get out of control, to rise and jerk and flood; the sea of sound became more manageable as she held herself quiet and contained. Yet even so, it was all she could do to hold on . . . her own body bucking and rolling under her; and words, shrieks, gunfire, explosions, sentences, came in, faded, or stayed. When something stayed then it, they, might develop or grow loud and accumulate around it other words, sounds, phrases, of the same kind or texture, like a bit of metal attracting to it particles of substances of a certain nature, so that a word, "bread," proliferated into the phrase "bread of life," burst into a pure high song like a thrush, from the Ninth Symphony, then jangled into banality with "you can't have bread with one meat ball," gave snatches of recipes for loaves as they were once made on a hearth, leered, jeered, threatened, on a wavelength of mockery, until suddenly— while Martha understood (again) how the words, phrases, sounds, came in from that sound-length in an exact relation to some mood or impulse in herself. (*FGC*, pp. 473-74)

Martha's intuitive powers reach their climax with her achievement of extrasensory perception, but she had shown indications of an ability to perceive spontaneously and insightfully into the essence of a situation or character long before she embarked on that program of rigorous training (being alone, not eating, not sleeping, in order to make her mind completely open and sensitive to stimuli). Since adolescence she had been able to hold many perceptions in her mind at once and to understand immediately the significance of a complex aggregation of details. These intuitive powers are remarkably similar to those which Dorothy Richardson allowed for Miriam Henderson in *Pilgrimage* and which she ascribed to the functioning of a "feminine consciousness." Miriam achieved what she called "featureless Freedom,"[13] a sense of oneness with a universe that ultimately seemed to lack the concept of evil, predicated as it was upon the Quaker belief in the basic goodness of human beings. But Doris Lessing does not allow her characters this kind of religious alternative. For Martha Quest, responding to the horrors of mid-twentieth-century history, such a view would be too simplistic.

Martha's adolescent moment of insight early in the *Children of Violence* series, however, does share some of the features of a mystical experience (especially the clarity of vision, the sharply delineated objects). The language is that of spiritual awakening: "it passed as lightly as the shadow wing of a bird"; "she knew that the experience associated with that emotion was not to be courted. One did not lie in wait for it; it was a visitor who came without warning" (*MQ*, p. 50). Martha recognizes the emotion as religious, yet she is no longer religious. The experience seems part of an innate capability, not related to belief. She stands looking across the dusty, African landscape, quietly, expectant, the air blue and the grass rustling, and she observes two bucks in the sunlight. She questions the usual terms for her feeling; "ecstasy," "illumination" both seem inadequate "because they suggest joy," and she perceives it as "a pain, not a happiness":

There was certainly a definite point at which the thing began. It was not; then it was suddenly inescapable, and nothing could have frightened it away. There was a slow integration, during which she, and the little animals, and the moving grasses, and the sun-warmed trees, . . . and the great dome of blue light overhead, and the stones of earth under feet, became one, shuddering together in a dissolution of dancing atoms. She felt the rivers under the ground forcing themselves painfully along her veins, swelling them out in an unbearable pressure; her flesh was the earth, and suffered growth like a ferment; and her eyes stared, fixed like the eye of the sun. Not for one second longer . . . could she have borne it; but then, with a sudden movement forwards and out, the whole process stopped; and *that* was "the moment" which it was impossible to remember afterwards. For during that space of time (which was timeless) she understood quite finally her smallness, the unimportance of humanity. (*MQ*, pp. 52-53)

---

[13] *Pilgrimage*, I, 43.

Martha's realization during "the moment" involves her insignificance in an "inhuman" universe. Her ego is inconsequential within "the chaos of matter." Her understanding involves an acceptance of the harshness of reality which, by contrast, makes Miriam Henderson's vision of immensity seem cozy. Moreover, it is not only the indifference of the universe to human desires that disturbs Martha, but that everywhere she looks she sees the indifference of one human being to another. There is a special warp to her consciousness; it has been affected by more than the philosophical theories about the absence of God and evolutionary determinism in the books she has read. The cataclysmic events of the twentieth century force her to see that the disorders in the political and social arenas are linked with universal forces which are revealed through the interactions of particles of matter, seasons, and movements of planets: massive powers that Martha intimated during her "moment." What is charging through them all charges through her own body: "Martha did not believe in violence. Martha was the essence of violence, she had been conceived, bred, fed and reared on violence" (L, p. 195).

The sexual dilemma which troubles Martha and Anna becomes part of this larger conflict as well. That "vision of some dark, impersonal destructive force that worked at the roots of life and that expressed itself in war and cruelty and violence" (GN, p. 164) is exemplified in the war between the sexes, which in Anna's own life comes to its climax in her violent struggles with Saul Green: "And I knew that the cruelty and the spite and the I, I, I, I, of Saul and of Anna were part of the logic of war . . ." (GN, p. 503).

The evolution towards a universal consciousness in Doris Lessing's novels appears to begin with an approach to reality centered in the physical body and its relationship with nature. It is no wonder that Martha's first overwhelming experience of "the moment" occurred during adolescence—the period of awakening sexuality. Sexuality itself becomes inescapably linked with the search for knowledge in these novels. Even though Martha's rebellion started initially on the basis of abstract ideas, yet it was surely through her body—as she later experienced sexual relationships, pregnancy, and childbirth—that her most profound discoveries were achieved.[14] By way of contrast, one might note that Miriam Henderson's "knowing" through her body was quite limited. Her "pilgrimage" depended to a much greater degree on the faculty of vision—perceiving through the eyes—which makes of

---

[14] See in particular the descriptions of Martha's pregnancy and labor in *A Proper Marriage*.

reality a subjective phenomenon. But carnal knowledge brings one away from the particularities of consciousness related only to the individual and into a "knowing" that is approachable for every human being.

In the earlier novels Martha fears being dissolved during sex. She fears reaching that level in herself which she shares with all living creatures. She is still caught up in her need to identify herself as a separate ego; her disassociation of mind and body then typifies the alienated condition of modern life. This disassociation (and the accompanying objectification of the body itself) complements the increasing objectification of people which takes place as the violence of modern life increases. Martha objects when a man refers to her breasts as "*Them*—just as if they had nothing to do with me!" (*MQ*, p. 220), but she still resorts to sex manuals for guidance, which only increases her real belief that the body is something that has a value of its own, separate from her as a person. It must be "handled" and "used" properly:

It was almost with the feeling of a rider who was wondering whether his horse would make the course that she regarded this body of hers, which was not only divided from her brain by the necessity of keeping open that cool and dispassionate eye, but separated into compartments of its own. Martha had after all been provided with a map of her flesh by "the book," in which each area was marked by the name of a different physical sensation, so that her mind was anxiously aware, not only of a disconnected partner, a body, but of every part of it, which might or might not come up to scratch at any given occasion. (*PM*, p. 63)

The young Martha fears losing her ego during sexual intercourse: "No, it was too strong . . . much easier to live deprived, to be resigned, to be self-contained. No, she did not want to be dissolved" (*L*, p. 99).

Martha is afraid that if she lets go she will confront the true nature of herself: a self that is not a unity at all, but a combination of fragments. To let herself be carried away on the tide of primal drives, joining her with the forces of nature—these might make her realize that reality itself is chaos. But much later, in *The Four-Gated City*, Martha realizes that the very dissolution through sexuality she once feared is only a dissolution of what is, in reality, already in fragments. On the contrary then, what seems like dissolution during complete sexual experience works paradoxically as a bringing together, a unifying function:

She had never really seen before how the separate parts of herself went on, working individually, by themselves, not joining: that was the condition of being "normal" as we understand it. Breath flows on, blood beats on, separately from each other; my sex lives on there, responding or not; my heart feels this and that, and my mind up here goes working on, quite different from the heart; yet when the real high place of sex is reached, everything moves together, it is just that moment when everything does move together that makes the gears shift up. Yet people regarded sex as the drainer, the emptier, instead of the maker of energy. (*FGC*, p. 61)

Although Martha finally becomes able to be drawn into an encounter with these greater forces, it is interesting to find that she must still objectify other human beings in order to do so. She becomes conscious that it has "nothing to do with Jack the person, he's the instrument that knows how to reach it" (*FGC*, p. 59). The word "instrument" leads us back again to the imagery of electronic technology. In fact, objectification has now gone so far that individuals may actually consider other people "instruments" to help them "tune in" to different wavelengths of experience. Thus, the imagery of sex also moves out of the mechanical (an earlier and simpler form of objectification) into the electronic—and finally to the telepathic. The lovers "came to themselves light and easy, and as if they had been washed through and through by currents of energy. She felt as if she had been connected to a dynamo, the centre of her life" (*FGC*, p. 61). Much later in the novel, when Martha becomes aware of her own extrasensory powers, she realizes that there is an interchangeability between one person and another possible in sex as well as through minds alone. She speaks of the energy two lovers make "like conductors of conduits for the force which moved them" (*FGC*, p. 470). And she is made aware of "an impersonal current which she brought from Mark, who had it from Lynda, who had it from . . . the impersonal sea" (*FGC*, p. 471). "Impersonal," of course, is the essential word. And it defines, at the last, the relationship of human being to human being, and human being to nature: "Great forces as impersonal as thunder or lightning or sunlight or the movement of the oceans being contracted and heaped and rolled in their beds by the moon, swept through bodies, and now she knew quite well why Mark had come blindly upstairs to the nearest friendly body, being in the grip of this force—or *a* force, one of them. Not sex. Not necessarily. Not unless one chose to make it so" (*FGC*, pp. 470-71).

In *The Four-Gated City* Doris Lessing may use the power of sexuality to provide the dramatic physical manifestations of unity, but it is only one of the steps in her movement towards a recognition of the mental unity that is most fully revealed through the consciousness of Charles Watkins in *Briefing*. Another step is the analysis of dreams —of the archetypes symbolized by images pulled from the collective unconscious that we experience through Anna Wulf's psychoanalysis in *The Golden Notebook*. Martha, of course, goes even further. At the end she recognizes the existence of a truly diffused consciousness and a heightened notion of what is not either particularly "masculine" or "feminine," but human: "the sense of herself which stayed had no sex" (*FGC*, p. 221).

Charles Watkins is considered insane according to his doctors' definitions, but those definitions result from a scientific mentality which expresses its own limitations through its "inability to see things except as facets and one at a time" (*B*, p. 42). Charles, on the other hand, sees now all at once, and not only are his concepts of time and space altered, but he begins to understand the interrelationships between all things: "I watched a pulsing swirl of all being, continually changing, moving, dancing, a controlled impelled dance, held within its limits by its nature" (*B*, p. 107). Once inside this other dimension he understands how individual minds "lay side by side, fishes in a school, cells in honeycomb, flames in fire," and perceives a "fusion with the people who were friends, companions, lovers and associates, a wholeness because I was stuck like a bit of coloured glass in a mosaic" (*B*, p. 106).

Consequently, that individual consciousness which Anna Wulf in *The Golden Notebook* saw as "a pulse in a great darkness" loses its connotations of alienation. Although Charles's own mind might be felt as "a pulse of individuality," yet "pulses of mind lay beating and absorbing beside my own little pulse, and together we were a whole" (*B*, p. 112). Moreover, in itself "humanity was a pulse in the life of the Sun" (*B*, p. 116), thus again extending the dimensions of the metaphor and using it to serve as the connection between the single consciousness and the evolving consciousness of the world.

Structure and Theme in *Briefing for a Descent into Hell*

Douglass Bolling

Of the major fiction writers now on the Anglo-American scene, it is perhaps Doris Lessing who best sustains James's faith in the novel as "the most independent, most elastic, most prodigious of literary forms."[1] We know that James would find much to dispute in Lessing's handling of her narrative materials; but we may be certain that he would applaud her visionary fullness, concern for form, and willingness to be difficult in order to engage the moral urgencies of a complex age. Lessing's stature rose greatly with the publication of *The Four-Gated City*, and the praise given her earlier for such works as *The Grass Is Singing, Martha Quest*, and *The Golden Notebook* seemed by 1969 fully justified.[2] Where the middle volumes of the *Children of Violence* series sometimes lack textural vigor and heightening (as in *A Ripple from the Storm* and *Landlocked*), *The Four-Gated City* restores the promise of the project's inception through its richly conceived and executed resolution. The novel at once concludes the *Bildungsroman* motifs and transcends them in a profound exploration and indictment of the age. Lessing's Stony Brook disclaimers notwithstanding, I believe that the work reveals an artistry and sense of form which match, and even surpass, the brilliance of *The Golden Notebook*.[3] The very ambitiousness of *The Four-Gated City*, its uncompro-

---

[1] "Preface" to *The Ambassadors, The Art of the Novel* (New York: Scribners, 1934), p. 326.

[2] See, for example, Paul Schlueter, "Doris Lessing: The Free Woman's Commitment," *Contemporary British Novelists*, ed. Charles Shapiro (Carbondale: Southern Illinois Univ. Press, 1965), pp. 48-61.

[3] Jonah Raskin, "Doris Lessing at Stony Brook: An Interview," *New American Review*, No. 8 (1970), p. 170.

mising quality and its demanding rhythms that separate and yet bring
together intensities of meaning and low mimetic surfaces—all these
evoke a concentrated response from the dedicated reader. Some critics
of Lessing's fiction have approached this novel with too little patience
for its sheer massiveness, its mimetic strategies, and its turn to the
apocalyptic at the price of the "personal."[4]

Both *The Four-Gated City* and the more recent *Briefing for a
Descent into Hell* indicate that their creator is ahead of her critics in
several healthy ways; for one thing the fiction reveals an artist astutely
aware that, as Wayne Booth argues, "though the author can to some
extent choose his disguises, he can never choose to disappear."[5] For
another, it evidences Lessing's commitment to innovation and challenge of entrenched critical notions—reminding us of Leon Edel's
comments that "Art is never static. It neither accepts conformity nor
does it like repetition" and that "Art thrives best on the variousness
of life and on a search for new forms and new techniques."[6] Perhaps
even more importantly, the two novels present a writer now fully involved with the dehumanizing and life-negating realities of the time:
Martha Hesse's personal development and her political concerns become caught up in the cataclysmic events of the last years of the century and Charles Watkins, the protagonist of *Briefing*, symbolizes the
loss (perhaps irreversible) of psychic wholeness by modern-day Western man.

Lessing's two novels put her in profound agreement with observations made by Erich Fromm; in arguing that "war and robotism"
are the major threats of the present, Fromm says that inhumanity today "means schizoid self-alienation. The danger of the past was that
men became slaves. The danger of the future is that men may become
robots. True enough, robots do not rebel. But given man's nature,
robots cannot live and remain sane, they become 'Golems,' they will
destroy their world and themselves because they cannot stand any
longer the boredom of a meaningless life."[7] Ihab Hassan suggests that
criticism "may have to become apocalyptic before it can compel our
sense of relevance. In the very least, it will have to entertain some

---

[4] See, for example, Frederick R. Karl, "Doris Lessing in the Sixties: The
New Anatomy of Melancholy," *Contemporary Literature*, 13, No. 1 (Winter
1972), 26-33.

[5] *The Rhetoric of Fiction* (Chicago: Univ. of Chicago Press, 1961), p. 20.

[6] *The Modern Psychological Novel* (New York: Universal Library, 1964),
p. 142.

[7] *The Sane Society* (New York: Fawcett World, 1955), pp. 312-13.

sympathy for the metaphors of apocalypse."[8] Accordingly, we will do justice to Doris Lessing's fiction not by seeking to judge it within narrowed formalist bounds but by giving ourselves to its values and by keeping the mind's eye open to the sentence of death beneath which our age thinly lives. In the following pages I shall discuss *Briefing* by focusing upon its major movements as these develop thematic statement. *Briefing* is not a work of the caliber of *The Four-Gated City*, but it is an important work for the reader and doubtless for Doris Lessing's evolution as a writer; perhaps as Frederick McDowell has written, it is a "transitional" novel giving promise of greater achievements ahead.[9]

The thematic center of *Briefing* is found in its exploration of man's psychic depths; the richness, mystery, and vastness of "inner space"; and the suggestion of modern (Western, European, "civilized") man's deadly loss of energizing contact with his own deeper dimensions. Modern man lives not within the vital largeness of his psyche but rather within the constrictions and shallows of his socially conditioned roles and his ego; his is the hollowness and failure of spirit of the alienated and truncated. Profoundly cut off from himself, modern man is the victim rather than the guiding spirit of his own creations; he is the creature of words, norms, and impoverished rituals. Only rarely, in moments of "madness" (schizophrenia, for example) is such a man able to break through the barriers to a hint of his lost being; when this occurs, he is institutionalized and provided medical treatment (electric shock and/or drugs) until "normalcy" returns. So long as the individual sustains "normal" behavior patterns the encapsulating society permits him his "freedom" to go his way—that is, to continue to negate the psychic depths only from which authentic freedom and integration can arise. Unless the circle can be broken, Lessing says in *Briefing*, there can be little hope for the survival of spirit.

One sees at once that the thematic concerns of the novel are derived from the work of influential writers of recent years—from such thinkers as Erving Goffman, Carl Jung, Norman Brown, R. D. Laing, and others. I am interested not so much in the identification of these sources and the extent of Lessing's borrowings as in an examination of the ways they are employed for thematic and aesthetic ends.

---

[8] *The Literature of Silence: Henry Miller and Samuel Beckett* (New York: Alfred A. Knopf, 1967), p. 17.

[9] "Time of Plenty: Recent British Novels," *Contemporary Literature*, 13, No. 3 (Summer 1972), 389.

With some exceptions, I believe that the heavy intellectual weight of *Briefing* is expertly controlled, subordinated to narrative advance and symbolic rhythms—in short, transmuted sufficiently that the reader can respond aesthetically and emotionally rather than merely intellectually.

Possibly the most striking feature of *Briefing* is the manner in which theme and structure are so tightly joined. Lessing wishes us to see—to sense powerfully, rather—that the rich strata of the unconscious are everything and the thin layer of ego-identity very little indeed by comparison. Much of the novel comes to us through the voice of the protagonist, Charles Watkins; but the words arise from deep within Watkins' psyche and possess an oracular quality intended to dominate the work. With Watkins' voice as guide we range widely over the immensities of psychic space until, two pages from the novel's end, we surface with the protagonist upon his restoration to "normalcy." Even then, we are permitted to meet "Charles Watkins" only through two brief letters to friends and one to an admirer. Quite clearly, Lessing's fusion of form and theme is designed to tell us that the everyday, "normal" Charles Watkins is not worth knowing. The novel ends with something of the abruptness and finality of the electric shock by means of which Watkins' ego-identity was restored to itself and one is left with the likelihood that Watkins will not again elude his surface self for the archetypal voyage into the core of his being.

Watkins' psychic voyaging is mediated for the reader by several devices: reports by the attending physicians; dialogue involving Watkins and the hospital staff; a series of letters, some written by Watkins, some written to him, some written by his wife and others to the physicians; an account of his war experiences (as transformed by latent psychic needs and goals) written by Watkins while in Central Intake Hospital; dialogue between Watkins and his wife; and exchanges between Watkins and the young patient, Violet Stoke. These devices, some more subtly than others, all emphasize the gap between man's psychic plenitude on the one hand and the impoverishment of "normal" human consciousness and institutional procedures on the other. They also offer some relief from the intensities of the archetypal "descent" and provide recognizable guideposts lest the reader lose his way in the "darkness" of the unconscious. What we see in *Briefing* is a novel which plunges deeply into the illogicality of the psyche but which is itself tightly structured and controlled.

Perhaps the best description of the form of *Briefing* is that of the left-turning or contracting spiral, with its implications of "destructiveness," in contrast to the expanding or "creative" spiral.[10] The action begins, by this analogy, at the outermost circle or spiral of the unconscious and contracts toward its termination, like the whirlpool, in Watkins' recovery of a fatal normalcy. The major movements of the novel take the reader progressively through the psychic levels of the protagonist and at last into his normal consciousness. Both the title and structure of this suggest the pessimism behind the novel's conception. For unlike traditional treatments of the descent into hell (the descent into the unconscious), such as Dante's, Watkins' is shaped so as to lead back to the protagonist's original state of sterility and spiritual dearth. Watkins is not redeemed by his archetypal quest; as ignorant as ever of his psychic potencies, he remains cut off from the knowledge that, for example, the "Journey into Hell symbolizes the descent into the unconscious, or the awareness of all the potentialities of being—cosmic and psychological—that are needed in order to reach the Paradisiac heights."[11] Similarly, his return to normal is largely a death-in-life rather than a completed journey "expressive of resurrection and the overcoming of death"[12] as in the Night Sea Crossing. Lessing's protagonist is a member of the elite (a professor of Classics at Cambridge) but he is clearly intended to be more—to be in fact Everyman of the twentieth century, a thin ghost of himself severed from the archetypal foundations of his being.

The first movement of *Briefing* presents the narrator-protagonist adrift in the currents of the Atlantic; he is oarless and alone, unable to exert will or direction upon his surroundings; his thoughts are highly charged with symbolic import. The helplessness of the narrator (he is caught up in the circlings of the North Equatorial Current) symbolizes the loosening of ego-control necessary if the spirit is to achieve rebirth. In this connection one remembers that the ocean may symbolize the unconscious.[13] Significantly, the narrator (or, more precisely, the "voice" of the psyche) perceives that there is great danger in remaining at but one level of the oceanic unconscious—he must seek to progress to other dimensions lest he "drown." The introduction of sea horses and the storm[14] suggests the operations of Neptune and the

---

[10] J. E. Cirlot, *A Dictionary of Symbols*, trans. Jack Sage (New York: Philosophical Library, 1962), p. 291.

[11] *Ibid.*, p. 158.

[12] *Ibid.*, p. 218.

[13] *Ibid.*, pp. 217, 230.

[14] Doris Lessing, *Briefing for a Descent into Hell* (New York: Alfred A. Knopf, 1971), pp. 5, 31, respectively. Subsequent page references in the text will be preceded by *B*.

"negative aspect of the spirit."[15] Thus the narrator wishes to find his way into the South Equatorial Current and then to the Brazilian coast (*B*, p. 38); his is an authentic navigation myth rather than the meaningless journeying of the *stultifera navis*; the latter "expresses the idea of 'sailing' as an end in itself, as opposed to the true sense of 'sailing,' which is transition, evolution and salvation, or safe arrival at the haven."[16]

To the confusion of the hospital staff, the narrator associates himself with such archetypal seafarers as Sinbad, Jason, and Odysseus as well as Jonah. In the irony (heavy-handed, perhaps) of the exchange between the narrator and Doctor Y, the latter fails to understand Watkins' cryptic comment that "We are all sailors" (*B*, p. 8); the physician—a symbol of the demythologized and dehumanized society—has lost touch with the archetypal dimensions of personal identity and thus defines himself by his social role: he says that he is not a sailor but "a doctor in this hospital" (*B*, p. 8). The designation of the physicians simply as Doctors X, Y, and Z suggests the depersonalized relationships holding between healer and sufferer in modern society and, perhaps more significantly, the final inadequacy of the verbal apparatus to do justice to the mysteries of spirit. The "real" Charles Watkins begins, we are meant to see, where X, Y, Z end.

In the first movement the motif of sleep and waking is introduced, and this motif deserves special attention. In the exchanges involving the nurse, physician, and Watkins (as yet identified only as "patient"), the latter rejects the alleged curative effect of sleep and instead associates sleep with "death" (*B*, pp. 8-11). For the staff members sleep is seen essentially as a restorative aid in the process of returning the patient to normal, to his recognizable "waking" self. In contrast, Watkins's oracular comment that he will die if he sleeps carries far beyond behavioral and conventional therapeutic considerations. At one level the narrator's fear of sleep symbolizes the fear of the unconscious depths by the "upper" strata of the psyche; as Watkins tells Doctor Y, "I'd slide off into the deep sea swells" (*B*, p. 8). In the wisdom of his "madness," the protagonist perceives (with Dante, Aeneas, Orpheus) both the great value of his dark descent and the dangers attached to it. Mythic associations of death with sleep (Thanatos with Hypnos) provide another level of meaning; relevant here is the Socratic insistence upon "waking" earthly sleepers from their deathly

---

[15] Cirlot, p. 217.
[16] *Ibid.*, p. 282.

ignorance as is the notion that such an activity is a "holy" one.[17] Similarly, gnostic ideas enrich the implications of the motif: as opposed to the deprivations of earthly sleep, waking "implies *anamnesis*, recognition of the soul's true identity, that is, re-cognition of its celestial origin."[18] And Biblical, hermetic, and primitive tribal sources see the ability to remain awake as part of the individual's initiation discipline and as proof of "spiritual strength."[19] At novel's end Watkins "awakens" to the sterile "hell" of modern society—and thus exemplifies R. D. Laing's description of the normal state of modern man as "the condition of alienation, of being asleep, of being unconscious, of being out of one's mind."[20]

Allusions to the "crystalline hush" (*B*, p. 18) and "organs made of crystal sound, of singing light" (*B*, p. 30) initiate patterns of imagery that are central to *Briefing*. Similarly, imagery of earth, air, fire, and water circulates through the first movement of the novel in an evocative way. Since no single element, but rather a dynamic interplay of all four, constitutes the norm, the narrator must emerge from the "water" in order to participate in the richness of being. (One thinks of the Jungian conception of the four functions of the psyche and the four archetypes deployed about the *selbst*.[21]) The crystal disk is probably the most complex symbol in *Briefing*, and its richness defies any easy enumeration of meanings. The disk operates at the anagogical level with its evocations of a universal splendor and harmony and at the psychic level with its implications of internal wholeness and integration for the narrator. It serves to unite patterns of solar symbolism and illumination and the norm of psychic illumination sought

---

[17] Mircea Eliade, *Myth and Reality* (New York: Harper Torchbook, 1968), p. 126.

[18] *Ibid.*, p. 129.

[19] *Ibid.*, pp. 130-31.

[20] *The Politics of Experience* (New York: Pantheon, 1967), p. 12. Laing's work, especially the above title, is central to *Briefing*. Chapters 5 ("The Schizophrenic Experience") and 6 ("Transcendental Experience") provide the core of meanings in Lessing's novel. Laing's outline of inner space voyaging ("from outer to inner"; "from life to a kind of death"; "from mundane time to eonic time"; "from outside [post-birth] back into the womb of all things [pre-birth]") is followed virtually step by step in *Briefing*. The tragic loss in the novel comes with the failure of the society to provide a successful return to outer space for the protagonist (in Laing's words, a return "from a cosmic fertilization to an existential rebirth"). Laing's schema appears on p. 89 of *The Politics;* the "ten-day voyage" of Jessie Watkins (chapter 7) throws further light on Lessing's indebtedness to Laing.

[21] Cirlot, p. 258.

by the narrator. Of great interest is the fact that often in dreams "the nuclear center, the Self . . . appears as a crystal . . . [and] evokes in us the intuitive feeling that even in so-called 'dead' matter, there is a spiritual ordering principle at work. Thus the crystal often symbolically stands for the union of extreme opposites—of matter and spirit."[22] The symbolism is further enriched by traditional associations of unity and perfection with the circle.[23]

The second movement of *Briefing* opens with the narrator on the Brazilian coast. Appropriately, Watkins' means of leaving the sea was a porpoise, a creature well-adapted to both air and water and thus a kind of transition between states of being. The narrator finds himself in natural surroundings of paradisal beauty and splendor (*B*, pp. 40-44), but he must seek out higher levels and attempts to climb the forbidding rock. The dark and glassy surface of this rock reminds him of the ocean waves of his earlier experience; like the waves and unlike the crystal disk, the rock's surface is opaque and menacing (*B*, pp. 48-49). Significantly, he is unable to "think" his way into a plan for climbing the steep wall but instead must be shown the secret by two friendly leopard-like creatures. Possibly, the animals symbolize "the non-human psyche . . . the world of subhuman instincts . . . the unconscious areas of the psyche."[24] The self acquires the animal's "connectedness with its surroundings. (That is why there are so many helpful animals in myths and fairy tales.) This relation of the Self to all surrounding nature and even the cosmos probably comes from the fact that the 'nuclear atom' of our psyche is somehow woven into the whole world, both outer and inner."[25]

The narrator next comes upon the ruins of an ancient city, which, despite its age and condition, possesses a beauty and harmony for him, and he chooses to remain there. The man-made structures and surrounding flora serenely blend together: the city has "an atmosphere as if it were inhabited. . . . More, as if this city was itself a person, or had a soul, or being. It seemed to know me. The walls seemed to acknowledge me as I passed. And when the moon rose for the third time since I had arrived on this coast, I was wandering among the streets and avenues of stone as if I were among friends" (*B*, pp. 57-58). In presenting here a conception of the city as an organism, with

---

[22] M. L. von Franz, "The Process of Individuation," in *Man and His Symbols,* ed. Carl G. Jung (New York: Doubleday, 1968), p. 209.

[23] Cirlot, pp. 44-46.

[24] *Ibid.*, p. 13.

[25] von Franz, p. 207.

its corollary of exchange and mutuality between the individual and his environment, Lessing implies a contrast to the mechanized and de-humanized modern city of Western capitalism.[26]

The narrator finds at the center of the city a great square with a circle within it and knows intuitively that he must clean the expanse of stone, restore the mandala to its rightful condition, and thereby come nearer the truths it symbolizes (*B*, pp. 58-59). At one level his action symbolizes the quest for the sacredness lost to modern man:

Whether in classical or in primitive foundations, the mandala ground plan was never dictated by considerations of aesthetics or economics. It was a transformation of the city into an ordered cosmos, a sacred place, bound by its center to the other world. And this transformation accorded with the vital feelings and needs of religious man. Every building, sacred or secular, that has a mandala ground plan is the projection of an archetypal image from within the human unconscious onto the outer world. The city, the fortress, and the temple become symbols of psychic wholeness, and in this way exercise a specific influence on the human being who enters or lives in the place.[27]

The last two sentences of the quotation bear especially on the deeper level of the narrator's psychic "descent" into the unconscious. His attempt to enter into the ancient society's symbols of wholeness com-plements his journey into his unconscious. Of the possible interpreta-tions of Lessing's mandala (the circle within the square), perhaps the most thematically charged one would be that the circle represents the psyche and the square the material principle of earth or body; the implication is clearly that soul and matter are to be seen as profoundly one rather than as estranged. In contrast to the mandala's harmonious placing of circle and square, we learn from Aniela Jaffé that "In most modern art, the connection between these two primary forms is either nonexistent, or loose and casual. Their separation is another symbolic expression of the psychic state of twentieth-century man: His soul has lost its roots and he is threatened by dissociation."[28] (Joseph Camp-bell's discussion of the Hebrew bifurcation of sacred and secular comes

---

[26] Frederick Karl's discussion of the enclosure theme in Lessing's work is relevant here. See also John D. Rosenberg's perceptive survey of the shifting conceptions of the city in "Varieties of Infernal Experience," *The Hudson Review*, 23 (1970), 454-80.

[27] Aniela Jaffé, "Symbolism in the Visual Arts," in *Man and His Symbols*, p. 243.

[28] *Ibid.*, p. 249.

to mind here.[29]) The narrator's experiences in the ancient city are ultimately psychic transformations of his conscious or "normal" interests in older civilizations and languages.

Other major rhythms of the second movement include the alternating influences on the narrator's psyche of moon and sun archetypes; his loss of innocence and knowledge of evil; chthonic incursions into the psyche; the appearances of the great white bird; and the arrival of the crystal (*B*, pp. 60-100). The narrator is not a detached observer of the sun and moon but, far more profoundly, is caught up in their pervasive presences and energies.[30] His recognition of the evil within himself comes with the slaughter of one of the cattle from the "ghostly herd" grazing on the plain (*B*, p. 66). A bonfire and accompanying orgiastic behavior symbolizes his deepening guilt and fear; the children and women (one of them being "Felicity," Watkins' wife) reflect his "normal" awareness of his inadequacies in personal and social relationships and his need to project these onto others. Now deeply within his psychic layers, he sees the savagery and "animality" latent in human behavior, including his own "civilized" behavior (*B*, pp. 66-72). The Adamic fall is echoed in his new awareness of his nakedness and effort to clothe himself (*B*, p. 72).

Before Watkins can be taken up into the crystal (the presence of which is felt increasingly in this part of the movement [*B*, pp. 76-78]), he must experience yet another dimension of the unconscious, that symbolized by the rat-dogs and apes. Most obviously perhaps, the rat-dogs point to the rigors of the evolutionary process as it struggles from an earlier to a more advanced stage; the creatures strain to "talk" and to stand upright but do so under great discomfort. The description of fighting between members of the same species (*B*, p. 97) points to the insanity of modern warfare and to Lessing's apocalyptic vision in *The Four-Gated City*.

More important thematically, the rat-dogs symbolize the psyche's need to come to terms with its dark dimensions in order to grow into stability and wholeness. Not only the peace of the mandala but the turbulence of the "underworld" must be fully experienced. As Joseph L. Henderson informs us, "the symbols that influence man vary in their purpose. Some men need to be aroused, and experience their

[29] *The Flight of the Wild Gander: Explorations in the Mythological Dimension* (New York: Viking Press, 1969), p. 204.

[30] For discussions of solar and lunar symbolism, see Cirlot, pp. 302-4, 204-6, respectively.

initiation in the violence of a Dionysiac 'thunder rite.' Others need to be subdued, and they are brought to submission in the ordered design of temple precinct or sacred cave, suggestive of the Apollonian religion of later Greece. A full initiation embraces both themes."[31] The rat-dogs are symbols of "transcendence" which liberate the psyche from fixation at immature or inadequate levels; as such they carry "a special chthonic [underworld] message" from the collective unconscious.[32] In their connection with psychic liberation, the creatures prepare us for the appearance of the bird and the crystal.

The great white bird introduces yet another rich source of symbolism into the action of *Briefing*; most important is that it provides further psychic "liberation" for the protagonist.[33] The bird grants the narrator two flights: the first helps to allay Watkins' "despair" over the threatening rat-dogs (*B*, pp. 91, 95); the second overcomes his thoughts of regressing into the "sea" (*B*, pp. 95-96) and leads to his renewed affirmation of the mandala (*B*, pp. 99-100). The flights also introduce him to the element of air. When the bird places itself in the center of the mandala, we realize the narrator is ready to enter into the crystal.

The third movement begins with the initial experiences of the narrator inside the crystal and ends with his "rebirth" on earth (*B*, pp. 101-48). He is first granted a vision into the workings of reality and a view of earth from his celestial voyage aboard the crystal; then figures of Greek and Roman mythology appear to effect his "return" to earth. Lessing's use of the mysterious crystal seems to reflect her recent interest in science fiction.[34] Interestingly, "the exploration of inner space" has been recently identified as one of the major themes of science fiction; and the suggestion has been made that "science fiction will be rendering its best service when it seeks to renew the realm of art, that is, when it helps us to order and comprehend our 'inner space' and explore the vocabulary and visions of mythological dimensions."[35]

The great mythopoeic vision unfolded to the narrator within his

---

[31] Joseph L. Henderson, "Ancient Myths and Modern Man," in *Man and His Symbols*, p. 149.

[32] *Ibid.*, p. 154.

[33] See the discussion of bird symbolism in Cirlot, pp. 25-27.

[34] Raskin, p. 175.

[35] Lois and Stephen Rose, *The Shattered Ring: Science Fiction and the Quest for Meaning* (Richmond: John Knox Press, 1970), p. 110. See p. 19 for other science fiction themes.

crystalline vantage point conveys the immensity, indeed the infinite reaches, of both outer and inner space. Imagery of "singing light," "fluid joyful being," dancing, and "harmony" points to such sources as Neoplatonism, Hindu thought, and other Western and Eastern mythologies and mysticisms (see, for example, *B*, pp. 107-11); similarly, negative imagery of coldness, "compulsion," death, and "sorrow," indicating a "flaw" in the sublunary area of the cosmos, reflects the Christian Fall and other conceptions (*B*, pp. 117-19). We see that the beauty and splendor of the cosmic "light" does not always inspirit the farther reaches of "cold" and "darkness." The narrator embraces the "harmony" of the universe seen as a whole but recoils from such specific manifestations as the moon's control over earthly and human rhythms. He cannot affirm the moon's "cold necessity" which so powerfully affects tidal, biological, and even psychological rhythms.

At the psychic level Watkins' vision suggests a contrast between the psyche's health and wholeness and an imbalance or pressure generated by one of its "parts" or functions—a failure to assimilate the maternal imago, for example. "Freedom" consists in surrendering one's self to the "laws" by which the psyche maintains its "harmony." At the social level the vision contrasts the "madness" of the egocentric —the "I, I, I, I,"—with the "sweet sanity of We" (*B*, pp. 120-21).

The final section presents a series of astronomical, mythological, and philosophical speculations, the dissemination by Watkins of visionary truths (*B*, pp. 123-30); dialogue involving Jupiter, Minerva, Mercury; a description of the conference of deities and a "film" of earth's activities (*B*, pp. 130-48). At the conclusion of the movement the "Descent Team" (including Charles Watkins) prepares for its drop to the "hell" of earth; its mission is to spread the truth (the seeing of "things as they are, in their multifarious relations," in their "Harmony" and "Unity") among the anarchical and violence-prone inhabitants of earth. In contrast to the oracular and heightened tone of the earlier parts of *Briefing*, the mood is at times jocular or witty, as in the pages of dialogue. The refractions of mythology should be taken as psychic transformations of Professor Watkins' "normal" interest in classical literature. Beneath his ego-driven, pedantic involvement in the latter, his unconscious seeks a dynamic and fecund metamorphosis.

Eliade writes that "the *regressus ad uterum* is accomplished in order that the beneficiary shall be born into a new mode of being or be regenerated."[36] Watkins' rebirth in the final section is only into the

---

[36] Eliade, p. 80.

sterile hell of a dubious normality. Modern society is indicted for
believing that sleep is an anodyne against the energies and potentials
of the human being from infancy onward. Watkins' "return" comes at
the midpoint of the novel and provides a transition from the depths of
the psyche to the surfaces of daily life and routine. The heightened
description of the first half gives way for the most part to the low
mimetic; we move, for example, from within Watkins' psychic vision
of himself as a celestial voyager among the gods to the "outer space"
of his mundane existence, from the visionary splendor of the singing
light to the secularized and diminished light of the modern world.[37]
Over and over the alert reader catches the unobtrusively employed
word or phrase which suddenly flashes with meanings developed in
the novel's first half.

The second half of *Briefing* is really a single long movement
counterpointed by an occasional excursus into Watkins' psychic
depths. Commentary and the series of letters provide insight into
Watkins' life prior to his attack of "madness" and also develop themes
of interest to Lessing—such as the deadening influence of modern
education upon the child's spontaneity and potential (*B*, pp. 175-83);
the indiscrimination of the media (such as television): "all events are
equally important, whether war, a game, the weather, the craft of
plant-growing, a fashion show, a police hunt" (*B*, p. 189); the highly
abstract and dubious nature of certain fashionable scholarly concepts
(Greece as the mother of Western civilization, for example), and the
dishonesties of some academics (such as the professor in Wiltshire).
These notions (*B*, pp. 199-202) become crucial when one realizes
that they are linked to an important phenomenon of modern civilization—that of historiographic *anamnesis*. Through this activity, Eliade
comments,

man enters deep into himself. If we succeed in understanding a contemporary Australian, or his homologue, a paleolithic hunter, we have suc-
ceeded in "awakening" in the depths of our being the existential situation
and the resultant behavior of a prehistoric humanity. It is not a matter of a
mere "external" knowledge, as when we learn the name of the capital of a
country or the date of the fall of Constantinople. A true historiographic
anamnesis finds expression in the discovery of our solidarity with these
vanished or peripheral peoples.[38]

---

[37] For an interesting attempt to deal with mental illness within the limits
of the low mimetic, see Melvyn Bragg's *The Nerve* (London: Secker & Warburg, 1971).
   [38] Eliade, p. 136.

As much of the second half of *Briefing* expresses the clutter, confusion, and equivocation of "normal" existence, so it provides a contrasting rhythm that invokes the beauty and fecundity of the unconscious and even, at times, of seemingly "deranged" expression. Charles Watkins' account of his alleged wartime experiences in Yugoslavia (*B*, pp. 246-73) violates fact but validates the truth of the heart. The letters which "frame" Watkins' account prove that he had not been in Yugoslavia and that Miles Bovey (who had been there) did not die in the war; within the frame, Watkins' psychic energies transform the literal into the imaginative truth of art. The episode may stand by itself, as a short story within the novel, but it is tied closely to the work's thematic center.

Perhaps revealing her most deeply felt values, Lessing indicates in this example how a personal relationship (the love between Konstantina and the narrator) may be joined to the social commitment of the group (the struggles of the Resistance) without itself being violated. Man is not a discrete mind or ego locked off from the world but rather is profoundly one with it; "mental" and natural rhythms interpenetrate. Thus Konstantina's death in the encounter with the deer is illuminated by von Franz's observation that we "have only to think of the fact that most grass-eating animals have their young at precisely the time of year when the grass is richest and most abundant. With such considerations in mind, a well-known zoologist has said that the 'inwardness' of each animal reaches far out into the world around it and 'psychifies' time and space."[39] It is this kind of deep wisdom that Watkins loses upon his return to normality.

Watkins' experiences with Violet Stoke (*B*, pp. 276-88, 298-304) provide a typical example of the way in which the psyche is freed from ego-domination. Both Watkins and Violet possess an "innocence" and openness which social conditioning destroys; they communicate from within themselves rather than across the barriers of their social roles. But the mutuality at the heart of their relationship is doomed: Violet probably will not find it without Watkins' continued presence, and Watkins loses his capacity for it after the electric shock treatment. The "restored" protagonist of the last two pages is the profoundly unenlightened creature of a diseased and darkened age, a man unable to "remember" that, as Jung says, "Light is always born of darkness."[40]

---

[39] von Franz, pp. 207-8.

[40] *Modern Man in Search of a Soul* (1933; rpt. New York: Harvest Book, n. d.), p. 215.

Some readers of *Briefing* may find the weight of psychological and mythic material to be either oppressive in itself or else insufficiently compensated for by other novelistic values; some may find the appropriation of concepts from R. D. Laing and others raising questions as to the writer's originality.[41] Other readers may find the projection of a protagonist such as Charles Watkins to be out of the important currents of modernism, preferring the greater authenticity of the Underground Man, for example. The latter, as defined by Maurice Friedman, is "the divided man who in probing to the depths finds antinomy and conflict rather than any single united self. He is the man who lives out the full tension of psychological compulsion and personal freedom."[42] One may also say that, with qualification, the limitations of *Briefing* are those of the lyrical novel, as that form has been described by Ralph Freedman: "an underemphasis on character and an overemphasis on image, dream-like encounter, or allegory. The excitement created by the plot is largely absent."[43] Despite these and other possible criticisms, I suspect that *Briefing for a Descent into Hell* will hold its own and will in time assume an especially interesting place in the Lessing canon. Northrop Frye's comment on the conclusion of *Finnegans Wake* bears directly on the ending of *Briefing*: "what happens there is that the dreamer, after spending the night in communion with a vast body of metaphorical identifications, wakens and goes about his business forgetting his dream, like Nebuchadnezzar, failing to use, or even to realize that he can use, the 'keys to dreamland.' What he fails to do is therefore left for the reader to do. . . ."[44]

[41] See, for example, Benjamin DeMott, review of *Briefing*, *Saturday Review*, 13 March 1971, pp. 25 ff; Joan Didion, review of *Briefing*, *New York Times Book Review*, 14 March 1971, pp. 1 ff.

[42] *Problematic Rebel: An Image of Modern Man* (New York: Random House, 1963), p. 257.

[43] *The Lyrical Novel: Studies in Hermann Hesse, André Gide, and Virginia Woolf* (Princeton: Princeton Univ. Press, 1963), p. 283.

[44] *Anatomy of Criticism* (New York: Atheneum, 1969), p. 354.

Doris Lessing and the
Sufi Way

Nancy Shields Hardin

Now the interesting thing is in twenty-
five years I haven't been asked the
right questions. The questions that I
am asked invariably are these: How
many hours a day do you write? And
do you write regularly every day or do
you write in a regular burst? These are
very unsophisticated questions and
they are asked by very sophisticated
people who might have studied literature for as much as fifteen years. . . .
Now the real question is this: Where
do you get your energy from? What
kind of energy is it? How do you husband it? How do you use it? . . .[1]

For more than ten years Doris Lessing has been a student of
Sufism and its impact on her fiction is evident. As with most forms of
mysticism, Sufism is extremely hard to define. The problem is intensified by Lessing's ambiguous use of what is already an ambiguity. In

---

[1] Doris Lessing, New School for Social Research (Sept. 25, 1972), one of
six talks given in September 1972. All quotations from this series are used by
permission of Doris Lessing.

Parenthetical page references in the text are to the following editions:
FC—*The Four-Gated City* (New York: Alfred A. Knopf, 1969). Copyright ©
1969 Doris Lessing Productions, Ltd.; B—*Briefing for a Descent into Hell*
(New York: Alfred A. Knopf, 1971). Copyright © 1971 Doris Lessing; T—
The Temptation of Jack Orkney & Other Stories (New York: Alfred A. Knopf,
1972). Copyright © 1963, 1964, 1968, 1969, 1971, 1972 Doris Lessing. The
first two works are used by permission of Alfred A. Knopf, Inc.; the third is
used by permission of John Cushman Associates, Inc.

the most general terms Sufism is a form of Islamic mysticism whose literature covers some 1,400 years, crosses a variety of nationalities (Near East, Africa, Europe), and includes scientists as well as philosophers and writers in its numbers. Such diverse people as St. Francis, Roger Bacon, and Denis de Rougement were influenced by Sufi ideas. Sufism is noted for its denial of codification of exact and prescriptive rules of behavior; indeed, it is a composite of anomalies and espouses neither ideology nor dogma. In the review, "What Looks Like an Egg and Is an Egg?" Lessing notes: "The Sufis themselves seldom conceal that they are concerned with presentation and effectiveness, not indoctrination. Hence their writings are littered with phrases like 'The color of the wine is the same as the color of the bottle,' or, 'Right time, right place, right people are necessary.' "[2]

For a non-Sufi to understand what it means to be a Sufi is perhaps impossible. What is possible and permissible is to endeavor to enlarge one's understanding of the term "Sufi." For those who seek information about Sufis, Lessing offers assurance that the best of contemporary Western sources of information is to be found in the books of Idries Shah. Her review of Shah's *The Sufis* some ten years ago not only gives the uninitiated reader a sense of the intrigue and mysteries to come, but perhaps as well offers valuable directives to the reading of some of her own works: " 'A Sufi, the Sufis, cannot be defined by any single set of words or ideas' and 'Sufism is known by means of itself,' says Idries Shah—who is master of the difficult arts of deliberate provocation, slight dislocation of an expected sense, use of the apparently banal—to make one read a thing again, and more carefully."[3] For the most part Idries Shah avoids the collective philosophical abstraction, Sufism, and would rather his audience understand the Sufi as individuals: "The Sufi's world has extra dimensions; to him things are meaningful in a sense which they are not to people who follow only the training which is imposed upon them by ordinary society."[4] The only way then to comprehend the Sufi mind is to shake loose from logical modes of thought. This theme is one that resounds time and again throughout Lessing's work.

However, the Sufi neither encourages disciples nor is there a guru to follow as in other Eastern ideologies. One is much more on his own and must assume responsibility for himself: "Man is the microcosm,

[2] *New York Times Book Review* (May 7, 1972), 6.

[3] "An Elephant in the Dark," *The Spectator* (Sept. 18, 1964), 373.

[4] *The Sufis* (New York: Doubleday, 1971), p. 39.

creation the macrocosm—the unity. All comes from One. By the joining of the power of contemplation all can be attained. This essence
must be separated from the body first, then combined with the body.
This is the Work. Start with yourself, end with all. Before man, beyond
man, transformation."[5] Furthermore, the Sufi is characterized by the
slogan: "Be *in* the world but not *of* it."[6] Participation in the world is
primary, for the Sufi is one who excels in a trade or a skill; although,
the individual student is offered a "secret garden,"[7] wherein he may
perfect his understanding and experience: "It is the development of
the human being which counts, nothing else."[8] Enlightenment comes
only through experience, not by way of intellect: "He who tastes not,
knows not."[9] Yet this is not to imply that the privacy of Sufi knowledge
is insurmountable: "Sufis are not secret: their work tends to be private
or ice-berg like because they believe that 'for every ounce which is
visible there must be a ton which is active, but not perceived by the
ordinary man.' "[10]

For those who do intuit this special perception in themselves and
who work to transcend the ordinary limitations of man, there is hope
for a further evolutionary stage of development: "The Sufis claim that
a certain kind of mental or other activity can produce under special
conditions and with particular efforts, what is termed a higher working
of the mind, leading to special perceptions whose apparatus is latent
in ordinary man. Sufism is, therefore, the transcending of ordinary
limitations."[11] While the Sufi stresses using one's mind in a new way,
he is to be distinguished from both mystic and magus: "the mystic
wants to 'be' and the magically minded wants to 'know.' The Sufi
attitude is undoubtedly that of 'being'; but, unlike the familiar type of
mystic, he will use 'knowing' as well. He distinguishes between the
ordinary knowing of facts and the inner knowing of reality. His activity connects and balances all these factors—understanding, being,
knowing."[12]

---

[5] *Ibid.*, p. 223. (Quoted from the Introduction to the *Perception of Jafar
Sadiq.*)

[6] Idries Shah, *Thinkers of the East: Teachings of the Dervishes* (Baltimore: Penguin Books, 1972), p. 198.

[7] Robert Graves, Introduction to *The Sufis*, p. xii.

[8] *The Sufis*, p. 225.

[9] *Ibid.*, p. 62. Rumi as quoted by Idries Shah.

[10] William Foster, *Sufi Studies Today* (London: Octagon Press, 1968),
p. 8.

[11] Idries Shah, *The Way of the Sufi* (New York: E. P. Dutton, 1970), p. 14.

[12] *The Sufis*, p. 381.

Encoded Sufi symbolism is to be found disseminated in a variety of sources: designs woven in carpets, poetry (Omar Khayyam, to name but one poet), Dervish tales and dances, Nasrudin jokes, *The Arabian Nights*, and Druid folklore. The Druids, for example, used mistletoe as a sacred and curative plant which symbolized their own mode of thinking. Robert Graves in an introduction to *The Sufis* notes: "The symbolism is exact, if we can equate Druidic with Sufic thought, which is not planted like a tree, as religions are planted, but self-engrafted on a tree already in existence; it keeps green though the tree itself is asleep, in the sense that religions go dead by formalism; and the main motive power of its growth is love, not ordinary animal passion or domestic affection but a sudden surprising recognition of love so rare and high that the heart seems to sprout wings."[13]

Certainly, one of the most unusual sources of Sufi information comes from the tales of Mulla Nasrudin. In *Landlocked* (introduction to sections one and four), Lessing uses the wisdom of Nasrudin teaching stories to underscore Martha's search for self-knowledge. Lessing comments about those basic Sufi attitudes toward life and self which may be found in Nasrudin subtleties: "But perhaps the most shocking to our assumptions about 'mysticism' is the corpus of Nasrudin 'jokes,' deliberately created to inculcate Sufic thinking, to outwit the Old Villain, which is a name for the patterns of conditioned thinking which form the prison in which we all live."[14] The legend itself of Nasrudin is an allegory of man's inability to perceive more clearly: "But they were like children born in a house from which they had never been allowed to stray, doomed to walk from one room to another without knowing that there could be another house, elsewhere, with different furnishings and a different view from its windows. . . ."[15] Nasrudin presents provocative situations whose unexpected juxtaposition of ideas is designed to jar the reader or listener from rigid thought patterns: "Mulla Nasrudin broke out of the net which had been cast by the old villain. For how can one burn a book which is not a book? How can one name a fool who is no fool? How can one punish a man who is a multitude? How can one strike a man who is oneself?"[16]

---

[13] *Ibid.*, p. xi.

[14] "What Looks Like an Egg and Is an Egg?" *New York Times Book Review* (May 7, 1972), 42.

[15] *Thinkers of the East*, p. 194.

[16] *Ibid.*, p. 195.

Consider Lessing's use of the Dervish teaching story which precedes *The Four-Gated City,* a tale about the fool who is sent to buy salt and flour and is cautioned not to mix the two. He places the salt on one side of the dish. When given the flour, he inverts the dish, thereby losing the salt. Likewise when he looks for the salt, on the other side of the dish, he loses the flour as well. At this point, Lessing ends the tale, letting the inner dimensions of the story reveal whatever the reader is ready to assimilate. Idries Shah's version of the same teaching story is more directive in its conclusion: "You have laughed at the joke of the fool. Now, will you do more, and think about your own thoughts as if they were the salt and the flour?"[17] Certainly, in *The Four-Gated City,* Lessing, as do the Sufis, stresses that whole areas of understanding must be examined afresh:

There is something in the human mind which makes it possible for one compartment to hold Fact A which matches Fact B in another compartment; but the two facts can exist side by side for years, decades, centuries, without coming together. It is a least possible that the most fruitful way of describing the human brain is this: "It is a machine which works in division; it is composed of parts which function in compartments locked off from each other." or "Your right hand does not know what your left hand is doing." (*FC,* p. 496)

Each of the Lessing protagonists must learn to accept and trust the evidence of his own senses: "We do not have opinions of our own. . . . It is becoming possible for people to trust their own experiences. There is no way of communicating this. What matters is to learn it for yourself."[18] The problem is to move beyond the education which has trained one "to believe that to put a label on a feeling, a state of mind, a thing—to find a set of words or a phrase; in short, to describe it—is the same as understanding and experiencing it" (*B,* p. 308). Lessing clearly wants the reader to consider her characters as experiencing their individual roles in a form of conscious evolution. One phase of this growth is an openness to extrasensory perception: "A man or a woman walking along a street gives no evidence of what he is thinking, yet his thoughts are playing all about him in subtle currents of substance. But an ordinary person cannot see these subtle moving thoughts" (*B,* p. 63). More recently in response to a question during her series of six talks at New School for Social Research, Lessing com-

---

[17] "Do More Than Laugh at Fools," *The Way of the Sufi,* p. 213.
[18] Doris Lessing, New School for Social Research (Sept. 27, 1972).

ments not only on her own abilities with ESP, but those of enormous numbers of people:

Well, it started off by my thinking how odd it was that a rationalist like myself should . . . have such a lively relationship with her dream life, for example, and take it for granted that I could pick up other people's thoughts, . . . I started to think about it . . . which took me a very long time to do. It's very hard to be a part of that complicated idea . . . that you are a rationalist and atheist and you don't believe and everything is already cut and dried and you already know everything and suddenly start throwing all that out the window and start thinking again. It was very hard for me to do that. . . . You can see someone pick up what you are thinking and start talking about it. It happens to everybody. . . . Or you will say something and someone will say that's funny I've been thinking about that. In actual fact what we are doing is using ESP. . . . What energy is reaching you? We don't know why, do we? There is something there to be explored . . . if we don't get upset. . . .[19]

The Sufis feel even more certain about the importance of this particular energy of ESP being used and developed:

Sufis believe that, expressed in one way, humanity is evolving to a certain destiny. We are all taking part in that evolution. Organs come into being as a result of a need for specific organs [Rumi]. The human being's organism is producing a new complex of organs in response to such a need. In this age of the transcending of time and space, the complex of organs is concerned with the transcending of time and space. What ordinary people regard as sporadic and occasional bursts of telepathic and prophetic power are seen by the Sufi as nothing less than the first stirrings of these same organs. The difference between all evolution up to date and the present need for evolution is that for the past ten thousand years or so we have been given the possibility of a conscious evolution. So essential is this more rarefied evolution that our future depends on it.[20]

The world through Lessing's eyes is not a commonplace sight even though she examines closely the most ordinary of things. She indicates clues for the reader, such as the signpost to be found in the passage quoted from Sage Mahmoud Shabistari's "The Secret Garden" which precedes *Briefing for a Descent into Hell*:

---

[19] *Ibid.*, Sept. 25, 1972.
[20] *The Sufis*, p. 61.

If yonder raindrop should its heart disclose,
Behold therein a hundred seas displayed.
In every atom, if thou gaze aright,
Thousands of reasoning beings are contained.
. . . .
Upon one little spot within the heart
Resteth the Lord and Master of the worlds.
Therein two worlds commingled may be seen. . . . (*B*, p. 1)

This then is followed by a passage from Rachel Carson: "This minuscule world of the sand grains is also the world of inconceivably minute beings, . . . all living, dying, swimming, feeding, breathing, reproducing in a world so small that our human senses cannot grasp its scale, a world in which the micro-droplet of water separating one grain of sand from another is like a vast, dark sea." Lessing does indeed look with her visionary imagination upon two worlds commingled in time and space. There is to her perceptions a fable-like content, somewhat resembling a Sufi allegory which conveys secrets to the elect and conceals them from others. One is reminded of Idries Shah's comments at the beginning of *Reflections: Fables in the Sufi Tradition*: "Do you imagine that fables exist only to amuse or to instruct, and are based upon fiction? The best ones are delineations of what happens in real life, in the community and in the individual's mental processes."[21] So it is with Lessing's writings in that her novels and her short stories partake of the two worlds—of real life on the one hand and of mental processes on the other. The secret is that Lessing, as the Sufis, does not see the two as separate: "it isn't either or at all, it's and, and, and, and, and, and. . . . Your dreams or your life. But it is not *or*, that is the point. It is an *and*. Everything is. Your dreams *and* your life" (*B*, pp. 165, 168).

It is Lessing's gift to stimulate the awareness of other possibilities in the minds of her readers. She, therefore, in a variety of ways, engages in explorations of space and time, journeying on occasion "into a totally uncharted interior" (*FC*, p. 507). In order to acquire this level of vision, frequently, a dissolution of the ordinary ego state becomes necessary. Lessing is not alone in speaking to this transcendental experience; R. D. Laing is equally concerned with other levels of consciousness. However, Lessing refers to Laing as "a peg": "All educated look for a key authority figure who will then act as a law giver.

---

[21] (Baltimore: Penguin Books, 1972), pp. 1-2.

Laing became that figure."[22] Yet, Laing speaks to the same issues that concern Lessing:

The fountain has not played itself out, the frame still shines, the river still flows, the spring still bubbles forth, the light has not faded. But between *us* and It, there is a veil which is more like fifty feet of solid concrete. *Deus absconditus.* Or we have absconded. . . . Already everything in our time is directed to categorizing and segregating this reality from objective facts. This is precisely the concrete wall. Intellectually, emotionally, interpersonally, organizationally, intuitively, theoretically, we have to blast our way through the solid wall, even at the risk of chaos, madness and death. For from this side of the wall, *this* is the risk. There are no assurances, no guarantees.

From the alienated starting point of our pseudo-sanity, everything is equivocal. . . . True sanity entails in one way or another the dissolution of the normal ego, that false self competently adjusted to our alienated social reality; the emergence of the "inner" archetypal mediators of divine power, and through this death a rebirth, and the eventual re-establishment of a new kind of ego-functioning, the ego now being the servant of the divine, no longer its betrayer.[23]

Lessing's protagonists are at various stages in "blasting" their way through the solid wall of the normal ego to the realization of "a new kind of ego-functioning." This secret knowledge "could not be sold, or taken: it could only be earned, or accepted as a gift" (*FC*, p. 135). Furthermore, there is a breakdown between those who achieve a level of heightened alertness as more knowledgeable protagonists and those who are naive recipients. Some participate on both levels. Energy, as a creative element, plays a significant role in each of these endeavors.

Lessing illustrates a variety of levels of wakefulness, whereby her protagonists attempt to energize themselves to trust and to maintain their altered experiences. She believes that such energy is much rarer than any other. Indeed, Lessing has suggested that accumulation of any creative energy is frequently done by means of physical ritual which enables one to move from one level of energy to another, as if changing gears.[24] Martha Quest uses "her body as an engine to get her

---

[22] Doris Lessing, New School for Social Research (Sept. 27, 1972).

[23] *Politics of Experience* (New York: Ballantine Books, 1967), pp. 143-45.

[24] In her Sept. 25, 1972, New School for Social Research talk, Lessing paraphrased Isadora Duncan as having described this rare form of creative energy: "Before I dance I have to switch a motor on . . . and if I can't switch the motor on, I can't dance." See Victor Seroff's *The Real Isadora* (New York: Avon Books, 1972): "Before I go out on the stage, I must place a *motor* in my

out of the small dim prison of every day" (*FC*, p. 472). This Lessing protagonist chooses to manipulate the energy generated by her anxiety and to use it in an exploration of self, in an attempt to bridge the gap within herself between the restrictions of acceptable knowledge and a deeper experience of knowing: "When people open up a new area in themselves, start doing something new, then it must be clumsy and raw . . . the new, an opening up, had to be through a region of chaos, of conflict. There was no other way of doing it" (*FC*, p. 176).

Martha challenges the narrowed set of ideas that society has comfortably conditioned most of the world into accepting: "There was something in the human mind that separated, and divided" (*FC*, p. 79). Having tried the channels of the culturally acceptable (Freud and Jung), Martha turns to the culturally suspect in her search for answers: "There were books on Rosicrucianism and the old alchemists; Buddhist books and the dozen or so varieties of Yoga; there were Zoroastrianism and esoteric Christianity; tracts on the I Ching; Zen, witchcraft, magic, astrology and vampirism; scholarly treatises on Sufism; the works of the Christian mystics" (*FC*, p. 486). Rather than relying on received knowledge that encourages pigeonholing of information and discourages confronting clues of destruction, Martha ultimately seeks an inward experiencing to give her understanding of a view of life she has glimpsed before, "a view of life . . . seen as a whole, making a whole" (*FC*, p. 191). Even as an adolescent on the African veld, Martha realized the painful quality of mystical participation in the world soul, an experience that left her reaching out after the moment, longing to try again: "There had been no ecstasy, only difficult knowledge."[25] As an adult in London, Martha holds tenaciously to those moments of wakeful insight which one cannot easily remember and as a consequence rejects any labeling of her experience. Her problem in part is that of trusting the validity of her unexpected knowledge since "she could not remember now what it was she had understood" (*FC*, p. 92). She comes to accept herself as one who must undergo the journey repeatedly in order to reach the moment of insight into her capacities: "There are people who know quite well that they are drugged and asleep, . . . We keep learning things and forgetting them so we have to learn them again" (*FC*, pp. 96-97). Dur-

---

soul. When that begins to work, my legs and arms and my whole body will move independently of my own will. But if I do not get time to put the *motor* in my soul, I cannot dance" (p. 123).

[25] Doris Lessing, *Martha Quest* (New York: Simon and Schuster, 1964), p. 63.

ing her voyage into her world of inner space stimulated by a lack of food and sleep, Martha begins "to see the way out, and forward?" (*FC*, p. 472). She begins to approach the Sufi concept of the whole person.

Periods of intensified awareness, then, seem to come only from the moments in which the receiver is receptive to the energizing force. Rosemary Baines, for example, finds herself "having been struck by a condition like extra wakefulness" (*B*, p. 192), which has been triggered by Charles Watkins' lecture. She attempts to describe the quality of the experience: "it was like suddenly touching a high tension wire. Of being, briefly, on a different, high, vibrating current, of the familiar becoming transparent" (*B*, p. 183). Yet later in the night when she struggles to hold on to the significance of the experience, in which the "day-by-day selves were held at bay for a moment" (*B*, p. 181), she acknowledges that the feeling has once again slipped from her grasp: "The time of being awake, of being receptive, of *being energetic*—had consumed itself. We don't have much energy. Your words—or rather, what you had put into the words—had fed us, woken us, made us recognise parts of ourselves normally well hidden and covered over . . ." (*B*, pp. 181-82). The problem becomes in part not only one of trusting the experience itself, but also of investing other stages of one's life with the same quality of energy. In her pragmatic acceptance of the fleeting quality of the knowledge of this particular energy, Rosemary writes Charles in the hope that he will join her small band of friends who have acknowledged the existence of this energy: "I suppose it won't seem much when I write it. Sometimes when you read a book or story, the words are dead, you struggle to end it or put it down, your attention is distracted. Another time, with exactly the same book or story, it is full of meaning, every sentence or phrase or even word seems to vibrate with messages and ideas, reading is like being pumped full of adrenalin. Ordinary everyday experiences can be like that" (*B*, p. 184).

Yet another of Lessing's protagonists in *Briefing for a Descent into Hell* who plunges outside the pseudo-ego as well as the more commonplace life experiences and voyages into inner space is Charles Watkins, who returns to everyday life, however, unchanged and unscathed. His inner world of experience, his altered world space, is authenticated by tape recorder during his experience, much as Martha Quest records her journey into other landscapes of mind by her notes. Watkins experiences a temporary but radical alteration of character and the subjective nature of his experience is of vastly different quality than his normal daytime ego would present. His return to alienated "sanity" is accomplished by electro-convulsive therapy, whereby he loses that part of himself earlier acknowledged, "part of ourselves knows things we don't know" (*B*, p. 301). Charles Watkins' "illness" does not establish a new kind of psychic energy change, but rather he is simply returned to where he was originally. The altered reality of his inner world is invalidated by his family and his physicians. Doctors X and Y examine and treat his "abnormality" as "bad" and something to rid him of. Watkins did not have the benefit of Bert Kaplan whom Lessing considers "every bit as revolutionary as Laing."[26] Kaplan reverses the concept of that which is abnormal in mental abberations:

the analogue for abnormality is not physical illness, but normal everyday action. . . . If abnormality is understood as action, certain immediate consequences are apparent, the most important of which is that the so-called "symptoms," rather than being ego-alien manifestations of a disease process that has somehow gotten a grip on the person, are instead purposeful acts of the individual which have intentionality and are motivated. The "illness" is something the individual "wills" to happen. Rather than belonging to a foreign process which has seized him, it belongs to him, and exists squarely within the regions of his responsibility . . . Our personal documents illustrate this very well. With few exceptions they reveal the authors as embracing their illnesses and identified with them. Although they suffer with them, there is also gratification, excitement, and meaning. . . .[27]

Other Lessing characters do not engage with the inner archetypal mediators so completely as Charles Watkins but approach altered states of consciousness through heightened awareness. Mark Coldridge of *The Four-Gated City* desires to know another form of reality but is trapped by his limited modes of perception. He can only glimpse the essence of other levels of knowledge through his love for Lynda which is the only genuine passion of his life. Beyond that he does not penetrate and rejects out of hand what he terms "that nasty mixture of irony and St. John of the Cross and the *Arabian Nights*" (*FC*, p. 613). A latter parallel with Coldridge is to be found in Jack Orkney, of "The Temptation of Jack Orkney," who is an intellectual and a writer.

Whereas Coldridge only begins to achieve enlightenment through his love, Orkney moves a step further along the way. Orkney, a successful journalist and socialist leader, has lived a life of concern "for

---

[26] Doris Lessing, New School for Social Research (Sept. 27, 1972).

[27] *The Inner World of Mental Illness* (New York: Harper and Row, 1964), p. x.

public affairs, public wrong and suffering" (*T*, p. 237). He is a rational twentieth-century man who

> travelling around the world as he had, he had long ago come to terms with the fact that certain cultures were close to aspects of life which he, Jack, had quite simply forbidden. He had locked a door on them. He knew that some people claimed to see ghosts, feared their dead ancestors, consulted witchdoctors, dreamed dreams. How could he not know? He had lived with them. But he, Jack, was of that part of mankind delivered from all that; he, Jack, did not consult the bones or allow himself to be afraid of the dark. Or dream. He did not dream. (*T*, p. 246)

Ostensibly his father's death and Orkney's ensuing dreams offer an insight to another level of meaning, an experiencing of a hidden world: "He was terrified. But that was not the word . . . he feared that the terror would fade, he would forget what he had dreamed; the knowledge that there was something that had to be done, done soon, would fade, and he would forget even that he had dreamed. What *had* he dreamed? Something of immense importance" (*T*, pp. 257-58).

A battle begins within himself between the urgent self who now dreams and "his daytime self" (*T*, p. 258), "his commonplace self" (*T*, p. 261). Concurrently he becomes more and more despondent at the futility of his own life and that of his friends, seeing his son and daughter's generation unable to learn from the experiences of their elders and to go on from there:

> But this time the "gap" was much worse because a new kind of despair had entered into the consciousness of mankind: things were too desperate, the future of humanity depended on humanity being able to achieve new forms of intelligence, of being able to learn from experience. That humanity was unable to learn from experience was written there for everyone to see, since the new generation of the intelligent and consciously active youth behaved identically with every generation before them. (*T*, pp. 273-74)

Orkney fantasies ways in which he can communicate with the young and convince them "that they had the chance to break this cycle of having to repeat and repeat experience: they could be the first generation to consciously take a decision to look at history, to absorb it, and in one bound to transcend it. It would be like a willed mutation" (*T*, p. 277). Orkney is another Lessing character who concerns himself with growth based on conscious recognition of need. One of the

Sufi writers, Rumi, whom Lessing quotes preceding section four of
The Four-Gated City, states it in this manner:

> From realm to realm man went, reaching his present reasoning, knowledge-
> able, robust state—forgetting earlier forms of intelligence. So, too, shall he
> pass beyond the current forms of perception. . . . There are a thousand
> other forms of Mind. . . .
>   But he has fallen asleep. He will say: "I had forgotten my fulfillment,
> ignorant that sleep and fancy were the cause of my sufferings."
>   He says: "My sleeping experiences do not matter."
>   Come leave such asses to their meadow.
>   Because of necessity, man acquires organs. So, necessitous one, in-
> crease your need. . . . (*FC*, p. 426)

Whereas Martha Quest undertakes to achieve that awakened
state through an inner landscape of pain, Jack Orkney accepts his
altered perception as gift: "His life had been set in one current, long
ago; a fresh current, or at least, a different one, had run into it from
another source; but, unlike the springs and rivers of myth and fairy
tale, it had been muddied and unclear" (*T*, p. 307). And one understands his acceptance is reluctant at best, but irrevocable nonetheless:
"for a gift had been made to him. Behind the face of the sceptical
world was another, which no conscious decision of his could stop him
exploring" (*T*, p. 308). The pathways into that awakened state are
varied, but recognition of one's mystical experience is not to be denied.
The metaphors change for the seekers; they may be that of a "crystal
visitor" (*B*, p. 65) of "another garden . . . hidden among trees" (*T*, p.
224) or of "the great roads running inwards. . . . Travelers coming in
from the desert found it hard to say when the exact moment was when
their feet found the right road. . . . For leagues of hot dusty traveling,
a silent yellow sand, and then the white city . . ." (*FC*, p. 135).

With Mihrène, of "Out of the Fountain," acceptance of that
which was outside of her ordered universe breaks the mold forever. By
taking the gift of "the single perfect pearl" (*T*, p. 209) from Ephraim
who was to her "like someone warning, or reminding, or even threatening . . ." (*T*, p. 211), she opens for herself unknown possibilities, none
of which can invalidate the experience with Ephraim: "it didn't make
any difference what she did. . . . She had been wrenched out of her
pattern, had been stamped, or claimed by the pearl—by something
else. Nothing she could do now would put her back where she had
been . . ." (*T*, p. 222). Neither can Ephraim's world ever be the same.
It would appear that he has spent his entire life preparing himself for

the intensity of his response to Mihrène without knowing it. Because he excels at his profession as a jeweller, he is called to Alexandria to cut the diamond for Mihrène's father; because of Mihrène, he dreams his bejeweled vision:

He imagined a flat bowl of crystal, which glittered like diamonds, in which were massed roses. But the roses were all white, shades of white. He saw roses which were cold marble white, white verging on coffee colour, greenish white, like the wings of certain butterflies, white that blushed, a creamy white, white that was nearly beige, white that was almost yellow. He imagined a hundred shades of white in rose shapes. These he pressed together, filled a crystal dish with them and gave them to—Mihrène? It is possible that already he scarcely thought of her. He imagined how he would collect stones in shades of white, and create a perfect jewel, bracelet, necklet, or crescent for the hair, and present this jewel to—Mihrène? Does it matter whom it was for? He bought opals, like mist held behind glass on which lights moved and faded, like milk where fire lay buried, like the congealed breath of a girl on a frosty night. He bought pearls, each one separately, each one perfect. He bought fragments of mother-of-pearl. He bought moonstones like clouded diamonds. He even bought lumps of glass that some one had shaped to reflect light perfectly. He bought white jade and crystals and collected chips of diamond to make the suppressed fires in pearl and opal flash out in reply to their glittering frost. These jewels he had in folded flat paper, and they were kept first in a small cigarette box, and then were transferred to a larger box that had been for throat lozenges, and then to an even larger box that held cigars. He played with these gems, dreamed over them, arranged them in his mind in a thousand ways. (*T*, pp. 212-13)

Ephraim's meeting Mihrène, collecting the jewels, and ultimately distributing them to the people of the village are linked by one element, timing. Each experience was related to moments out of the ordinary movement of everyday time. Each was precipitated by a wakefulness of self, more usually stifled, of moments stirred by passion. In *Briefing* Lessing notes: "It is only in love and in war that we escape from the sleep of necessity, the cage of ordinary life, to a state where every day is a high adventure, every moment falls sharp and clear like a snowflake drifting slowly past a dark glistening rock, or like a leaf spinning down to the forest floor. Three months of ordinary living can be not much more than the effort of turning over from one side to another in a particularly heavy uncomfortable sleep" (*B*, p. 255). And of the love that Charles Watkins describes, Lessing comments: "it was a love that flowered from the time and the place . . ." (*B*, p. 258).

Thus, for the four years that Ephraim is a sergeant in World War II, he pursues "a private interest, or obsession, which was, when he arrived anywhere at all, to seek out the people and places that could add yet another fragment of iridescent or gleaming substance to the mass which he carried around in a flat tin in his pack" (*T*, p. 215). His treasure is desired by a man in his company who follows him in a moment wherein all rules and order dissolve and tries to take it from him: "There are those who believe that this time out of ordinary order is the reason for war, its hidden justification, its purpose and law, another pattern behind the one we see" (*T*, p. 216). Ephraim hides his treasure in the fountain of a small Italian village and later returns to the rubble-filled fountain where that earlier "incident had disappeared, had become buried in the foreign texture of another time, or dimension" (*T*, p. 218). Here he meets Mihrène again and renews her faith in herself once more by his stern and questioning eyes: "Why are you content with the second rate?" (*T*, p. 211). Here, too, he distributes his treasure, this time to the people of the village: "Then he stood up and began flinging into the air pearls, opals, moonstones, gems of all kinds, to fall as they would . . . treasure that was ambiguous and fertile like a king's" (*T*, p. 221).

Timing appears thematically in a variety of instances in these last Lessing works. In Charles Watkins' observation of the honeysuckle tendrils and the camellia's rhythmical and persistent movement, which he notes before his electro-convulsive therapy, lies the clue to his return to his conventional self:

Sometimes, watching, I could feel the process on that wall as a unity: the movement of the honeysuckle spray, the waiting camellia, and the breeze which was not visible at all, except as it lifted the honeysuckle spray up and close to the camellia.
It was not: The honeysuckle spray swings and reaches the camellia.
It was not: The wind blows the spray on to its host.
The two things are the same . . .
Now I see a third part of the process . . .
Not only: The movement of the spray made it reach the camellia,
Or: The wind blew it so it could reach the camellia,
But: The further growth of the honeysuckle made it possible to reach the camellia.
But the element in which this process exists is—Time.
Time is the whole point. Timing. (*B*, pp. 297-98)

And timing is of course intermingled with the transcendence of ego.

Indeed, Dr. Rosen, the narrator of "Out of the Fountain," whose life has been irreversibly changed by the knowledge symbolized by the fragment of opal which he carries, tells the reader that given slightly different circumstances and a different moment in time, "this story will have a different shape . . ." (*T*, p. 223). So too is memory regarded as being on another level in time: "So each one of us walking or sitting or sleeping is at least two scales of time wrapped together like the yolk and white of an egg . . . when . . . you or I ask ourselves, with all the weight of our lives behind the question, What am I? What is this Time? What is the evidence for a Time that is not mortal as a leaf in autumn, then the answer is, That which asks the question is out of the world's time . . ." (*B*, p. 64).

Furthermore, Lessing, as the Sufis, sees that man's knowledge of perceptual energy is still in an evolutionary stage, even for the more advanced. Her ideas are very much in accord with those of the Sufis: "Sufism has two main technical objectives: (1) to show the man himself as he really is; and (2) to help him develop his real, inner self, his permanent part."[28] As with the "I" in Lessing's metaphorical garden, "it is not possible to see the shape of the whole . . . you can never see all of it at once . . ." (*T*, pp. 227-28). This persona of "The Other Garden" encourages the reader to assimilate the two worlds: "Of course, to see it in January means that you are imagining it in June; the dislocation you have suffered by seeing the garden there, where you didn't expect it, is sharpened by seeing two gardens at once, summer superimposed on this winter scene . . ." (*T*, p. 226). One cannot make out the plan of the place nor is the design evident: "Back through one circle after another, then across the grass that lies beyond the steps. As you leave, the place draws itself in behind you, is gathered in to itself, like water settling after a stone has disturbed it. There it is, whole, between its hedges, its bare trees, repeating and echoing like a descant, using every theme that is used in the great Park outside, but used there roughly, in crude form" (*T*, pp. 229-30). Indeed, given a slight warp in time or focus, even to turn your back or to turn a corner, "it is all gone" (*T*, p. 230). Thus Lessing focuses attention on shifting plays of light as that which moves across the fissures of an opal and directs us to fables that provoke the reader's knowledge of other levels of awareness:

It was clear to both by now that whatever events had taken place between

---

[28] Ustad Hilmi, Mevlevi, "The Sufi Quest," from *Thinkers of the East*, p. 198.

them, momentous or not (they are not equipped to say) these events were in some realm or on a level where their daylight selves were strangers. It was certainly not the point that she, the unforgettable girl of Alexandria had become a rather drab young woman waiting to give birth in a war-shattered town; not the point that for her he had carried with him for four years of war a treasury of gems some precious, some mildly valuable, some worthless, bits of substance with one thing in common: their value related to some other good which had had, arbitrarily and for a short time, the name *Mihrène*. (*T*, pp. 219-20)

A Doris Lessing Checklist

Agate Nesaule Krouse

The following checklist is highly selective because of limitations of space. In the *Selected Bibliography of the Works of Lessing,* I have included the first English and American editions of novels, plays, autobiographical narratives, and collections of short stories and poems. In addition, I have included those poems, essays, book reviews, and letters which remain scattered in various periodicals. Lessing's short stories present a special problem: a large number of them were originally published in periodicals and several of them remained relatively unknown until the publication of *The Temptation of Jack Orkney.* I have not attempted to list subsequently collected items since they are more readily available in book form. I have, however, included the titles of all collections, even though many of the same stories appear in them more than once. Thus, for example, all the stories in *This Was the Old Chief's Country* and four of the short novels in *Five* appear in *African Stories*; *The Story of a Non-Marrying Man and Other Stories* is simply the English edition of *The Temptation of Jack Orkney.* On the same principle that Lessing's work is more readily available in book form, I have eliminated a number of excerpts from her work which have appeared as separate entries of articles in previous bibliographies and checklists. I have also excluded translations, the numerous reissues and paperback editions of books, and the growing number of short stories on their way to becoming standard anthology pieces. Items are arranged chronologically within the following categories: articles, essays, and letters; autobiographical narratives; book reviews; novels; plays; poems; and short story collections.

In the *Checklist of Lessing Criticism,* I have included books, critical articles, interviews, bibliographical materials, and dissertations entirely devoted to Lessing. Since relatively little criticism exists, I have also included several books and articles which deal briefly but interestingly with Lessing's work. In a few instances where the nature or usefulness of the material may not be immediately apparent, I have included a short parenthetical note. All items are arranged alphabetically. Because of limitations of space, I have not been able to list the vast number of reviews of individual works. Since these vary greatly in scope and quality, I hope a complete, accurate, and annotated checklist of reviews will appear in the future.

I. *A Selected Bibliography of the Works of Doris Lessing*

Articles, essays, and letters:

"Being Prohibited." *New Statesman,* 51 (April 21, 1956), 410, 412.
"The Kariba Project." *New Statesman,* 51 (June 9, 1956), 647-48.
"The Small Personal Voice." In *Declaration,* ed. Tom Maschler. London: MacGibbon & Kee, 1957, pp. 12-27.
"London Diary." *New Statesman,* 55 (March 15 and 22, 1958), 326-27, 367-68.
"The Fruits of Humbug." *Twentieth Century,* 165 (April 1959), 368-76.
"Ordinary People." *New Statesman,* 59 (June 25, 1960), 932.
Letter to the Editor. *New Statesman,* 62 (November 3, 1961), 651.
"Smart Set Socialists." *New Statesman,* 62 (December 1, 1961), 822, 824.
"What Really Matters." *Twentieth Century,* 172 (Autumn 1963), 97-98.
"Zambia's Joyful Week." *New Statesman,* 68 (November 6, 1964), 692, 694.
"Afterword." In Olive Schreiner, *The Story of an African Farm,* ed. Irving Howe, The Masterworks Series. Greenwich, Conn.: Fawcett Premier, 1968, pp. 273-90.
"A Few Doors Down." *New Statesman,* 78 (December 26, 1969), 918-19.
Letter to the Editor. *New York Review of Books,* 15 (October 22, 1970), 51.
"An Ancient Way to New Freedom." *Vogue,* 158 (July 1971), 98, 125, 130-31.
"In the World, Not of It." *Encounter,* 39 (August 1972), 61-64.
"Vonnegut's Responsibility." *New York Times Book Review* (February 4, 1973), p. 35.

Autobiographical narratives:

"Myself as Sportsman." *New Yorker*, 31 (January 21, 1956), 92-96.

Going Home. With drawings by Paul Hogarth. London: Michael Joseph, 1957; Rev. ed. London: Panther Books, 1968; Rev. ed. New York: Ballantine Books, 1968.

In Pursuit of the English: *A Documentary*. London: MacGibbon & Kee, 1960; New York: Simon and Schuster, 1961.

Particularly Cats. London: Michael Joseph, 1967; New York: Simon and Schuster, 1967.

Book reviews:

"Desert Child." *New Statesman*, 56 (November 15, 1958), 700.

"African Interiors." *New Statesman*, 62 (October 27, 1961), 613-14.

"An Elephant in the Dark." *Spectator*, 213 (September 18, 1964), 373.

"Allah Be Praised." *New Statesman*, 71 (May 27, 1966), 775, 778.

Novels:

The Grass Is Singing. London: Michael Joseph, 1950; New York: T. Y. Crowell, 1950.

Martha Quest. [*Children of Violence*, Vol. I.] London: Michael Joseph, 1952; New York: Simon and Schuster, 1964.

A Proper Marriage. [*Children of Violence*, Vol. II.] London: Michael Joseph, 1954; New York: Simon and Schuster, 1964.

Retreat to Innocence. London: Michael Joseph, 1956.

A Ripple from the Storm. [*Children of Violence*, Vol. III.] London: Michael Joseph, 1958; New York: Simon and Schuster, 1966.

The Golden Notebook. London: Michael Joseph, 1962; New York: Simon and Schuster, 1962.

Landlocked. [*Children of Violence*, Vol. IV.] London: MacGibbon & Kee, 1965; New York: Simon and Schuster, 1966.

The Four-Gated City. [*Children of Violence*, Vol V.] London: MacGibbon & Kee, 1969; New York: Alfred A. Knopf, 1969.

Briefing for a Descent into Hell. London: Jonathan Cape, 1971; New York: Alfred A. Knopf, 1971.

The Summer Before the Dark. London: Jonathan Cape, 1973; New York: Alfred A. Knopf, 1973.

Plays:

"Mr. Dolinger." Unpublished play, 1958. [See John Russell Taylor, *The Angry Theater*: *New British Drama*. Rev. ed. New York: Hill & Wang, 1969, p. 145. See also Myron Matlaw, *Modern World Drama*: *An Encyclopedia*. New York: E. P. Dutton & Co., Inc., 1972, p. 456.]

Each His Own Wilderness. In *New English Dramatists: Three Plays,* ed. Elliot M. Browne. Harmondsworth, Middlesex: Penguin Books, 1959, pp. 11-95.

"The Truth About Billy Newton." Unpublished play, 1960. [See review by A. Alvarez, *New Statesman,* 59 (January 23, 1960), pp. 100-101. For a brief discussion, see Allardyce Nicoll, "Somewhat in a New Dimension," in Stratford-Upon-Avon-Studies 4, *Contemporary Theatre.* London: Edward Arnold Publishers Ltd., 1968, pp. 82-83, 92.]

Play with a Tiger: A Play in Three Acts. London: Michael Joseph, 1962.

Poems:

Fourteen Poems. Ed. limited to 500 copies. Northwood, Middlesex: Scorpion Press, 1959.

"Here." *New Statesman,* 71 (June 17, 1966), 900.

"A Visit." *New Statesman,* 72 (November 4, 1966), 666.

"Hunger the King." *New Statesman,* 74 (November 24, 1967), 731.

"A Small Girl Throws Stones at a Swan in Regents Park." *New Statesman,* 74 (November 24, 1967), 731.

Short story collections:

This Was the Old Chief's Country: Stories. London: Michael Joseph, 1951; New York: T. Y. Crowell, 1952.

Five: Short Novels. London: Michael Joseph, 1953.

The Habit of Loving. London: MacGibbon & Kee, 1957; New York: T. Y. Crowell, 1957.

A Man and Two Women: Stories. London: MacGibbon & Kee, 1963; New York: Simon and Schuster, 1963.

African Stories. London: Michael Joseph, 1964; New York: Simon and Schuster, 1965.

The Black Madonna. London: Panther Books, 1966.

Nine African Stories. Selected by Michael Marland [from *African Stories*]. With illustrations. London: Longmans, 1968.

The Story of a Non-Marrying Man and Other Stories. London: Jonathan Cape, 1972.

The Temptation of Jack Orkney and Other Stories. New York: Alfred A. Knopf, 1972.

II. *A Checklist of Lessing Criticism*

Alcorn, Noeline Elizabeth. "Vision and Nightmare: A Study of Doris Lessing's Novels." *Dissertation Abstracts,* 32 (1971), 1500A. (Univ. of California)

Allen, Walter. *The Modern Novel in Britain and the United States.* New York: E. P. Dutton & Co., Inc., 1964. Pp. 197, 276-77.

Anon. "The Fog of War." *Times Literary Supplement* (April 27, 1962), p. 280.

Anon. "The Witness as Prophet." *Time*, 94 (July 25, 1969), 75-76. [An interview with Lessing included with the review of *The Four-Gated City*.]

Bannon, B. A. "Authors and Editors." *Publishers' Weekly*, 195 (June 2, 1969), 51-54. [An interview.]

Barnouw, Dagmar. "Disorderly Company: From *The Golden Notebook* to *The Four-Gated City*." *Contemporary Literature*, 14 (Autumn 1973), 491-514.

Bergonzi, Bernard. "In Pursuit of Doris Lessing." *New York Review of Books* (February 11, 1965), pp. 12-14.

———. *The Situation of the Novel.* London: Macmillan, 1970. Pp. 69, 80, 200-204, 209, 212.

Bolling, Douglass. "Structure and Theme in *Briefing for a Descent into Hell*." *Contemporary Literature*, 14 (Autumn 1973), 550-64.

Brewer, Joseph E. "The Anti-Hero in Contemporary Literature." *Iowa English Yearbook*, 12 (1967), 55-60.

Brewster, Dorothy. *Doris Lessing.* Twayne's English Authors Series. New York: Twayne Publishers, Inc., 1965.

Brooks, Ellen W. "Fragmentation and Integration: A Study of Doris Lessing's Fiction." *Dissertation Abstracts*, 32 (1971), 3989-90A. (New York Univ.)

Burgess, Anthony. *The Novel Now.* New York: W. W. Norton, Inc., 1967. Pp. 99-101.

Burkom, Selma R. "A Doris Lessing Checklist." *Critique*, 11, No. 1 (1969), 69-81.

———. " 'Only Connect': Form and Content in the Works of Doris Lessing." *Critique*, 11, No. 1 (1969), 51-68.

———. "A Reconciliation of Opposites: A Study of the Works of Doris Lessing." *Dissertation Abstracts*, 31 (1971), 5390A. (Univ. of Minnesota)

———. "Wholeness as Hieroglyph: Lessing's Typical Mode and Meaning." Unpublished paper for MLA Seminar 46: The Fiction of Doris Lessing (1971).

Carey, Alfred Augustine. "Doris Lessing: The Search for Reality. A Study of the Major Themes in Her Novels." *Dissertation Abstracts*, 26 (1965), 3297. (Univ. of Wisconsin)

Carey, John L. "Art and Reality in *The Golden Notebook*." *Contemporary Literature*, 14 (Autumn 1973), 437-56.

Churchill, Caryl. "Not Ordinary, Not Safe." *Twentieth Century*, 168 (November 1960), 443-51. [Discussion of plays by Lessing and others.]

Drabble, Margaret. "Doris Lessing: Cassandra in a World Under Siege." *Ramparts*, 10 (February 1972), 50-54.

Ebert, Roger. "Doris Lessing: An Idol on a Mercurial Pedestal." *Louisville Courier-Journal and Times* (June 22, 1969), sec. G., p. 4., cols. 5-6. [An interview.]

Ellmann, Mary. *Thinking About Women.* New York: Harcourt Brace Jovanovich, Inc., 1968. Pp. 142, 197-99.

Enright, D. J. "Shivery Games." *New York Review of Books* (July 31, 1969), pp. 22-24.

Ferguson, Mary Anne. "Sexist Images of Women in Literature." In *Female Studies V: Proceedings of the Conference, Women and Education,* ed. Rae Lee Siporin. Pittsburgh: Know, Inc., 1972. Pp. 77-83. [Discussion of the value of a feminist approach to "To Room Nineteen," p. 80.]

Gindin, James. "Doris Lessing's Intense Commitment," *Postwar British Fiction: New Accents and Attitudes.* Berkeley: Univ. of California Press, 1962. Pp. 65-86.

Graustein, Gottfried. "Entwicklungstendenzen im Schaffen Doris Lessings." *Wissenschaftliche Zeistschrift der Universität Leipzig,* 12 (1963), 529-33.

Halliday, Patricia. "The Pursuit of Wholeness in the Work of Doris Lessing: Dualities, Multiplicities, and the Resolution of Patterns in Illumination." Diss. Univ. of Minnesota, 1973.

Hardin, Nancy S. "Doris Lessing and the Sufi Way." *Contemporary Literature,* 14 (Autumn 1973), 565-81.

Hartwig, Dorothea. "Die Widerspiegelung Afrikanischer Probleme im Werk Doris Lessings." *Wissenschaftliche Zeitschrift der Universität Rostock,* 12 (1963), 87-104.

Hinz, Evelyn and John J. Teunissen. "The Pietà as Icon in *The Golden Notebook.*" *Contemporary Literature,* 14 (Autumn 1973), 457-70.

Howe, Florence. "A Conversation with Doris Lessing." *Contemporary Literature,* 14 (Autumn 1973), 418-36.

———. "Doris Lessing's Free Women." *Nation,* 200 (January 11, 1965), 34-37.

———. "A Talk with Doris Lessing." *Nation,* 204 (March 6, 1967), 311-13. [Excerpts from an interview.]

Ipp, Catharina. *Doris Lessing: A Bibliography.* Johannesburg: Univ. of Witwatersand, 1967.

Kaplan, Sydney. "The Limits of Consciousness in the Novels of Doris Lessing." *Contemporary Literature,* 14 (Autumn 1973), 536-49.

Karl, Frederick R. "Doris Lessing in the Sixties: The New Anatomy of Melancholy." *Contemporary Literature,* 13 (Winter 1972), 15-33.

———. *A Reader's Guide to the Contemporary English Novel.* Rev. ed. New York: Farrar, Straus, & Giroux, 1972. Pp. 291-312 and *passim.*

Krouse, Agate Nesaule. "A Doris Lessing Checklist." *Contemporary Liter-*

ature, 14 (Autumn 1973), 590-97.

———. "The Feminism of Doris Lessing." Diss. Univ. of Wisconsin, Madison, 1972.

Lang, Frances. "Doris Lessing: Madness as Ideology." *off our backs* (December 1972), pp. 10-11.

Lodge, David. *The Novelist at the Crossroads and Other Essays on Fiction and Criticism.* Ithaca, New York: Cornell Univ. Press, 1971. Pp. 17, 24.

Marchino, Lois A. "The Search for Self in the Novels of Doris Lessing." *Studies in the Novel*, 4 (Summer 1972), 252-61.

———. "The Search for Self in the Novels of Doris Lessing." *Dissertation Abstracts*, 33 (1972), 2384-85A. (Univ. of New Mexico)

McDowell, Frederick P. W. " 'The Devious Involutions of Human Character and Emotions': Reflections on Some Recent British Novels." *Wisconsin Studies in Contemporary Literature*, 4 (Autumn 1963), 339-66. [Discusses Lessing, pp. 346-50.]

———. "The Fiction of Doris Lessing: An Interim View." *Arizona Quarterly*, 21 (Winter 1965), 315-45.

———. "Recent British Fiction: Some Established Writers." *Contemporary Literature*, 11 (Summer 1970), 401-31. [Discusses Lessing, pp. 424-28.]

———. "Time of Plenty: Recent British Novels." *Contemporary Literature*, 13 (Summer 1972), 361-94. [Discusses Lessing, pp. 387-89.]

Morgan, Ellen. "Alienation of the Woman Writer in *The Golden Notebook.*" *Contemporary Literature*, 14 (Autumn 1973), 471-80.

Morris, Robert K. "Doris Lessing, *Children of Violence*: The Quest for Change," *Continuance and Change: The Contemporary British Novel Sequence.* Carbondale: Southern Illinois Univ. Press, 1972. Pp. 1-27.

Mulken, Anne M. "Twentieth-Century Realism: The 'Grid' Structure of *The Golden Notebook.*" *Studies in the Novel*, 4 (Summer 1972), 262-74.

Newquist, Roy. "Doris Lessing." In *Counterpoint*, ed. Roy Newquist. Chicago: Rand McNally & Co., 1964. Pp. 414-24. [An interview.]

Nicoll, Allardyce. "Somewhat in a New Dimension." In Stratford-Upon-Avon-Studies 4, *Contemporary Theatre.* London: Edward Arnold Publishers Ltd., 1968. Pp. 82-83, 92.

O'Fallon, Kathleen. "Quest for a New Vision." *World Literature Written in English*, 12 (November 1973), 180-89.

Porter, Nancy. "Lessing's Recovery of Silenced History." *World Literature Written in English*, 12 (November 1973), 161-79.

Pratt, Annis. "The Contrary Structure of Doris Lessing's *The Golden Notebook.*" *World Literature Written in English*, 12 (November 1973), 150-60.

———. "Introduction." *Contemporary Literature*, 14 (Autumn 1973), 413-17.

———. "Women and Nature in Modern Fiction." *Contemporary Literature*,

13 (Autumn 1972), 476-90. [Discusses Lessing, pp. 487-88.]

Rabinovitz, Rubin. *The Reaction Against Experiment in the English Novel, 1950-1960.* New York: Columbia Univ. Press, 1967. Pp. 29-30, 78, 86.

Raskin, Jonah. "Doris Lessing at Stony Brook: An Interview." *New American Review,* 8 (1970), 166-79.

Schlueter, Paul. "Doris Lessing: The Free Woman's Commitment." In *Contemporary British Novelists,* ed. Charles Shapiro. Carbondale: Southern Illinois Univ. Press, 1965. Pp. 48-61.

———. *The Novels of Doris Lessing.* Carbondale: Southern Illinois Univ. Press, 1973.

———. "A Study of the Major Novels of Doris Lessing." *Dissertation Abstracts,* 29 (1968), 3619-20A. (Southern Illinois Univ.)

Seligman, Dee. "The Sufi Quest." *World Literature Written in English,* 12 (November 1973), 190-206.

Smith, Diane S. "Ant Imagery as Thematic Device in the *Children of Violence* Series." Unpublished paper for MLA Seminar 46: The Fiction of Doris Lessing (1971).

———. "A Thematic Study of Doris Lessing's *Children of Violence.*" *Dissertation Abstracts,* 32 (1971), 1530A. (Loyola Univ.)

Sukenick, Lynn. "Feeling and Reason in Doris Lessing's Fiction." *Contemporary Literature,* 14 (Autumn 1973), 515-35.

Taylor, John Russell. *The Angry Theater: New British Drama.* Rev. and expanded ed. New York: Hill & Wang, 1969. Pp. 37, 145.

Trussler, Simon. "Arnold Wesker: An Interview Given to Simon Trussler in 1966." In *Theatre at Work: Playwrights and Productions in the Modern British Theatre,* ed. Charles Marowitz and Simon Trussler. New York: Hill & Wang, 1967. Pp. 78-95. [Wesker discusses Lessing's role in organizing playwrights, p. 86.]

Webb, Marilyn. "Feminism & Doris Lessing: Becoming the Men We Wanted to Marry." *The Village Voice,* 18, No. 1 (January 4, 1973), 1, 14-17, 19.

Wellwarth, George. "Doris Lessing: The Angry Young Cocoon," *The Theater of Protest and Paradox: Developments in the Avant-Garde Drama.* New York: New York Univ. Press, 1964. Pp. 248-50.

Wiseman, Thomas. "Mrs [sic] Lessing's Kind of Life." *Time and Tide,* 43 (April 12, 1962), 26. [An interview.]

Zak, Michele Wender. "*The Grass Is Singing*: A Little Novel about the Emotions." *Contemporary Literature,* 14 (Autumn 1973), 481-90.